THE MYSTERY RIVERS OF TIBET

Also available in the Plant Hunters series
with introductions by Geoffrey Smith:

THE DOLOMITES by Reginald Farrer

THE VALLEY OF FLOWERS by F. S. Smythe

PLANT HUNTING ON THE EDGE OF THE WORLD
by E. Kingdon Ward

THE RAINBOW BRIDGE
by Reginald Farrer

A NATURALIST IN WESTERN CHINA by E. H. Wilson

THE
MYSTERY RIVERS OF TIBET

BY F. KINGDON WARD
INTRODUCTION BY GEOFFREY SMITH

CADOGAN BOOKS
LONDON

First published in Great Britain in 1923
by Seeley Service & Co. Ltd.

This edition published in 1986
by Cadogan Books Ltd
16 Lower Marsh, London SE1 7RJ

ISBN 0 946313 52 0

Printed and bound in Great Britain by
Redwood Burn Ltd, Trowbridge, Wiltshire

INTRODUCTION TO THIS EDITION

'The Mystery Rivers of Tibet' was for me both a surprise and a source of pleasurable anticipation: surprise in that there was a book by Kingdon Ward which I had not even heard of; and anticipation in that, instead of re-reading already familiar passages, 'The Mystery Rivers of Tibet' offered the prospect of a completely new adventure in print with the author. As always before reading a book which deals with unfamiliar country and places I look up the area concerned on a map. Fortunately, on this occasion the map needed is conveniently to hand at the end of the book. The tiny square dotted in on the top North East corner gives some indication of the vast distances involved.

The area botanised by the author takes in a part only of three rivers – Salween, Mekon, and from the map a meandering loop of the Yangtze, so it was with a keen sense of anticipation that I settled down to the first stage of a journey through a land which, even today, is still veiled in mystery. All three rivers share the same point of origin on the desolate, vast, frozen wasteland, the Chang Tang Plateau of North Central Tibet – a wild, dangerous land with weather conditions at times so severe that any slight misjudgment could have the direst consequences. Even the natives were at times victim to sudden changes in climate, as the author relates on his return to Tra-Mu-Tang when three porters, out of a party of ten travelling on a journey from Taron, were frozen to death in a snowstorm.

'The Mystery Rivers of Tibet' differs in several respects to Kingdon Ward books which deal specifically with one or more of the large-scale expeditions he undertook. These books – 'Pilgrimage for Plants', 'Plant Hunting in the Wilds', 'Romance of Plant Hunting', and 'Plant Hunting on the Edge of the World' are, as the titles suggest, accounts of Kingdon Ward's insatiable quest for new species of plants.

Unlike many of the other famous plant hunters who trained local people, and used them as collectors of plants and seed, Kingdon Ward preferred to work alone, finding, evaluating, and making his own selections, while keeping detailed descriptive botanical notes which are a tribute to his powers of observation. I particularly remember the description from another well-used book of his in my library of the Chinese and Tibetan Alps where he describes the seasons: ". . . though the summers are wetter, the autumns sunnier, and the winters colder the seasons are as distinct as they are in Great Britain. In autumn the berries of Cotoneaster and Berberis, crimson, scarlet, coral, and carmine, make a brave display before the snow comes at Christmas and spreads a white carpet over the world. Whole mountainsides run blood-red with leaf and berry, while at lower altitudes the evergreen forest is laced and mottled with vermilion and orange." There must have been something in the very air of the Himalayas that tapped deep wells of poetry hidden inside those who searched out the deep valleys, and held silent communion for long periods with soaring mountain peaks.

Reading this book I could sense that, though serious in purpose, on this expedition at least, there was a relaxed, almost holiday approach. In one other respect, also, the conduct of the plant hunting enterprises is in contradiction to the observation I made that Kingdon Ward preferred to do his own collecting. For crossing the Sierra on the way to A-tun-tzu he gives the following description: "I sent two of my Tibetan collectors back to Do-kar-la to see what they could find, and report on what seeds were ripe, telling them to be back in ten days".

As in all the books I have read which deal with the border between Tibet and China, there runs an undercurrent of lawlessness, curiously intermingled with simple hospitality which can change almost as quickly as the weather to suspicion and outright hostility. A description of how the author climbed up the W1 ridge in order to see night creep down once more over the savage landscape in which the twin peaks of Orbor were set like diamonds, together with the news that he had just been given most comfortable quarters in rooms, swept and garnished, create a picture of peace-filled security. This is sharply contrasted on the next page by descriptions of war, alarms and desperate situations.

However, the theme which runs continuously throughout the book is one of plants growing wild in some of the grandest scenery in the world, described with the facile pen of a plantsman. Unlike Farrer, whose plant geese were smothered in such expansive terms that by the magic of prose they were transformed into swans, Kingdon Ward debates on the merits of a flower before passing judgment. "The *Meconopsis delavayi*, a shimmering bluish violet flower with the texture of Japanese silk, is a plant of only 3 to 6 inches high when in bloom, growing closely under quite small rocks but in fruit the peduncles elongate several inches, bringing the capsule out of hiding place that they may the more freely scatter their seeds on the wind" – a description there not just of floral beauty and botanical features, but one which is sufficiently detailed on choice of habitat to give any gardener reading it a clue to cultivation also.

The long journey is nearly at an end. A twenty-five mile march through rippling hills brings Kingdon Ward's expedition on to the edge of the plains. Next morning they cover the remaining ten miles before the sun gains power, then to Rangoon by train, a terse, almost laconic finale to a journey which refers to three great Asiatic rivers. In the very last paragraph Kingdon Ward notes that the exploration of the upper Salween still remains to be done. Indeed, sixty-three years later a bamboo curtain adds a further restriction to potential explorer plant hunters.

GEOFFREY SMITH

THE
MYSTERY RIVERS
OF TIBET

A DESCRIPTION OF THE LITTLE-KNOWN LAND WHERE
ASIA'S MIGHTIEST RIVERS GALLOP IN HARNESS
THROUGH THE NARROW GATEWAY OF TIBET,
ITS PEOPLES, FAUNA, & FLORA

BY

Captain F. KINGDON WARD, B.A., F.R.G.S.

*Late Indian Army Reserve of Officers, attached 1/116th Mahrattas,
Indian Army.*

AUTHOR OF
"THE LAND OF THE BLUE POPPY," "IN FARTHEST BURMA"
&c., &c., &c.

London
Seeley Service & Co. Limited
196 Shaftesbury Avenue
1923

AUTHOR'S NOTE

PROFESSOR JAMES WARD, of Cambridge, did me the honour to read through the original manuscript of this book. As a result, I rewrote it. Any merit which may thereby have crept into it, is due to his teaching; those faults which still remain are due to my lack of learning. The debt I owe him will long remain unpaid.

The spelling of Chinese place-names is that used by General H. R. Davies in his map of Yun-nan. (Wade's system.) The spelling of Tibetan places which I visited is transliterated, as accurately as possible, from the Tibetan; for places which I did not visit, I have adopted Mr. Eric Teichman's spelling.

My thanks are especially due to my wife who undertook the laborious and uninteresting task of compiling the index.

F. K. W.

LONDON.

CONTENTS

Contents

14 MAPS

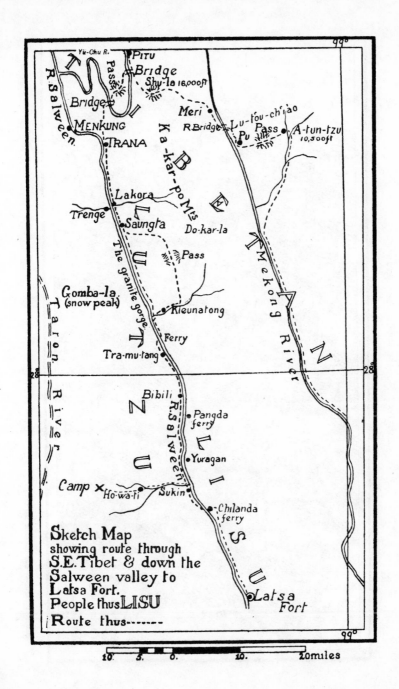

Sketch Map
showing route through
S.E. Tibet & down the
Salween valley to
Latsa Fort.
People thus LISU
Route thus ------

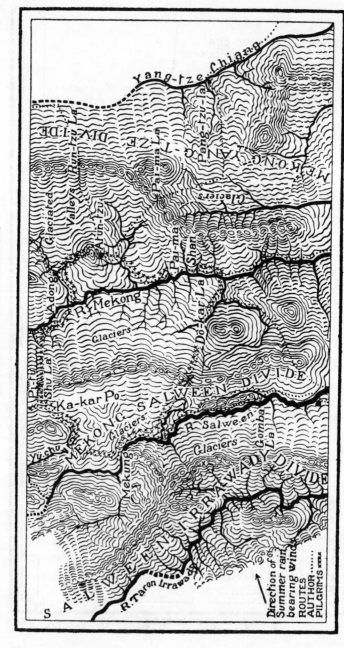

Scale, 1 inch = 12¾ statute miles

Yang-tze Chiang

MEKONG-YANG-TZE DIVIDE

Fun-tzu-La

Pang-tzu-La

Valleys Fun-tzu La

Glaciers

Glaciered

Pai-ma La

Pai-ma Shan

A-tun-tzu

Adong

Glaciered

R. Mekong

Glaciers

Dô-kar La

Pê-ma Shu La

Ka-kar Po

MEKONG-SALWEEN DIVIDE

Glaciers

R. Salwe.en

Gomba La

Yu-chu

Mekong

Glaciers

IRRAWADY DIVIDE

SALWEEN

R. Taron Irrawady

Direction of
Summer rain-
bearing winds
ROUTES
AUTHOR ....
PILGRIMS ×××

The Mystery Rivers of Tibet

I

Through the Kachin Hills to China

IN February, 1913, I left England on a plant-hunting trip to Eastern Tibet, travelling via Burma and so by Yun-nan to the belt of deep gorges which stripe the country called Kam. April had come when we crossed the mile-broad Irrawaddy at Myitkyina, northern terminus of the Burma railway, and headed towards the blue mountains which guard the China frontier. Now the pack-mules settled down to the steady two-and-a-quarter miles an hour of Asian travel, and for three days we plodded up through the monsoon forest. The hot weather was upon us, and many of the trees stood naked in the white sunlight. A breeze springs up, whirling down leaves and winged fruits. One of the latter, a species of Hiptage, mimics the flight of a butterfly, and suggests that certain butterflies, noticing this, may have modelled their flight to correspond with the motions of spinning fruits, thereby escaping detection.

There was a flattened leguminous pod commonly seen on the ground, which never contained more than one fertile seed; thus it was practically a winged one-seeded fruit. The fertile seed was always situated at the base of the pod, the rest of which formed the wing;

the seed end of the pod was clothed with a stiff pile of orange-coloured bristles, but the wing was glabrous. Every pod on the ground had been bored through by some insect, and its seed destroyed. Thus had a samara been evolved from a many-seeded pod, perhaps by a gradual seed reduction in order to concentrate protection on a single pod, partly in the form of this hairy envelope. Not that success had yet been attained.

An interesting shrub commonly met with is a species of Clerodendron. In the bud the long stamens and style are curled up together like a watch-spring. As the flower opens wide its jaws, however, the ripe stamens curve upwards, and the style downwards, carrying the still unripe stigma out of the way. Presently the stigma ripens, and the style curls upwards towards the entrance, thus coming into contact with insect visitors attracted by the sweet fragrance. Meanwhile the withered stamens, having performed their task, take the place of the style, the two pairs crossing each other so as to form an X as they bend downwards.

By day blood-sucking flies annoyed the mules, settling on their necks and bellies, making them stamp and start and toss their heads angrily.

One morning we halted for lunch on a hill overlooking the forested valleys beyond the 'Nmai hka, where dwell the dog-eating Marus. The river itself was hidden in a maze of hummocky country, dominated by a high sugarloaf peak. Here and there thin columns of smoke rose into the still air, and beyond were the dim outlines of great mountain ranges ; below lay the parched lands of the Irrawaddy plain, sunk in the curdled mist, and around us were the jungle-clad Kachin Hills growing bluer and bluer towards the China frontier.

Passing through Szi villages we saw women seated on the ground outside long low grass-thatched huts weaving cloth. Dirty, ugly, stunted, they gaily decorated themselves with monstrous bamboo neck rings, metal bangles, tubes thrust through the distorted ear lobes, numerous black rattan rings round the calf, and other uncouth ornaments.

On the 9th April we began the ascent to Kambaiti Pass. The Bauhinia trees, though leafless, were in full bloom, painting the hill-side with lilac smudges. There was a handsome species of Cornus with compact hemispheres of waxy looking flowers, which are bright orange when they first open, fading as they die. Thus each ball of flowers is orange in the centre, growing paler and paler towards the circumference, giving a very pretty effect.

Another shrub found here is *Agapates Wardii*, which grows on granite rocks or in the boles of big trees. It has curious swollen enlargements of the stem, composed of water-storing tissue, which is eaten by insects, and worn away leaving large cavities.

The top of the pass (about 10,000 feet) was purple with Primula sp. This is the frontier. Crossing over, we entered Yun-nan and descended to the Ta-ho, here spanned by a steep bamboo bridge. The mules crossed by a ford higher up. We now found ourselves amongst rolling hills covered with short springy turf and scattered pines ; tucked away in sleepy hollows were Lisu villages.

At dusk we reached Ku-yung-kai, a Chinese market town, but the mule inns were yet a couple of miles off across the paddy fields. Reluctantly we set out to pick our way through the swamps, and in the growing darkness were soon utterly bogged ; to make matters worse it

began to rain furiously. There was nothing for it but
to return the way we had come, which we did ; the last
part of the journey being made a little easier for us by
some good people who came out carrying torches.
Eventually we crowded into the single room of a solitary
hut, the mules lying on top of each other in the pig-
sty.

On the following day our road lay across a flat cultivated valley, through lanes of yellow dog roses, scarlet
japonica and snowy apple blossom, by hill-sides covered
with pink Camellia and crimson Rhododendron, with
porcelain-blue gentians underfoot. Trees of feathery
Cryptomeria watch over the graves of the dead, and in
the wayside marshes, whorls of orange-flowered *Primula
chrysochlora* are unfolding. *P. chrysochlora* is very like
P. helodoxa from the same district. The latter is in
cultivation.

At last the bare volcanic hills of T'eng-yueh rose into
view. We trod a narrow stone-flagged path, hedged
with sprawling bushes of large pink roses ; emerged on
to the downs, speckled with tombstones of grey lava,
where the wind sighs through the grass and the cuckoo
calls from the alder copse ; and so by peaceful temples
and happy villages we came to the noisy little waterfall
outside the West Gate. Under the shadow of the city
wall my friend, Mr. E. B. Howell, Commissioner of
Customs, was awaiting me ; and with him I spent three
pleasant days.

On April 16th we set out for Tali-fu, through lanes
of spring flowers.

Now the muleteers amused me. One of the animals
suffered from a " hot stomach " and drastic action was
taken. First his belly was pierced, a metal tube thrust

through the hole, and some fluid drawn off; then blood-letting was resorted to, the mule standing helpless on three legs.

But the men did not confine such gentle attentions to their animals, and one victim of fever was quickly cured by his mates. Taking off his coat he was soundly smacked on the chest and back, in order to drive the bad blood into his extremities; then his arms were roughly massaged, his fingers rubbed down, and finally pricked above the nail. And as the blood oozed out, the fever left him. We passed a wedding procession, the saucy banging of a gong warning us to get out of the way. The bride, with her doll's face thickly powdered, was dressed in new silk trousers and shapeless jacket, with tiny triangular shoes above which bulged her maimed ankles. A thick black veil concealed her from view, for she was sick with shyness, so that a man must walk alongside her pony to hold her on. Followed a tawdry cabinet containing gifts of food, borne at a shuffle by ragged coolies.

We reached Tali-fu on April 27th to find the great fair just over, and the plain rich with colour; fields of green wheat and scented beans, the blue lake crested with frothing waves, the dark mountains glazed with snow, all drenched in golden sunshine.

Northwards we travelled, to the fringes of agricultural China. Everywhere prosperity smiled at us from the brilliant fields; yet everywhere the spectre of want lurked beneath the surface. Beyond the busy city of Chien-ch'uan it poked up its ugly head, and straightway we marched through a moaning avenue composed of human derelicts, maimed, blackened, yet still moving creatures who had once been human beings. Some were

seated, and in jarring notes, with hands clasped, begged
alms of the passer-by ; most were prostrate, too weak
even to look whether any have troubled to drop a few
" cash," a few scraps of food, fit only for starving dogs,
into the little bowl set beside each ; some, whose skeleton
forms partly concealed by dreadful rags showed sores and
wounds still more ghastly, were already dead.   What
a terrible contrast between prosperity and utter destitu-
tion !   A sea of crops, and along the shore this flotsam
thrown up to suffer and die !

Poor wretches !   They must needs sleep this night
in ditches, or among the graves on the hill-side, with the
pariah dogs.   Just beside them stands the city of Chien-
ch'uan with its teeming population ; but the homeless
are not allowed inside the city walls, and the people
daily give food to the outcasts, at least sufficient to prevent burial of the whole crowd falling on the public
purse at once !

Soon the snowy Li-kiang range rose into view.   At
first sight it appears that the Yangtze river, finding the
way barred by this range, had turned back on itself,
seeking another route, and had flowed northwards in
a U-loop round the end of the range.   But it is not so.
The Yangtze flows north-north-east, and cuts clean
across the snowy range, whose axis is continued beyond
Chung-tien.

We reached Li-kiang next day.   It is a small unwalled
city of steep cobbled streets, situated in a bowl amongst
the hills.   Near by is the Temple of the Water Dragon,
where a stream of pure water gushes from beneath a
rock ; more picturesquely, a dragon lives beneath the
rock, and from his cavernous jaws the water flows out
forming a small pond.   Here water-lilies float over a

bewitching reflection of the old temple against a background of snowy peaks.

A fair was in full swing and the city was crowded in consequence. Surrounding lake, temple and spring is a grove of trees, and here within earshot of the gurgling water, the crowd surged round the open stage opposite the temple, where a strolling company was about to perform one of those tedious domestic dramas beloved by the Chinese. Open-air stages are found in attendance on Buddhist temples all over China, inside the courtyard if the temple is a big one, but often outside. Originally there was a close connection between religion and the drama ; the earliest plays were no doubt always religious. However, they are now so far divorced that in England, even in this so-called enlightened age, many self-righteous people look with horror on the stage. When I asked why temples in China always have stages attached to them I was told it was a matter of convenience. " The temple belongs to the people," said my acquaintance, " and so does the drama ! " What more natural than to associate the two !

In a far corner were dwarf Azaleas in pots, massed with crimson and terra-cotta coloured blossom, dwarf pines, and a few orchids of the genus Cymbidium. The Chinese, too, love flowers, in an aimless sort of way.

Across the lake was an open meadow, surrounded by booths, and here a motley crowd had assembled. There were sallow-cheeked Chinese traders, fair-skinned Moso in pleated skirts, tall Tibetans from Chung-tien, lanthorn-jawed Lisu with hooked noses, and round faced Minchia come out of the west, arguing, expostulating, pleading, bargaining, as Asiatics do.

All the goods exposed for sale were of European or

Japanese manufacture—clocks, knives, needles, mirrors, and so forth. There was not a single article of Chinese workmanship on view. And why? Because the Chinaman is satiated with them. What *he* wants now is a Homburg hat, a watch, and a pair of leather boots—something *useful*, not merely ornamental. So he looks on apathetically while his country is denuded of its treasures, which become the playthings of a London drawing-room, and imports the machine-made article instead. Presently he will import the machine. Each copies the other, thrice denying his own. And yet it is not *ideas* which are elegant or vulgar, but the things which represent those ideas. The idea of wearing a dressing-gown at the opera sounds bad form—but no, it is the dressing-gown, not the idea that is bad form; for if the dressing-gown is made in Japan instead of in Manchester, you may wear it. Many ladies of my acquaintance wear hat-pins and brooches inscribed with Chinese characters, but if these words, simple little messages like " happiness " and " good luck," were written in English, they would go without rather than wear them; for no person of taste places a sea-shell painted "A present from Margate" on the drawing-room shelf. And the moral of it all is that China will cut as incongruous a figure misusing our muskets as we figure miscutting her embroideries.

One evening after dark I walked over to the fair when the tumult of business was hushed, and found a group of Tibetans seated round their fire, preferring to sleep beneath the stars they knew and love so well rather than sleep beneath an alien roof. It is very peaceful under the dark pines, where the breeze stirs the big red and yellow lanterns which flicker over the tranquil water.

Next day I visited the horse bazaar, where fat Chinese merchants were to be seen riding Tibetan ponies up and down the meadow, before purchasing. The rider seated himself on a pile of bedding, thrust his heels into the stirrups, and balanced thus precariously with his knees under his arm pits, started off at a rapid trot.

It was now time to continue our journey, and having secured the services of a caravan returning to Chung-tien, I hired fifteen mules, bought loads of tea and sugar for barter among the Tibetans, and changed my Indian rupees for Chinese silver. Two days later, therefore, on May 16th, we left Li-kiang, and crossing the narrow plain, began to climb up out of the bowl. The snowdrop-trees rained silken petals on us, and the fragrance of many flowers saluted the nostrils. A chain of shallow valleys, linked together by wooded passes, led us in the evening to an open meadow, flanked by a group of snowy peaks. This place was called Kan-hai-tzu, or " dry lake " ; soon it would be converted into a marsh by the melting of the snow above, but now herds of sheep, goats and ponies wandered over the emerald-green turf. All round us surged the forest foaming into leaf, the shrill greens of cherry, birch and willow mingling kindly with the jealous yellows of maple and the generous wine-red of rowan ; sombre conifers chequered the bright slopes with shadow.

Camp was pitched on a knoll, during the passage of a severe thunder-storm ; the altitude was 10,616 feet.

Continuing our journey northwards, next day we descended by a steep stony path to the Yangtze. In the forest, the mule I was riding bolted and leapt down the narrow track, colliding with trees, and dashing violently in amongst the pack mules, causing considerable confusion and not a little pain to the rider.

The great river here flows north-eastwards, presently to hurl itself into the heart of the Li-kiang range, a spur of which we had just crossed. The steep slopes which confine it are dotted with villages, and cultivated below ; above are pine woods, and still higher, forests clothe the mountains.

On May 18th we crossed to the left bank in the ferry boat, a triangular flat-bottomed scow, large enough to take our fifteen mules, with their loads, and a dozen men across in one trip. However, the muleteers had a job to goad the last half-dozen animals into leaping the high gunwale. The ferry boat was now hauled up-stream under the lee of the bank, and launched into the river, where, caught in the swift current, it went spinning down-stream. Now the men sang in chorus, as they jerked the big fore and aft sweeps ; leaking badly, with the mules doing their best to capsize us, the clumsy scow was wafted slowly across and swung into slack water under the opposite bank, a hundred yards below the starting-point.

The ferry is a new one, started in connection with the telegraph line which runs from Li-kiang northwards to A-tun-tzu.[1]

We now left the Yangtze and turning up the gorge of the Chung river camped below the village of Chao-ch'iao-to. On May 19th, still following up the same turbulent stream, we camped on the wet hill-side at an altitude of 8101 feet, and next day crossed a pass, 10,605 feet, descending through forest bordered with tall scapes bearing whorls of golden flowers. This was *Primula chungensis*.

[1] The line was destroyed by the Tibetans in 1917, and has not been restored.

We camped in a clearing where stood two Lisu mat huts, scant protection against the cold wind; the temperature fell to within a few degrees of freezing in the night, and two of the mules wandered away and lost themselves.

Just below our camp a torrent rumbled through a narrow cleft between steep rocky slopes, to which sturdy pines clung like fur. On the rocks were purple orchids (*Pleione yunnanense*).

We had to start without the missing mules on May 21, leaving one of the men to prosecute the search. Ascending through pine woods, we came upon fragrant bushes of *Daphne calcicola* closely hugging the crumbled limestone cliffs. Anon the valley broadened, whimsically, and we entered undulating country, crossing sandy moors carpeted with pink and lavender-blue dwarf Rhododendrons; the latter *Rh. hyppophaeoides*, was not previously known. Later it was introduced into this country by Mr. George Forrest, and may be seen in many gardens. The highest point reached during this march was 11,688 feet. Nowhere was there a sign of human habitation; across the river gorge to the west, dreary firs stood with their feet in the snow, under a lowering sky.

We camped in an open meadow backed by a park of pine trees, with the Rhododendron moor beyond. There were patches of dwarf blue iris (*I. kumonensis*) in the park, and masses of snow-white *Primula chionantha* in the bogs, besides many other flowers; even the continuous drizzle could not dim the beauty of this spot.

II

Across the Chung-tien Plateau

THE missing mules turned up next morning, and we made a late start. After marching a few miles we left the wooded moorland and entered upon wide pastures, where herds of yak grazed. Presently, crossing a low spur, we found ourselves close to the Chung river again, now flowing swiftly between high banks of gravel. Here and there stood massive houses, surrounded by fruit trees. We were on the Chung-tien plateau.

The house in which we slept the night, and to which we were made welcome by the inmates, was scrupulously clean, the brass cooking pots and tea churns brightly polished. Not so the Tibetans themselves.

On May 23rd we traversed a series of shallow valleys hollowed out of the limestone. Here grew species of Meconopsis, Incarvillea, Iris, Morina, Pedicularis, and other alpines, but they were not yet in flower. Clearly the plateau is an old lake bottom—perhaps at one time a chain of lakes. Streams from the wooded slopes on our right had cut deep chines in the gravel terraces; to the west rose bold rocky ranges.

It was dusk when we reached the city of Chung-tien. After the cold ride across the grassland it was pleasant to enter the kitchen of the inn and warm oneself at the crackling fire. The leaping flames, curling round an immense iron pot in the centre, afforded the only illumination, and indistinctly lighted up the central pillar —a pine trunk so stout that I could not clasp my arms round it.

Presently a Chinese officer, followed by two soldiers, one of whom swung a gauze lantern a yard high, entered and accosting me with scant ceremony, spoke thus :

" Do you understand Chinese ? "

" Yes, a little."

" Where are you going ? "

" To A-tun-tzu."

" Have you a passport ? "

" Yes, from T'eng-yueh ; it is in my box ; I will send it to the *Yamen* to-morrow."

" You are stopping here to-morrow then ? "

" Yes, I have no mules yet ; the Li-kiang men do not wish to go any further."

The officer bowed and withdrew, and I was left to my own reflections.

Chung-tien is a quaint little city. The high-walled houses, roofed with shingles kept in place by stones, jut out irregularly into the narrow cobbled streets, which thread their crooked way through them. There are some three hundred Tibetan families here, and the great monastery, with several thousand lamas, is a few miles distant. A small Chinese garrison, nominally one hundred men, serves to keep those truculent people in check.[1] Chung-tien would be a splendid place at which to collect transport for a descent upon the fertile plains of Yun-nan, being 11,000 feet above the sea ; there is good grazing, but little agriculture.

---

[1] Ching-tien was captured by the Tibetans in 1917, during the war of independence. The Chinese have not yet recaptured it—or tried to.

The local Tibetans are cheerful, nice-looking folk. The women do their hair in three plaits, and a triangular cloth cap, like a baby's sun bonnet, is tied on the top of the head. On feast days, a gorgeously coloured apron is hung over the back and tied across the chest.

Most of the hills round the city are bare, though some are clothed with larch (*Larix tibetica*) and gnarled oak. Eastwards a limestone bulkhead rises to a height of several hundred feet, and behind this range is another broad valley through which a stream meanders northwards to a lake at the head of the plateau ; beyond that again are higher ranges, some of them where the Chung river has its source, covered with eternal snow. The striking yellow blossoms of *Daphne calcicola* gilded many of the limestone outcrops in the neighbourhood.

On May 23rd we started northwards once more, passing round extensive swamps gemmed with clusters of rose-pink *Primula fasiculata*. This little bog plant ramps over the black slime, smothering everything in its way. Through a valley to the east the sunshine glittered on the brazen domes of the great monastery, all red and white against the emerald-green turf.

At the extreme head of the plateau we came to a small lake, remnant of an extensive sheet of water ; but even this disappears in the winter. That was the last we saw of the verdant Chung-tien plateau with its marshes and flowers, its herds of yak, and its kindly Tibetans. Crossing a well-wooded pass, 12,535 feet, we left the high limestone ranges behind us and descended through lanes of golden-flowered pæonies to the village of T'an-tui, veiled in peach blossom ; then on through fragrant pine woods, still descending into drier regions, till the snow-crested Yangtze-Mekong divide filled the horizon.

We had women porters now, strangely clad in coarse trousers so baggy that they resembled skirts, an effect heightened by an apron hanging down back and front. The pig-tail is grotesquely swollen by the addition of wool which is plaited in with the hair, and the whole is bound on top of the head where it bulks large.

After two days we began to drop down more rapidly to the arid gorge of the Yangtze, the rusty red soil of the cultivated uplands giving place to barren gravel and rock, scantily clad with thorny bushes. Here grow *Indigofera calciola*, *Jasminum nudiflorum*, and *Clematis Delavayi*, its silken perianths just pouting their lips as they nodded on slender pedicels ; also ash-coloured twiggy bushes of *Justicia Wardii*, *Buddleia eremophila* and *Spiraea sinobrahuica*, all gasping for water. Shrivelled plants of *Campanula colorata* flowered listlessly in the dust with species of Lychnis and Arisaema.

At the dun-coloured village of Hsien-to, invisible against the sterile background, save for splashes of green walnut trees and pink peach blossom, we crossed a big tributary of the Yangtze ; then climbing a high spur, dropped into the long corridor of the great river itself.

The Yangtze here flows due south, so that it was difficult to convince oneself that it was the same river we had crossed ten days earlier. Eventually we reached the ferry at Pang-tzu-la and crossed to the right bank, where we found the people already reaping the spring wheat.

On May 31st we began the ascent of the formidable mountain barrier which still separated us from the Mekong, our baggage being carried by donkeys. Near the monastery of Tung-ch'u-ling the hill-sides were dappled with bushes of *Berberis concolor* which rained gold dust on the wind. It is a new species. There are many species of Berberis in western China, but none of them as fine as the Andine species—*B. Darwinii*, in depth of colour. Next day we entered the forest, following a stony track which grew rapidly steeper. The pines and stubby oaks of the dry forest were gradually replaced by fir trees, the tips of whose branches were trimmed with emerald-green bearing, like fat candles, the sappy purplish red cones; these in turn gave way to tree Rhododendrons, larch, and finally dour-looking junipers, their tawny masts often broken off short.

We camped that night at 13,000 feet amidst patches of melting snow and frozen-looking Rhododendrons, where tortured larch trees wrestled to the death with the inhospitable climate. On June 2nd we crossed a pass and reached the rolling plateau at the top of the Yangtze-Mekong divide. The summit of the range is conspicuously glaciated. It was a dreadful day, swift showers sweeping up the valley on the wings of the wind; eastwards the snowy peaks of the Pai-ma-shan range were muffled in cloud.

Tramping through snow, we crossed several streams which, flowing from the high rocky spurs to the east, trench deeply through the plateau to join the main glacier stream of Pai-ma-shan. By the roadside two dead mules, with frozen lips parted, grinned at us fixedly.

In the afternoon we crossed the Pai-ma-la, 14,800 feet, and struck the telegraph line to A-tun-tzu, erected in 1912.

There are two distinct passes here, one at either end of the plateau summit. According to Captain Gill, the northern pass is the lower. On General H. R. Davies' map only one pass, the Pai-ma-la, is shown, and that considerably higher than either of Gill's. It is not clear from the latter's route map which is the pass over the main watershed. Certainly there are two passes, and it is the northern pass, the Pai-ma-la, which crosses the main watershed; but I doubt if General Davies' map is correct when it shows the snowy range as a spur of the main divide. It appears to be the divide itself. The stream rising from the east flank of the snowy range, marked on Davies' map as flowing to the Mekong, really flows due south, and is the source of the Kari river. It flows therefore to the Yangtze.

Camp was pitched on a grassy alp at 12,000 feet. The rain continued all night; and when day broke, puling like a child, we could scarce see a hundred yards through the dense cloud.

Still crossing streams which flowed from the east, we traversed the slope high up, amongst ruby and emerald-budded woods, where cherry, maple, oak, currant, poplar, barberry, willow and Rhododendron were frothing into leaf. Underfoot mauve Primulas (*P. minor*) were opening their sleepy eyes and stretching themselves eagerly.

The mountain sides in many places presented a dismal aspect, for they were covered with charred pine forests, only the gaunt and blackened trunks still standing. In the bank numerous charcoal pits had been dug.

Ascending towards the last pass, which crosses a spur whence you drop down into the A-tun-tzu valley near its head, we halted for lunch in a grassy dell, where masses of white-flowered Rhododendron shone like snow. An Arisaema was in flower beneath the bushes, its tightly compressed leaflets not yet plucked from the ground by the growing stem. When at last the hoop is

c

dragged forth and straightens itself, the solitary leaf expands into an umbrella composed of numerous radiating spear-shaped leaflets, beneath which the spathe shelters itself. Many flies lay dead at the bottom of the mottled cup, imprisoned by the swelling ovules, and an enterprising spider was reaping a rich harvest among the victims.

Early in the afternoon we stood on the pass and looked down on the pale-coloured village of A-tun-tzu, nestling in a horseshoe of mountains. Picture the scene on a radiant afternoon, the barren valley, all steeped in sunshine, chequered with houses surrounded by shady trees and barley fields, little oases which gleam now like emeralds in a base setting, and in autumn one by one turn to gold as harvest time creeps up the valley; the flat-topped hill, full-fledged with flowering shrubs and crowned by the white buildings of the monastery; the crescent of mud-walled houses divided by a single cobbled street rising step by step to the little fort which forms the northern gateway; the whole embraced by high mountains, their lower slopes green with a patchwork of cultivation, their summits rising amongst the frayed clouds which sail across the azure sky.

Due west of the village rises A-tun-tzu mountain, well-timbered below; most of the surrounding slopes are, however, brush clad, being exposed to the hot dry wind which blows up from the Mekong gorge. Here are birch trees and silvery leafed Hippophäe, trembling poplars, willows, honeysuckle, currant, Desmodium, Indigofera Philadelphus, barbery, Cotoneaster and Rhododendron to mention a few.

Descending from the pass we presently reached a house over which a magnificent maple, breaking into

vivid leaf, threw a delicious shade. Its massive trunk
and wide-spreading branches bespoke age ; subsequently
I learnt that a Chinaman had offered the owner a hundred
taels of silver—about £12—for the tree as it stood. He
wished to make *tsamba* bowls out of it. Happily the
Tibetans, being fond of their trees and flowers, have
not yet reached that restless state symptomatic of
the materialistic mind, which wants to turn every natural
object into something manufactured, bought for cash.
He refused to trade.

A purple-flowered Buddleia (*B. incompta*) which grows
on the low gravel cliffs by the stream-side was in full
bloom. In the spring its leaves are like lacquered silver
beneath ; but in autumn the silver changes to gold.
However most Buddleias are very much alike.

I now settled down in A-tun-tzu and began to make
preparations for going into camp on the surrounding
mountains, there to search for new flowers. First I
engaged the services of a Chinese speaking Tibetan as
interpreter, besides two other Tibetans as collectors,
who, however, only worked for me intermittently ; these
three with my Chinese cook, Lao-wu, and my " boy "
Li, formed the staff.

One evening I sat down on the mountain slope beneath
bushes of Rhododendron aflame with blossom ; numbers
of tits chirped and hopped from bush to bush, poking
their heads inside the blotched corollas, seeking small
beetles. When the dazzle of sunset had been replaced by
violet dusk, I looked westwards across the Mekong valley
to the sacred mountain of Ka-kar-po,[1] and saw cataracts

---

[1] ᠊᠊᠊ "The white mountain." This is a famous sacred
mountain of eastern Tibet. "Kar-po" is a common name for snowy
peaks in this part of the country.

of splintered ice frozen to the cliffs over which they plunged ; close to the foot of the biggest glacier were several houses scattered over terraces of shining corn. My first journey, I decided, should be to the glacier valley.

N.W. Yun-nan had suffered from an exceptionally severe winter, and spring was late. Though the fine weather had at last begun, the average minimum temperature in A-tun-tzu for nine days (June 4th–12th) was only 43·4° F. (lowest 38·1° F. on June 4th) and the average maximum 66·1° F. (highest 70·5° F. on June 10th). Consequently I could not expect to find very much in flower yet at 13,000 or 14,000 feet, where snow still lay in many places.

There is a much-eroded limestone spire jutting up from the ridge behind A-tun-tzu among an ocean of Rhododendron and Abies. At its foot the snow lay in deep drifts down by the stream, where hemispheres of *Primula sonchifolia* gleamed blue in the cool shade. Pale-pink spikes of *Souliaea vaginata* were also in flower, though the leaves still slept in each other's embrace underground, and the sulphur-yellow poppywort, *Meconopsis integrifolia*, dared not show itself as yet. But the hill-sides were a maze of colour. Birch and maple trees breaking into bright green leaf vied with the wine-red foliage of trembling poplars, and surging round all the Rhododendrons were frothing into flower, whipped into waves of purple and ivory-white. Beneath golden barberry nodded grotesque slipper orchids, the liver-coloured *Cypripedium tibeticum* and the primrose *C. luteum ;* long tresses of snowy *Clematis montana* hung from the trees. Already the meadows were one gorgeous cohort of colour.

The summer solstice was celebrated in the village with

feasting and revel. After great preparations the previous night, the street was early deserted, everyone going off into the mountains to picnic. At dusk the happy people returned singing, with bunches of flowers; and the children played games in the mule square till the silver moon set and purple night enfolded the tired village in its embrace.

III

Flowers & Glaciers

WE did not wait to see the end of the festival, which lasted several days; but set out on June 12th for the Mekong, following a small track almost due west. This path crosses the southern spur of A-tun-tzu mountain, and after traversing the mountain side for some distance drops suddenly down into the Mekong valley.

Looking across the gorge from the pass, we caught a glimpse of vast forests yearning upwards towards the numb white silence, and of mute snowfields gradually quickening to riotous rivers of ice. It was our hunting ground.

After quitting the conifer forest, the hill-sides, at first dotted with magnificent flowered specimens of pink Azalea (*Rhododendron yunnanense*) rapidly became drier and more open, till finally, as the stream approached the Mekong, it fell over a precipice and shouldered its way noisily through a deep limestone gorge. Below this we again found ourselves in a region of extreme aridity, tree growth being confined to a narrow belt hugging the stream.

We slept the night at a village called Pu, where twenty or thirty houses are jammed together anyhow, leaving narrow dark lanes between. It was hot in the valley, for the breeze had died down and the minimum that night was 67° F.

Next morning we passed by a grove of fine junipers—
the *hsiang-mu-shu* or "scented-wood tree " of the Chinese.
Close by was the rope-bridge over the Mekong. The
two ropes, one slanting each way, are slung high above
the gorge, the steep and rocky cliffs of which, in the bed
of the river, are composed of greyish-green and red
shales, standing vertical and striking nearly north and
south.

While the loads and men were travelling across the
rope, a business which took an hour or more, I collected
plants and later seated myself on the rocks as close to
the river as possible, for I never wearied of watching
the rush of water. Here the surface heaves, and great
pustules swell up as though gas were being rapidly gener-
ated inside them, burst with a hiss, and pass on in swim-
ming foam ; there a ridge of water dances over a hidden
rock and breaks suddenly, and a little frothing wave
tries to crawl back by itself over the hurrying water, but
is swept hastily away, to re-form below ; a stick comes
frolicking down on the roaring tide, is buried for a
moment, and reappears a dozen yards away ; waves
spring up suddenly and slap insolently against the smooth
rock slabs, scored with grooves and pot-holes when the
flood rose higher than it does now ; and whirlpools dart
gurgling from place to place like will-o'-the-wisp. It is
a fascinating pastime to sit and watch all these ever-
changing tricks of the gambolling, shouting Mekong
waters, their voice rising throughout the summer, and
dying away to a whisper in winter as the red mud sinks
out of sight, and the water reflects the blue of heaven.

A climb of about a thousand feet up the steep cliff-side
brought us into the glacier valley, the roar of the Mekong
growing fainter as we ascended, till suddenly, crossing the

spur, it ceased altogether. Now our ears detected only
the shriller rattle of the glacier torrent. In front of us,
guarded by a white *chorten*, were the scattered houses of
Milong, the little path threading its way amongst
cultivated terraces, whose banks were smothered beneath
masses of golden St. John's wort, white jasmine and pink
Deutzia. Arrived at the chief's house, I sat down under
a weeping willow and had lunch while we changed porters
and made enquiries about reaching the glacier.

Above Milong a path led up the stony valley, crossed
the torrent by a wooden cantilever bridge, and ascended
great mounds of earth and rock fragments, covered with
flowering shrubs and trees—roses, barberry, Hippophaë,
Euonymus, Ailanthus, poplar, maple, willow, hazel and
many more. We were walking along the summit of an
ancient moraine 350 feet above the present ice level
and nearly a mile below the snout of the glacier.

Presently we entered the forest. Here one of the most
conspicuous features was a magnificent conifer with
very much the habit of a pine, and bearing small spherical
cones. The path skirts the extreme edge of a tremendous
precipice, at the foot of which flows the glacier, rent
by many longitudinal crevasses and numerous shallow
grooves cut out by streams, though otherwise the gently
curved surface of the ice was remarkably smooth. An
occasional echo as rocks and stones clattered into a crev-
asse was the only sound which floated up from below.

In some places the path was hacked out of the cliff
on our right, in other places it followed a natural ledge,
or a few logs were thrown across a gap in the cliff. Suddenly we came out into a small open space where stood
a *mani* pyramid, its base lapped by a surf of blue irises
frothing into flower. Here, on the very brink of the

precipice, stood a dilapidated temple, its courtyard overgrown with rank weeds, and round the wall, rows of leather prayer drums from which the stuffing had burst out in many places. The roof was of wooden slats, kept in place by stones.

So far the forest was composed very largely of conifers, with little undergrowth, but above the wooden temple, henceforth called the lower temple, we entered mixed forest. This is indeed the most conspicuous formation on the Mekong-Salween divide from Ka-kar-po southwards, and here a rich undergrowth surged round the trees.

The path no longer follows the cliff edge, but winds its way up the steep slope of the mountain. Just above the temple, many hundreds of feet above the glacier, is an unmistakable fragment of moraine, buried in the forest, evidently a continuation of the moraine below.

Numerous streams, at first sliding stealthily down bare rock slabs, presently leap over the precipice on to the glacier below. Finally we emerged on to a natural platform, where, on the very brink of the chasm, stood a second wooden temple.

Below, the cliff fell away sheer for hundreds of feet to the glacier, and we had a superb view of the snow peaks at the head of the valley, and of the wonderful ice-fall opposite : even as we looked there came a crack which brought us all to our feet in time to see a huge ice pillar sway for a moment, totter drunkenly, and fall with a roar that went bellowing down the valley, frightening a cloud of green parrots from the trees. So that was our greeting ! and indeed the thunder of avalanche and crumbling sérac was with us day and night, becoming more continuous as the summer advanced. By mid-summer the glacier for a long way below the fall was white with splintered ice as a rocky coast with salt sea spray. It seemed to me that the glacier must be moving at a fair pace to judge by the frequency with which these séracs toppled over the brink.

Behind the temple, thin rock bulkheads separating steep ghylls, develop into an array of pinnacles on the skyline as seen from below, though in reality they are not more than half-way to the ridge. The ridge itself, which was between four and five thousand feet above our platform, was invisible from below on account of the abrupt slope.

The path ended at the temple, and the sheer cliffs soon forbade any attempt to progress further up the valley or descend to the glacier. Consequently, movement in any direction except by the path down the valley, by which we had come, was cramped ; the climb behind the temple, in spite of a steep zigzag path leading up the ridge to a hermit's cave, a thousand feet above, was of the most arduous and sometimes hazardous description. As for the ramshackle temple, henceforward distinguished as the upper temple, it comprised but a single flat-roofed hall with a trinity of mud Buddhas at the back, and behind them, lining the wall, a wooden frame-work containing in pigeon-holes the bulky board-bound volumes of the Tibetan Buddhist scriptures ; a row of squeaky prayer drums outside, a cluster of poles from which fluttered the ragged remains of prayer flags, and an incomparable view of the snow peaks and the ice cataract below.

Of the glacier I must now proceed to give a more detailed account, because it is in itself evidence of a great change which is taking place in this region. To the

north rose the steep spur just described ; across the
glacier to the south, the view was shut in by the next
spur, covered with dense forest. Eastwards, down the
valley, we had a view of A-tun-tzu mountain, framed
between the two spurs and rising like a wall from the
Mekong gorge, while beyond that peeped up the jagged
crest of the Yangtze-Mekong divide.

One day I descended from the path, which, as already
explained, at first follows the crest of an old moraine,
and reached the foot of the glacier. This ends in a taper-
ing snout with several projecting tongues, a little over
a thousand feet above Milong village. The face of the
ice, where it had caved away, presented a curious honey-
comb appearance, the ridges being clearly outlined in
dirt, and except for small lateral crevasses, the surface for
the last few hundred yards of the glacier, though undulating, was peculiarly smooth ; above that, in the gorge,
where the moraine came to an end till the lower temple
was reached, longitudinal crevasses of great length
became prominent, and the surface was billowy. The
crevasses, no doubt, engulf everything which falls on
to the ice from the cliffs above ; there was not the vestige
of a moraine in the gorge itself, the ice flowing against
the cliff.

The surface of the glacier is distinctly convex in transverse section, owing to the more rapid melting of the
ice in proximity to the bare cliffs, especially on the left
or north bank, where the cliff faces due south. On this
bank, reaching from a point a little above the present
ice foot to within half a mile of the village lies the ancient
lateral moraine by which we had ascended. It exhibits
a double step structure, no doubt indicating two distinct
phases in the retreat of the ice to its present level.

From the base to the lower step, A in the sketch (p. 53), the moraine is bare of vegetation; then comes a narrow belt which is, so to speak, under cultivation; here plants are beginning to gain foothold, mostly small bushes of Hippophaë, Pyracantha, and Rubus with tufts of grass. The second ledge, A in the sketch, is 150 feet above the glacier, and the summit of the moraine B which is thickly overgrown with forest and traversed by the path between Milong and the lower temple, is 200 feet above the upper ledge. The fact that there is such a sharp distinction between the forest-clad moraine above, where vegetation has firmly established itself, and the bare earth slope below, suggests a periodicity in the retreat of the ice, to which the ledges referred to may be due. Beneath the trees, scratched stones occur, and on the other slope of the moraine, not yet obliterated by debris fallen from the cliffs above, deeply scored rocks may be seen.

Two or three hundred yards below the foot of the glacier, mounds of earth and rocks are piled high, but beyond that the material of the terminal moraine has been sorted and cut into gravel terraces by the stream, though the valley still preserves the deep U-shape in section associated with ice work, and evidence of the previous extension of the ice can be traced at least as far as the village, two miles away.

I asked the local people if the ice had ever extended further and they replied that forty or fifty years ago it had come further down the valley.

Crossing over to the right bank, facing north, there is no moraine to speak of either above or below the glacier foot, nor is there any sheer cliff; instead, the ice extends as a thin coating protected by earth only a little higher up the sloping wall, and above that comes bare rock and forest, or, towards the head of the glacier, alpine turf. The gulleys on both sides, however, debouch into the main valley high above the glacier, particularly on the left bank, where we were.

At the lower temple the glacier surface begins to grow very irregular, being ruckled by half-healed transverse crevasses formed at the ice-fall, with pressure ridges between them. The great ice-fall itself is situated far up the valley and ends almost opposite the upper temple.

The question one naturally asks is—how has this tremendous chasm been formed? Has it been laboriously ground out by the ice itself or was the mould ready prepared when the ice was first poured into it? The fact that the glacier once filled the gorge as shown by the moraine on the edge of the cliff near the lower temple, probably a thousand feet above the glacier of to-day, goes for little in face of the fact that the glacier is also proved to have retreated two miles, and as shown by its snout and terminal moraine, to be still retreating ; for it may merely have sunk passively to its present level owing to diminution in thickness of the ice, without ever having carved out the gorge at all. In fact, it is obvious that it must also have grown thinner while it was growing shorter.

It is a difficult problem. If the ice did not carve out the gorge, then it must either have been done by water or have a tectonic origin. Personally, I doubt if either water or ice could do the work alone.[1]

We stayed only three days at the upper temple as

[1] For a fuller account of this glacier see " Glacial Phenomena on the Yun-nan-Tibet Frontier," *Geographical Journal*, July, 1916.

facilities for exploring the valley were so extremely limited ; moreover the season was still too early for the spring flowers, many of the gullies above the upper temple being choked with snow. Yet the day temperatures were warm enough, the maximum shade temperature varying between 75° F. and 80° F. and the average minimum for the four days (June 14th–17th) being 56·1° F.

Meanwhile I had established myself in the main hall of the temple—not at all an imposing place—behind which were several other smaller rooms where the two or three priests dwelt. Buddhist hells, products of the fertile imagination of some Asiatic mind other than that of Gaudama, who preached no such doctrine, disfigured the wall above my bed, and the trinity of mud idols looked down on me throughout the night watches, without disturbing my slumbers ; sleep was broken only by the thunder of some falling sérac bursting like a shell in the brilliant moonlight.

At dawn the view eastwards to the orange sky beyond the black curtain of the Yangtze-Mekong divide, and the sun shafts presently spraying out behind its highest peak and darting across the Mekong valley, was a sight to sit and dream over.

So far I have said little about the flora of the glacier valley, between 10,000 feet (altitude of the lower temple) and 11,000 feet (altitude of the upper temple) and from 11,000 feet to the crest of the ridge overlooking the temple, about 4000 feet higher; except that it was composed chiefly of mixed evergreen and deciduous forest, rather open on the steeper slopes, with thickets of small trees and shrubs in sheltered places.

Many of the plants here mentioned were not yet in

flower, being, indeed, only discovered on a subsequent visit to the temple ; but it will be best to review here, however briefly, the vegetation as a whole.

On the first day of our visit we tried to reach the summit of the ridge behind the temple, soon discovering that, as already stated, what appeared from below to be the crest, though by no means easily attained, was in reality a long way from the top.

The start was made up a spur following a path through the forest, but when the path came to an end, we scrambled into a dry grassy gulley beyond. Thus we worked our way diagonally up the main valley in which direction the climbing became as a matter of fact more and more difficult, and incidentally, the crest of the ridge further and further above us. The almost vertical strata, striking north and south, had given rise to razor-edged ridges cut into shark-toothed pinnacles, and it was up and across these we had to find a way.

Once while resting our attention was drawn to the cliffs across the gulley, by a shower of rocks which fell suddenly from the precipice, and looking up, we saw several wild sheep, little dots high up on the cliff, nimbly leaping from rock to rock.

Round the temple were larches and huge Pseudotsuga trees, besides many shrubs, including *Celastrus spiciformis*, *Hydrangea heteromalla*, *Lonicera Henryi*, *Deutzia purpurascens*, and roses. Best of all was a superb Enkianthus massed with little bell flowers. In the open were patches of blue irises, and in the shade clumps of rose-flowered *Primula likiangensis*. About 12,000 feet the forest, at least on this side of the valley, facing south, became much thinner and more localised, small shrubs, especially barberry, occupying the steep broken ridges, with meadow flowers in the gullies ; but the meadow still slumbered and the rocks were dotted with tussocks of dry grass, hiding here and there a white-flowered Lloydia (*L. yunnanense*) or yellow lily. Later in the season there were all kinds of flowers here—Nomocharis, fragrant *Stellera chamaejasme, Morina Delavayi,* blue monkshood, Allium, *Primula pseudocapitata* and grass-of-Parnassus—to mention only a few. Still higher, where deep patches of snow lay in the shelter of the rocks, scattered fir trees alone survived of the forest, and the thickets of barberry were replaced by a tanglewood of Rhododendron.

After six hours' climbing, which I had found rather exhausting, for the day was hot and the work arduous, we halted at about 14,000 feet, just above the tree limit and a few hundred feet from the crest of the ridge.

The rock, like the vegetation, had changed, granite replacing slate. The spurs became broken up into fantastic tors separated by narrow chasms. On their sheltered sides, wet from the trickle of melting snow, were signs of a rich alpine flora, the few plants that were already in flower, such as the lovely little butterwort *Pinguicula alpina* and *Diapensia himalaica,* both pink and white varieties, occurring in such masses as to colour the rocks. This Diapensia is equally abundant on the Yangtze-Mekong divide, but the butterwort is more typical of the rainy Mekong-Salween divide, being common at the Do-kar-la, though it does lurk, a reluctant fugitive, on A-tun-tzu mountain ; whence, together with certain other living fossils making up a sort of floristic island, it has not yet been hunted by the changing climate. Here, in full daylight, the butterwort grew so thickly that the summit of one tall granite stack was painted a bright canary yellow.

The descent by a different route to that which we had followed on the way up was fairly easy, and we found ourselves on the path again in two hours; then, instead of dropping straight down to the temple, the grey wooden roof of which rose amongst the trees, a thousand feet below, we crawled round the base of a precipice and sought the hermit lama in his cave. Hither he retired periodically for contemplation. The lama received us hospitably, and offered us of his best buttered tea and *tsamba*. He had just finished his prayers, behind the curtain, and all the sorcery outfit—bell, book and candle, for exorcising devils and performing other miracles, was spread around the tiny cave where the lama slept and ate and prayed for days together. However, the outside of the cave was even more interesting than the inside, for on a slate cliff just above were great tufts of the lovely chrome-yellow *Primula pulvinata*, one of the Suffruticosa or woody stemmed section of perennial primulas. It lives to a great age, even perhaps for as much as a century, forming clumps as big as a cushion. The plant was in full bloom, the stems, each bearing an umbel of four or five fragrant flowers, scarcely rising above the dense cushions of dark green leaves which closely covered the matted stems below. The foliage is fragrant. This was a happy find, the species being previously unknown ; and seeds sent to England flowered at the Edinburgh Botanic Gardens in 1916.

With our backs to the cliff, we now looked down a steep gulley over the green tree-tops, straight to the glacier where it began to try and pull itself together at the foot of the fall. Séracs and fallen bergs were breathlessly jumbled together in boisterous confusion.

At night, in the glow of the full moon, the view of

D

the glacier from the temple was most impressive, the séracs looking like a long procession of ghosts, as they staggered one by one over the precipice, and slid from summit to base ; then I would start up from my sleep as the temple seemed to shake with the roar of an avalanche, and looking across the glittering gulf, see cascades of snow falling sheer for hundreds of feet from the hanging valley opposite, leaping from ledge to ledge and spattering the rocks below with frozen spume.

It was not till our second visit to the temple, at the end of July, that we succeeded in reaching the summit of the cliff above us. The gullies in July at 13,000–14,000 feet were full of meadow flowers, and the alpine region was carpeted with dwarf Rhododendrons, Cassiope, dwarf barberry, juniper and other plants similar to those found at Ka-kar-po camp.

On the crags at 14,000 feet we found a Meconopsis with rich purple flowers, but it was very rare, and always occupied places awkward to get at. A little lower down a dwarf Rhododendron with dull crimson flowers, a new species, was prominent on the rocks, and still lower was a red-flowered comfrey, whose stems, covered with long white silky hairs, made the plant very attractive.

Most beautiful of all were the forests below the upper temple, with the sunlight splashing between the trembling leaves and dancing with the shadows on the carpet of pale blue irises beneath. Here were maples and oaks, lindens, birch trees and a Pyrus, whose large silver-backed leaves turn glorious colours in the autumn. Other shade plants in the forest were Pyrola, *Vaccinium modestum* and a Spiranthes with variegated leaves, all of them uncommon. A feature of this forest was the number and variety of small birds which twittered amongst the trees. They were mostly dull browns, greys and blacks—not conspicuous, but none the less pretty, tits, fly-catchers, wrens, wood-peckers, thrush-like birds and many more. I have never seen so great a variety of birds before in one place. One had only to sit still under a tree for a few minutes and the curious little creatures came in numbers to look and chirp. One day I saw a troop of short-tailed monkeys, probably *Semnopithecus roxellanae*. Fancy monkeys at 10,000 feet!

On June 17th we started back for A-tun-tzu, and a little above the lower temple there stepped out on to the path to meet us, a black Himalayan bear. I was ahead of the porters at the time, and came straight upon him round the corner, only a few yards distant; but he quickly plunged into the forest where it was impossible to follow him.

We did not cross the Mekong at Milong, but continued down the valley high above the river, and descended to a village near the mouth of a stream, whence a path leads up the ridge to another temple, situated in a smaller glacier valley. The houses were scattered over a sickle-shaped platform bitten out of the bare river walls, with a few outlying farmsteads gleaming white between big shady walnut trees. Many little streams of crystal clear water are diverted from the mountain torrent and rattle down the stony paths, past hedges of pomegranate, all green and scarlet in summer, and pear trees whose fruiting branches are soon to be weighted to the ground between low stone walls covered with maidenhair ferns and polypodies, and through narrow lanes shaded by roses and scented jasmine, to the terraces below.

On every grey-white roof the golden corn is spread for threshing, and in the evening, men and women

stand round in a ring while the flails rise and fall rhyth-
mically.   Later on appears a solitary figure, dark against
the evening sky, holding a basket and whistling for a wind
to come and float the chaff away as she pours out the
grain in a thin stream.   At sunset, small grubby children,
scantily clad in goat-skins, like ancient Britons, idly drive
home the flocks of goats that have been feeding all day
on the stiff spiny shrubs of the arid valley.   It is all very
quiet and peaceful, with the thunder of the river instead
of the roar of traffic, mountains rising on every hand
instead of great buildings, travellers from distant parts
of Asia, with the far-away look of the wide world in their
eyes, leisurely passing to and fro instead of the constant
stream of preoccupied men hurrying by with bowed
heads ! What do they know of cities, these nomads !

There was a big famished mastiff tied up outside the
house where we spent the night.   This dog gave me
a hostile reception every time I ascended or descended
the ladder (for the ground floor was occupied by cattle)
till an old lady threw it some goat-skins and ragged
brown skirts to lick ; then he occupied himself hunting
for fleas and lice long treasured up in them, devouring
with relish such as he discovered !

Next morning we crossed the river.   The main rope
was partly under water, and where not immersed, vibrated
like a tuning fork with the rush of water.   But a
second rope had been rigged close by, and though we
went perilously close to the chocolate-coloured water
at the lower end, we got over without mishap.   Last to
be slung across the now sagging rope was one of the
ponies, and scarcely had he started when a plume of
smoke rose into the air from the slider, owing to the
tremendous friction against the splintered bamboo.

Flowers & Glaciers

It was touch and go, for the smoke column grew in volume every second. Would the unfortunate animal ever reach the far bank? Ten yards from shore he struck the hurrying water with a splash; the slider, now almost on fire, stopped dead, and the pony hung immersed to his belly, thoroughly frightened, churning the water ineffectually, till two men swarmed along the rope and dragged him safely ashore, none the worse for his adventure.

Crossing the high spur above us, we reached A-tun-tzu in the afternoon, having been absent a week.

There had been no rain here during our absence, and we stepped straight from grey skies into bright sunshine on the other side of the spur.

SECTION ACROSS GLACIER FOOT, KA-KAR-PO.
(MEKONG-SALWEEN DIVIDE)

The section is not drawn to scale and the slopes are exaggerated.

A B C Ancient moraine, A is 150 feet above the ice level at C and B is 200 feet above A.

A C Gravel and earth with scratched stones at the top. Bare below, shrubs higher up.

A Ledge or shelf

A B Boulders covered with forest.

Forest

Bare rock or earth

Ice level

IV

The Meadows of Do-kar-la[1]

IT was late in June when we started for the Do-kar-la, or "white stone pass," which is on the pilgrims' road round the sacred mountain called Ka-kar-po. Crossing the Mekong by the rope bridge we pitched camp below the forest, where on the dry ash-coloured limestone rocks, *Androsace coccinea* was in flower. It is a lovely plant with its tight rosettes of wee leaves, and close heads of rich cinnabar-red flowers. But it is not hardy.

On the following day we entered the pine forest, where oaks and milk-white Rhododendrons (*Rh. decorum*) also grew ; and in the afternoon, being held up by an avalanche which had ploughed across the path, camped by the torrent. All round us grew giant trees, most noticeable being the Conifers, Picea and Pseudotsuga. Crouching between them were many shrubs, species of Ribes, Hydrangea and Euonymus ; woody climbers flung their branches in every direction—here were *Aristolochia moupinense, Sabia yunnanensis,* Akebia, Actinidia, and others ; on the moss-grown boulders by the noisy torrent were Pyrola, Spiranthes and even a yellow-flowered Impatiens. A Crawfurdia with quaint polony-like fruits twined itself happily round the bamboo stems.

Next day we clambered across the wreckage piled up

---

[1] རྗེ་དཀར་འལ་ Written Doker-la on most maps.

by the avalanche and ascended through the heart of the forest. There were more flowers by the way-side— Corydalis, speckled cuckoo-pint and purple columbine, besides fragrant hyacinth, but the forest undergrowth was scarcely awake as yet. In September it stood six feet high ; while trumpet lilies towered above the ferns and meadowrue, whose purple-beaded flowers nodded amongst leaves of maidenhair which spread fanwise over them.

So we continued with many a check caused by fallen trees and avalanches, till the valley broadened out into sun-kissed meadows ; and here flowers clustered round red-stemmed birch trees. Frail yellow poppies curtsied to us as we passed, travellers' joy lolled over bushes, sprawling languidly here and there, and the purple panicles of tamarisk, in the pebble beds by the stream, waved in the breeze like plumes. Then came a heath composed entirely of dwarf Rhododendrons prostrate beneath the willow trees with pouting perianths borne single or in pairs on slender pedicels, rose-pink, purple and bright canary-yellow. They included several new species, as *Rh. chamaetortum, Rh. gymnomiscum.*

We pitched camp by the chattering stream where the meadow was blithe and gay ; higher up, bottle-necked gullies, choked to the mouth with rocks and snow, had vomited everything into it. Here dense bamboo brake disputed the ground with fir forest. Down below on the wetter ground bamboo prevailed, but amongst the tumbled boulders and on the precipices above, Abies, though ragged and forlorn, ever triumphed.

Immediately opposite the spot selected for our camp, the pilgrims' path left the main valley, and climbing steeply up the high granite wall in short zigzags, entered a broad hanging valley which led to the pass. But here the meadow was blanched and bleak, the flowers yet torpid ; snow lay in the corries, melting reluctantly.

August had come before the meadow reached its zenith. Then indeed we waded knee-deep through a sea of flowers. There were pink Nomocharis and mute bells of Codonopsis, lavender blue with crimson veining, *Primula pseudosikkimensis*, like stately cowslips of daffodil yellow, blue cowls of monkshood, purple columbine and the crowded corymbs of *Aster fuscescens*, which last has been raised in England from my seed. Here and there the band of meadow walled in by towering granite cliffs is interrupted by thickets of willow scrub and Rhododendron, or dotted with birch, alder and cherry trees ; the latter were now in bloom.

Above the meadow are alpine pastures strewn with jewel flowers. Here *Primula bella* stares at heaven with sightless violet eyes, and the porcelain-blue trumpets of *Gentiana heptaphylla* recline in nests of mossy foliage. The former belongs to a group of Primulas characterised by having the throat stuffed up with a wad of hairs. This doubtless protects the essential organs from damage by rain ; but were the plant less widely spread, one might suspect it of grievously interfering with pollination. Here also the neat rosettes of *Phlomis rotata* and *Primula brevifolia* cower against the grey gravel.

Trapped between granite cliffs several hundred feet high, the only way out was up one of the flues which slit the walls of our prison. These flues had vomited out cone-shaped screes which spread fanwise into the valley ; below were massive boulders, covered with a dense growth of shrubs ; towards the apex the carpet of vegetation was striped with long gashes, flogged raw by the continual rain of stones. To reach the topmost cliffs, one had to buffet a way through the bamboo brake, scramble from boulder to boulder amidst tangled shrub growth, and finally ascend the slipping gravel which grew ever steeper, to the broken rocks; then climb up by narrow chimneys, clinging precariously to dwarf bushes. Everyone's life hung on a chance. I have lain awake in my tent when moonlight flooded the meadow and listened to the roar of the rock avalanche rolling from cliff to cliff; and looking across the valley, all black and silver, when the frantic noise has died away to a whisper, and only the owl is hooting gently, and the stream humming to itself, seen the white fog of dust hovering over our own gully—the very one we had climbed that afternoon. And I have raced across the scree for my life, and ducked panting under the friendly shelter of a cliff.

In some places the shrub thickets were composed entirely of Rhododendron—*R. Wardii* with lemon-yellow flowers and *R. pagophilum* with rose-pink flowers. The former has flowered in England from my seed, and is highly spoken of, both for its fine foliage and for its flowers. It is quite hardy. Elsewhere grew species of Lonicera, barberry and willow, small maple and birch trees, a dwarf raspberry bearing a bumper crop of delicious fruit, and *Potentilla fruticosa*.

On the steep gravel the fat maroon poker-heads of *Polygonum Griffithii*, bowed amongst the polished sea-green leaves, and trusses of crimson *Rhododendron sanguineum* crouched against the rocks, were conspicuous.

The wet cliff ledges were lined with the creeping moss-like stems of *Cassiope palpebrata*, whose delicate milk-white corollas glance down shyly from their slender

stalks ; and from the crevices depended magnificent
bunches of pale violet *Isopyrum grandiflorum*, its shimmering flowers, like chalices of egg-shell china, far larger
than anything ever met with in this widespread plant
before. There is a much poorer variety found on the
drier limestone rocks of the Yangtze-Mekong divide.
My Do-kar-la plant has flowered in England ; some day
perhaps it will be known as *Isopyrum grandiflorum
magnificum*.

On the cliffs, too, was a carpet of dwarf Rhododendron,
including two pretty little species *R. oresbium*, with
lilac flowers, and *R. chryseum* with flowers of pale gold.
These grew like heather, their tangled stems interlocking
to form a continuous mat. *Rh. chryseum* has flowered
in this country, from seed collected by Mr. George
Forrest, who has introduced a large number of species.

A mile above our camp, the main valley was blocked
by a granite cliff over which water poured in a thin cascade ; but the stream had carved a passage through for
itself. From the valley above, which was reached by
climbing a gully, thus outflanking the cliff, we could see
down the valley, past the open meadow where the smoke
from our fires hung blue in the air, to the forest below.
Huge blocks of stone were perched here and there by
the stream. Above was the snout of the southernmost
glacier on Ka-kar-po, which had once upon a time tumbled
over this cliff and swept far down the valley, planing the
rocks, carrying those great erratics, and filling the valley
with ice to the level of the hanging valley opposite our
camp.

During a week (June 26th–July 2nd) spent in the
meadow, it rained every day—heavy drizzles sailing up
the valley, or sudden showers swooping down from the

pass ; yet the total rainfall was only 0·85 in. The average minimum temperature at 13,000 feet was 41·8° F., and the maximum 58·2° F., though one day it rose as high as 66·5° F. The barometer was always high in the morning and fell gradually throughout the day, the extremes noted being 20·12 in. and 19·74 in.

Many were the devices of the flowers to cope with the everlasting rain mists, which blanket the Do-kar-la in summer. In some genera, such as Nomocharis and Meconopsis, the flowers hang their heads ; or they are completely pendant, like tubular bells, as in species of Codonopsis, Cassiope, Lonicera, *Primula brevifolia* and others ; *Isopyrum grandiflorum* hangs head downwards from the cliffs ; the erect flowers of many gentians close when a cloud passes over the sun, and, their tubes being pleated, shut tightly as soon as it begins to rain ; sunshine opens them again. The throat of *Primula bella*, another erect species, is stuffed with a dense wad of hairs, and in some of the dwarf Rhododendrons, the flowers stand on edge.

Voles and pigmy hares abounded in the wooded meadow. The latter, like guinea-pigs, have no tail, and the soft grey fur and large ears give to the pinched little face a very hare-like expression.

Speckled sand-flies were a great plague by day ; the more it rained the more they bit, so that our necks and wrists suffered greatly.

On July 3rd we broke camp, reaching Londre, just above the Mekong, next day. Here I was invited to attend a small boy, who, while herding goats on the hillside, had been felled by a stone avalanche.

At first I could see nothing, but as my eyes became accustomed to the gloom I made out the patient lying almost naked, on a heap of filthy skins. His face was pale and drawn, his limbs wasted, his close-cropped hair appeared caked with dirt; otherwise I could see no sign of injury. It was stifling in the room, temperature over 80° F. and the polluted atmosphere was alive with flies; a loathsome sour smell clung to the dim place. I asked for more light and they slid back the wooden windows.

Presently came a wrinkled old woman, who seated herself beside the boy and fanned his head with a bunch of withered flowers. Instantly, with an impatient buzz, there rose into the air such a cloud of flies that I involuntarily recoiled, horrified, and saw exposed in the boy's head, a frightful wound. This, then, was the secret of the caked dirt, this gash which had been filled to the brim with hundreds of hungry flies jostling for a place. Even now they settled down again to their ghastly scavenging and rose momentarily at intervals as the old woman flicked them!

The wound was four days old, and all they had done was to plaster it with mud to stanch the flow of blood; there the boy lay on his poor dirty couch of rags, stiff with gore, while his old grandmother tried to afford him some relief by stirring up the flies! That was his one consolation—to hold the old lady's withered hand in his, while she soothed him in his agony. Then, opening a window which let in a flood of golden sunshine, I set to work.

The Londre river, formed by the confluence of two streams flowing from the Do-kar-la and the Londre-la, cuts its way through a narrow gorge to the Mekong. The village of Londre is situated at the bifurcation, about five miles back from the river. One more march up the Mekong valley, where the temperature did not fall below 71° F. at night, and the restless flies in the dark, sour-smelling Tibetan houses gave us no peace, and A-tun-tzu was reached on July 7th.

During our absence my room had been entered, a box forced, and some silver stolen. The incident leads me to comment upon the local authorities. A-tun-tzu was at this time a haven of refuge for black sheep along the border, the garrison especially being as scurvy a set of knaves as could be found in all the far west ; nor had the kuan-tai, or commander, himself a savoury reputation. Lin was his name, a tall man with arbitrary features and shifty eyes. He had recently burked a murder case, and was commonly reputed to have embezzled money intended for the soldiers, who were paid at irregular intervals. Being a man of volcanic temper and malignant disposition this tyrant amongst a rabble of soldiery was left to his own devices ; but being frequently impeached at the capital, he was finally cashiered. In order to avoid unpleasantness, he left quietly one summer night !

Chao, the civil mandarin, was a horse of another colour. Intellectual looking, with the air of an ascetic, he was always icily polite ; but his sour smile would have provoked mutiny in legions. As is commonly the fate of reformers, he was cordially hated by the merchant class, in that he waged incessant warfare against their opium smoking habits and had introduced a measure to tax all musk which passed through the village. Now the musk trade is by far the most important on the border.

During the next ten days I made several ascents of the limestone spire already referred to. From the cracked white cliffs facing A-tun-tzu hung bunches of *Isopyrum grandiflorum* and *Potentilla peduncularis*—an unlovely plant, but bountiful; and the honeycombed ridge bristled with squat bushes of Caragana whose flesh-pink flowers and bloated pods nestling in the silvery grey foliage, were pretty. The north side of the pinnacle was enveloped in Rhododendron and Abies ; this little wood was always full of pheasants, both tragopans and snow-cock (*Crossoptilum sp.*) They always went about in flocks of a dozen or more. Under the trees here grew the rosy *Primula likiangensis* and *P. septemloba ;* and on the limestone ledges I came across the creeping *P. annulata*, as well as the little canary-yellow alpine butterwort, *Pinguicula alpina*, already referred to. This lures me to make an observation.

Pinguicula alpina is common on the Mekong-Salween divide, but so far as I know occurs nowhere on the Yangtze-Mekong divide save on this outlying peak.

Now the floras of these two parallel ranges, separated only by the gorge of the Mekong river, are strikingly dissimilar. The much heavier rainfall of the Mekong-Salween divide sufficiently accounts for this. And yet cowering away on this outlier of the Yangtze-Mekong divide we do find a few plants, properly reckoned among those of the Salween divide—this butterwort for example, with species of Ribes and Euonymus.

The explanation seems to be—and this idea is borne out by the retreat of the ice from the eastern ranges— that the Yangtze divide once supported a flora similar to that of the Salween divide (both being derived from a common source), and that as a result of increasing desiccation it has lost it, evolving a flora of its own in harmony with the drier conditions. These living fossils are the remnants of this earlier flora which elsewhere has disappeared from the range. There is certainly no reason to regard them as directly derived from the western range. If such transport of seeds from range to range took place, we should expect to find in favoured localities on the Yangtze range Salween plants whose seeds are better adapted to long journeys than those enumerated—the wind-borne seeds of *Primula Franchettii* for instance. Yet they have not been found. It may indeed be questioned whether the seeds of alpines are ever capable of transport over big distances.

Moreover if seeds can reach the distant Yangtze divide from the Salween range, how much easier for the Salween plants to travel northwards along the same range! Yet north of Ka-kar-po the Salween flora more closely resembles that of the Yangtze range than it does that of the Salween range south of the snowy mountains. At this point we must seek the dividing line further west, between the Salween and the Irrawaddy.

The plants peculiar to the ranges east of the Mekong are such as enjoy a dry climate, for example, *Primula septemloba, Androsace spinulifera, A. coccinea, Delphinium yunnanense, Meconopsis Prattii* and *Codonopsis convolvulacea.* Those confined to the western ranges are, on the contrary, plants of wet meadows and moist rocks— *Primula Franchettii, P. serratifolia* and *Cassiope palpebrata.* Plants which are as common on one range as on the other, for instance *Primula brevifolia, Meconopsis speciosa, Cassiope fastigiata* and *Diapensia himalaica,* are all high alpines ; and it is at very high altitudes that conditions on the two ranges most nearly approach each other. Many of the alpines are indeed identical, while others are represented by microforms, that is closely related species, on the two ranges ; for example, *Primula dryadifolia* on the Yangtze divide is represented by *P. philoresia* on the Salween divide. Doubtless the similarities outweigh the differences, and we may regard the floras of these twin ranges as being in a condition of progressive differentiation.

One evening I was invited to dinner with the local Chinese merchants. At five o'clock we sat down ten at a table, some thirty guests in all. Everyone was provided with a pair of chop-sticks and a china wine cup, but there were no napkins, and the Chinamen used their sleeves freely. No ladies were present ; they are as rigorously excluded from these functions as from a college " hall " at Cambridge. Half-naked cooks now came dashing in from the kitchen next door with steaming bowls full of chopped liver, sprouting beans, pickled eggs, sea-cucumbers, birds' nests, sharks' fins, bamboo shoots, and other exotic delicacies. Then armed with chop-sticks, we all set to, finicking in the bowls for tit-bits like a flock of sparrows. Presently the wine began to circulate, and to the business-like clapping of chop-sticks, and curious noises made by obese Celestials shovelling hot rice into capacious mouths was added uproarious laughter. I say wine, but that is a poetic licence. It is called *shao-chiu* or burning spirit ; it is the colour of gin, and tastes like methylated spirit. Luckily the wine cups are no bigger than liqueur glasses, since you must drink ; to refuse would be a serious breach of etiquette. Moreover it is necessary to play for drinks three rounds with each guest at your table : a strange game, showing fingers and shouting a number. Every time you shout the number corresponding to the

total of fingers shown, you lose—and drink forfeit.
A rapid calculation assured me that I was in imminent
peril of twenty-seven drinks ; but happily I won several
times. The fun waxed fast and furious. Men were
shouting across the room to each other, rocking with
helpless laughter. At this point the tables were cleared
and the cooks came rushing in again with what at first
I mistook for clay-coloured pancakes ; however, they
turned out to be only hand towels dipped in hot water
and wrung out. Each guest received one, and now red-
faced men mopped their fevered brows. Finally chop-
sticks were wiped clean on sleeves and put away, and the
guests, talking and laughing noisily tumbled out into
the street ; as for me I went to bed and stayed there
quite a long time.

Rain began to fall in A-tun-tzu now, though the total
for nine days, July 7th to 17th, was only 0·26 in., and
we enjoyed plenty of sunshine. The average minimum
temperature during the same period was 52·7° F., the
average maximum 68·7° F.

There were many butterflies abroad during the summer
but mostly of widely spread genera and indeed species—
familiar chalk-blues, orange-tips, Apollo and tortoise-
shell. To obtain the large and more brilliant Papilios,
bugs, beetles and praying mantises, one must go down
into the hot Mekong valley.

Crossing the mountains into the Salween valley,
however, one steps into quite a new world ; here insect
life is far more prolific, showing relationship with that
of India and Burma. The Mekong-Salween divide in
fact is a barrier of some significance ; not only does it
separate a flora mainly Indo-Malayan from another

E

which is mainly Chinese or Eastern Asiatic ; it also marks the boundary between the Oriental and Palaearctic zoological regions.[1]

On July 15th we left A-tun-tzu once more, this time to attack the Ka-kar-po glaciers again.

[1] See "The Mekong-Salween Divide as a Geographical Barrier," *Geographical Journal*, July, 1921.

V

Ka-kar-po, the Sacred Mountain

IMAGINATION, taking to flight, is prone to outstrip probability, so that the traveller readily entertains a pleasant, yet often quite groundless thrill of anticipation at the discoveries he expects to make. This was my experience when, from the top of the pass, I once more looked across to those cold white peaks and thought of all the floral treasures which might lie concealed amongst their steep glaciers, poised above the Mekong valley.

Following the same route as on our previous journey, we crossed A-tun-tzu mountain and descended to the scorching valley, to find bare fields and women threshing the corn at Pu. The people of this village are extremely dirty and goiterous. Though friendly, they are rather shy with strangers. Yet what good-hearted creatures they really are! Shall I ever forget the scene in the *visi's* house, where I was invited to stay! A small naked child sat by the fire nursing a sick goat, on one side of him a big grey cat gazing through half-shut eyes at the embers, on the other a small wire-haired dog, like an Aberdeen terrier, half asleep; and scuttling to and fro, now into the cool darkness of the room, now out again into the sunshine, a number of tiny fat porkers which were only just learning how to grunt in a tone calculated to disclose contentment. I have frequently seen Tibetan children hugging puppies, baby pigs, or cats, and carrying them about like dolls ; for they are fond of animals, and, with the exception of their pack-donkeys, which they work to death, treat them kindly on the whole.

Next day, July 16th, we crossed the river and ascended to Milong, where the people collecting round the *visi's* house, again welcomed me in the most friendly spirit. Here stood a weeping willow whose graceful and homely appearance were delightful, though my pleasure was not unalloyed with a feeling of respect, since the tree attracted thousands of bees, which were engaged in imbibing honey-dew from the foliage.

After changing porters at Milong, we crossed the glacier stream and began the direct ascent of the opposite spur. Everywhere the lower slopes reflected in their crumbling stony soil, dotted with compact blue-green bushes of Sophora, the aridity of the valley below. Presently the shrub growth became thicker and with it there appeared small trees of the feathery five-needled Yun-nan pine (*Pinus excelsa*) as well as the three-needled species (*P. longifolia*), and scrubby oaks infested with bunches of Loranthus ; till after a climb of some 2000 feet we finally entered real forest on the crest of the spur, and threw ourselves under the trees for a rest.

We were now on a shoulder of that same spur whose crest I had already tried to reach from the upper temple. Eastwards it fell away steeply to the Mekong, while by travelling along the crest I hoped to reach a camping ground near the snow-fields and directly above the great ice-fall on the temple glacier.

At first it looked as though we might succeed, for there was quite a good path along the crest of the spur ; however, my hopes were dashed, for the path ended presently by a tiny pool of very muddy water, and I realised that this was probably all the water we should find. There was just enough room by the water-hole to pitch the tents, but it was obvious that we were still some distance from that point on the ridge immediately overlooking the temple, and certainly several thousand feet below the alpine region ; so I pushed on, and at once began to encounter difficulties. Tree growth was displaced by a dense tangle of bamboos festering in a damp lichen-haunted darkness ; their dead haulms stretched out in every direction across a track which rapidly became more and more obscure ; their living stems grew so thickly as to confuse one's sense of direction.

After picking and pushing my way through this for half an hour, the growth became so dense that, reconnoitring ahead of the porters, I had to confess to myself, not only was there really no path at all, but that I might even experience some difficulty in finding my way back ; for I had abandoned the crest of the ridge altogether in order to follow the line of least resistance. However, shouting to the porters below, I presently picked up the trail again, and we all reunited at the water-hole to discuss matters. Dusk had now fallen.

It was evident that we should never reach our goal by following this spur, for the porters with their loads would not be able to break through the bamboo fence I had encountered above. Even had they been able to do so there was the further difficulty of obtaining water, and finally it was doubtful whether we should find any place to pitch our tents. The Tibetans, too, half of whom were women and girls, were becoming mutinous and wanted to camp where we were, saying that there

was a path up the next spur to the north, and that it
would be much easier to reach the alpine regions I sought
by that route ; so having firmly black-balled the pre-
posterous suggestion to camp by the water-hole, I rather
disgustedly gave the order to retire, and we descended
almost to the Mekong again. We did not, however,
recross the glacier stream to Milong, but continued
down the spur to the next village above Milong called
Silong, in anticipation of our attempt on the glacier to
the north.

It was long after dark when we got in, and but for the
brilliant moonlight, we should certainly have found the
steep rock-strewn path difficult ; as it was, we stumbled
and blundered into each other in the narrow lanes, and
were glad enough when our whoops elicited in reply the
barking of dogs. Presently the unbarring of a gate,
followed by the flare of pine torches, burning pale in
the silver moonlight, announced our arrival.

Next day we continued up the left bank of the Mekong
for a short distance, ascending to a considerable height
above the river, and then turned up another valley.
Across this, perched on the opposite spur, we caught
sight of a small village. The path—I might almost say
road here—was, like all Tibetan paths in the arid Tsa-rong
regions I have ever travelled over, excellent and con-
toured the mountain side for over a mile. Alongside
the path a channel had been dug, and water led from the
stream higher up flowed swiftly on its way to the village
several miles distant. The slope was well wooded, and
shading the aqueduct were many spindle trees (Euonymus).
Descending steeply to the torrent, we crossed by a
cantilever bridge, as it was impossible to get any further
up the valley, towards the fir forests whose spires grizzled

the sky, nor could we from here see either glacier or snow peaks, all being hidden by a big shoulder.

The climb up to the village in sunshine was hard work, for the path went almost straight up a spur ; even the sturdy little ponies found it steep, and frequently halted gasping. However, towards the top we found shade beneath oaks and pine trees, and soon after reached the village—half a dozen houses huddled together in the midst of a few cultivated fields. Here we rested for lunch.

The path through the forest above followed the crest of the spur, and though steep in places, was quite good enough for ponies as far as our first camping ground. This was situated in a meadow shut in all round by pink-flowered Rhododendrons and conifers, some of which were very fine trees. A Pseudotsuga I measured was 19 feet in circumference, 5 feet from the ground, and many of them must have been upwards of 120 feet high. The birches and maples too were magnificent, finer than anything I had seen at the Do-kar-la, though the undergrowth which was now just coming into flower was less luxuriant. It is worthy of remark that in these forests the undergrowth flowers in the summer, after the trees are fully clothed with leaves, and not, as in English woods, during the early spring when the trees are first fledged.

We pitched camp early in the afternoon at an altitude of 12,692 feet, and the Tibetans, promising to rejoin us early next morning, returned to the village below with the riding ponies, which they said we could take no further. It was a lovely evening, the moonlight filtering through the forest into our flowery retreat, and sprinkling the meadow with silver ; but the sand-flies were very bad, making sleep for a long time impossible.

On the following day, July 18th, the porters turned up in good time, bringing two or three ponies after all, and we continued the ascent by a steep path through the forest, keeping along the crest of the granite spur ; there was only one place where we had any difficulty with the pack animals, their loads having to be taken off and lifted over a ledge of rock. Gradually maples, Rhododendrons and Picea trees gave place to silver fir which alone composed the upper forest ; the undergrowth too had changed.

And then, quite suddenly as it seemed, the phalanx of trees broke, struggled forward in dismayed attack, and was finally wiped out altogether. We had crossed the frontier of another world. Now we found ourselves on a rocky shoulder of the spur. Flower-starred rock mounds alternated with deep hollows full of scarlet scrub Rhododendron ; *Rh. sanguineum* and *Rh. gloccigerum*, and the banks grew *Primula bella* and the rare *P. albiflos*, a mangy looking species which I had discovered in 1911, hiding under bushes of pink Rhododendron ; nests of staring crimson *Primula philoresia* coloured the rocks, and large white-and-gold flowered poppyworts were scattered about—this last evidently a pale form of *Meconopsis speciosa*.

Then we turned the corner and there, right above us, rose the snow mountains of Ka-kar-po, buttressed by great rocky saw-edged spurs whose feet stood in the Mekong ; far below on our left, crawling down from the snow-fields, which foamed in frozen fury between the peaks, tumbled the riven glacier, disfigured at one spot where the ice had peeled off the precipitous rock bed, by an ugly black lozenge-shaped scar. Northwards, across a valley stuffed with moraine material half burying

a remnant of glacier, where the Ka-kar-po range begins
to drop to the 16,000-foot notch of the Shu-la, affording
easy access into Tibet, the sunshine glowed hot on the
red cliffs of Tsa-rong ; and behind us, over the slanting
forests and across space, the Yangtze-Mekong sierra
stood out bold as a castle wall for a distance of fifty mile
from Pai-ma-shan in the south, to beyond Tsa-ka-lo in
the north.

Though the wild array of ragged ridges and bludgeon-
headed towers which splinter the skyline are no longer
snow-clad, yet through the glasses I could recognise many
a barren cirque and valley through which glaciers had
once forced triumphant passage. At dawn the scene
is superb. As the faltering light gradually grows brighter
behind it, straining the heavens, every peak and pass
stands out like cut card, black as ink ; presently golden
beams flicker between the peaks and slanting across the
slumbering valley, glitter on the snows of Ka-kar-po.
And the mountain world awakes.

We pitched camp at an altitude of 14,136 feet right
on the side of the spur where the trees died out, in a
meadow of blue Primulas and white Anemone. There
was a rude hut here—four low walls of piled stones roofed
with branches, built by the herdsmen who bring their
yak up to these pastures in the summer ; and just
sufficient level ground to take my tent. A path led down
the slope on our left to a spring some distance away, and
we were protected to the north by the crest of the spur
rising a hundred feet or so above camp.

It had taken us only two hours to reach this place,
and the Tibetans after helping us to arrange the new
camp, returned to their village, leaving us in possession—
two Chinamen, two Tibetans and myself. The day was

dull and chilly, a raw wind blowing up from the valley carrying rain and smudging the snow peaks with cloud.

After a preliminary excursion up the ridge in the afternoon, I turned in early, and was startled out of my sleep about one o'clock in the morning, as the tent was flapping violently ; just then a rope gave way, and one end of the tent threatened to collapse altogether. It was blowing a gale from the east, the full fury of which caught us in our exposed position, and the rain was coming down in sheets, accompanied by lightning ; pitch darkness completed the confusion. As my tent was in danger of giving way altogether and the rain was being flung inside, I slipped on a dressing-gown and dashed across the intervening space to the hut, only to find the fire almost out and my men sleeping like children, though water was pouring through the flimsy roof in a dozen places ! However, I roused the slumberers, and while two of them went out into the storm and secured my tent, others lit the fire and made me a cup of tea. Presently the storm began to die down, and I returned to bed and broken sleep ; when I awoke again it was very still outside, and I could hear the faint roar of the glacier torrent away below us.

The storm, however, cleared the atmosphere, and the crystal morning greeted us. Snow lay not far above the camp, and the whole line of the Yangtze-Mekong divide was freshly powdered. Very nearly an inch of rain had fallen during the two hours the storm lasted. Throughout the day we had brilliant sunshine, a few wisps of cloud eddying around the snow peaks, and disappearing to re-form elsewhere.

Almost daily, after dawn, one would see clouds rising up from the valley in columns, formed in mid-air out of nothing, as it seemed. At first these embryo clouds were of extreme tenuity, visible only as a slight fogginess of the atmosphere, dulling the view across the valley, but gradually they condensed and took ephemeral shape as puffs and plumes, or became drawn out into bands lying against the mountain side.

The explanation is, that a considerable vacuum being formed in the Mekong valley by day, cold air carrying whatever moisture there may be in the atmosphere pours down from the snow mountains after sunset to fill it ; for every evening I noticed that my camp fire was blown down the mountain side by the rush of air into the warm valley, the clouds above gradually dissolving till the sky was perfectly clear. At sunrise next morning the upper strata of air, warmed by the first rays of the sun, even while the valley below is still in deep shadow, begin to ascend again, followed, of course, by the lower strata, which at once rise up to take their place. Owing to irregular warming of the valley, this air rises in detached columns, and as soon as it is sufficiently cooled by contact with the snow peaks the water vapour is squeezed out and appears condensed as cloud.

Immediately after sunset a heavy dew is deposited, and it is this dew which supplies the vegetation with water.

Along the rocky ridge above camp grew a tangle of Rhododendron, of all colours ; but the most remarkable one appeared to have black or deep plum-coloured flowers. When, however, the sun shone through them, the flowers were seen to be blood red, which is how they would appear to their bee visitors, since the flowers stand horizontally. Thus they are really far more conspicuous than might be supposed from their small size (the plant stands barely four inches high) and dull colour as seen from above. A Rhododendron four inches high is probably a novelty to many people acquainted with the Rhododendron as a big bush at home, or a tree in the Himalaya, and is the more remarkable that no one would ever mistake it for anything but a Rhododendron. There are a large number of these dwarfs characterised by flowers standing horizontally, borne in pairs instead of in trusses, which gives each flower more room to develop, hence they are usually borne on long pedicels and are not markedly zygomorphic.[1]

The style in *R. Mombeigii* is bent downwards and closely adpressed against the corolla, the stigma, which is very viscid, just projecting beyond the lip, while the pollen is in threads, one complete thread in each other, resembling the pollinia of some orchids ; so that it is evident we have here a rather remarkable plant.

Another jolly little shrub, a real dwarf, with the habit of ling is Gaultheria, though perhaps it is prettier, and certainly it is more conspicuous in fruit, as the flowers are small, and of the palest pink.

The north side of the ridge, which was much broken up, abounded in flowers, mostly such as I had seen before —clumps of glossy-leaved *Saxifraga purpurascens*, white-flowered *Cassiope fastigiata* growing much as heather does in Scotland, the Cambridge blue poppy (*Meconopsis speciosa*), primulas, gentians and clusters of Rhododendron ; on the south face, that overlooking the glacier, there was a good deal of barren scree, and here beneath the shelter of the cliffs grew *Meconopsis Delavayi*,

---

[1] They belong chiefly to the two sections, *Campy-logynum* and *Forrestii*. The latter are a group of creeping Rhododendrons, discovered by my friend, Mr. George Forrest.

a shimmering bluish-violet flower with the texture of
Japanese silk : it is a plant of only three to six inches
high when in bloom, growing closely under quite small
rocks, but in fruit the peduncles elongate several inches,
bringing the capsules out of their hiding place that they
may the more freely scatter their seeds on the wind.

The ridge now became more broken. After climbing
steeply up and down over several sharp peaks, we came
to a knife-edged wall of rock with sheer precipices on
either side, and at one point interrupted by a projecting
rock round which it was necessary to climb cautiously,
since it was impossible to climb over it ; otherwise one
might have crawled along the wall on all fours. Two
of my men walked upright along the narrow way, and
were rewarded for their temerity with a beautiful little
rose-red Saxifrage. But I made a detour, followed
by my Tibetan interpreter, who was no gymnast either,
climbing down a steep grassy gulley on the left, and
keeping round the base of the precipice till it seemed
reasonably safe to climb up to the crest of the ridge
again. But it was not easy work even here, as it was
everywhere very steep and there was plenty of loose rock
about.

From this point onwards progress up the ridge was
slow, with steep ascents over scree here and there, and
sometimes a deep-cut narrow chasm which cleft the
ridge, to cross or turn ; it was such a chasm, too broad
to jump and too deep to turn, that finally made me
abandon the last steep climb up a gable-like mountain,
to the snow, our altitude then being 15,739 feet, or
1603 feet above camp. There were, however, deep snow
drifts even here, on the north side, and massive cushions
of the brilliant golden-yellow *Draba alpina*—one of the

few really beautiful alpine Cruciferae—showed that we were close to the limit of plants. The last shrubs— dwarf barbery, Rhododendron and Cotoneaster had been left behind some time since.

The glacier below our camp to the south was very like the temple glacier, only smaller—little more than an ice-fall, in fact, throughout its course. From our camp it was possible to reach a small moraine which flanked the glacier for a short distance ; further up the valley, however, the ice comes right up to the cliff. The upper part of the glacier is confined in the usual gorge. I descended to the moraine—a double one— and found the outer practically bare of plants, though there was a considerable growth of shrubs on the inner and older one. From this point I ascended the valley as far as the moraine and, unable to proceed further, climbed a gully, wading knee-deep through flowers to the crest of the ridge, and so back to camp.

It is evident that the Ka-kar-po peaks can best be climbed from the Mekong valley. There is choice of at least three routes (i) via the Do-kar-la, by keeping up the main valley and over the waterfall, instead of turning off to the pass. This is certainly the best, perhaps the only, route by which to attempt the highest peak of all ; (ii) by the ridge and gable just described, which appears to afford an easy route up the second highest peak, by keeping to the ridge most of the way, and then traversing in snow to the northern or western face of the peak, which to the east rises from the glacier in an almost sheer precipice ; and (iii) from the Shu-la, the pass at the northern end of the snowy range corresponding to the Do-kar-la at the southern end. I think a route could be found from here up the northernmost snow-peak—which, however, is not amongst the highest—though there is tremendous snow slope to climb. It must not be imagined that this list exhausts the possible routes. However, I would recommend the above to anyone who wished to attempt an ascent without spending a lot of time looking for the best possible route. I am certain that climbing on the Ka-kar-po range is best undertaken from the Mekong, not from the Salween, and that, with the exceptions of the Do-kar-la valley at the southern end, and the Shu-la at the northern end, the approach must be made by a spur, on account of the tremendous ice-falls in the valleys. From A-tun-tzu as a main base, an ascent would require about a week, with four days for the return journey; or, from a secondary movable base at one of the villages on the right bank of the Mekong, the climb and return need not occupy more than five or six days.

By far the best climbing season is the autumn and early winter, from the middle of October till the middle of December, when, in spite of the cold, fine weather can be almost guaranteed. In summer, though there is often fine weather for a week or ten days at a stretch, especially in June, climbing is probably more difficult, if not impossible, on account of avalanches.

I had no particular ambition to set foot on any of these virgin peaks myself; yet I sometimes wondered, as I gazed on them in the pink glow of sunset, when the lightning rippled across the sky far down the valley, and the setting planets glowed big, whether their future conqueror would ever think of me, follow my routes, and find my camping grounds. Sitting thus, outside my tent under the brilliant stars, I watched the moon rise over the Pai-ma-shan, till, from high in the heavens,

it shed a ghastly radiance on the tortured glacier below ;
and as I mused, the dead heroes of the mountains seemed
to wander out of the night into the glow of the firelight,
and pass silently before me—Mummery, hero of a hundred
climbs, Whymper, whose name is imperishably associated
with the disastrous triumph on the Matterhorn, and
many others, men whose iron nerve had never deserted
them in the supreme moment ; they were, I thought,
kindred spirits in this madness of the mountains ; but
looking up from the flickering fir-logs I found myself
alone . . . an ice pillar crashed to ruin, with a tremendous
roar, and the dog star rose under Orion, scintillating like
a diamond.

I may here draw attention to the interesting fact that
on the three parallel ranges hitherto denoted as the
Yangtze-Mekong, Mekong-Salween and Salween-Irrawaddy divides, the highest peaks occur on transverse lines,
a tendency pointed out by Colonel Sir Sydney Burrard
in connection with the Himalayan and Trans-Himalayan
ranges.[1] Thus, the Pai-ma-shan group on the Yangtze-
Mekong divide stands opposite the Ka-kar-po group
on the Mekong-Salween divide, and the latter nearly
opposite Gompa-la on the Salween-Irrawaddy divide.

We suffered from two pests at Ka-kar-po camp.

The first was a big green blood-sucking fly, which
came into my tent in scores on sunny days. He was
a clumsy great insect, sluggish in his movements and as
a rule easily dealt with, for he gave plenty of warning,
always settling heavily with a loud buzz, though when he
did bite he stabbed hard with a proboscis like a needle
that made one jump. I think he must have been sent

[1] *A Sketch of the Geography and Geology of the Himalayan Mountains
and Tibet.*   Part III.

into this world to annoy the yak ; but as they had not yet arrived at this altitude, he paid his attentions to us as passable substitutes. The second was the sand-fly we had already encountered at the Do-kar-la. Luckily there were no nocturnal pests.

Of all the plants which clothed the spur round my tent, none was more curious than a small fungus [1] which grew up from the short alpine turf like a black finger ; for each was the living tombstone of a caterpillar, out of whose decayed body it grew.

The Chinese, who set a high value on it as medicine (for which excellent reason my " boy " spent all his spare time lying on his belly looking for these little curiosities to sell for a fabulous sum on his return to Tali-fu) call it *chung-ts'ao*, that is, "insect plant." Naturally they believe that the insect turns into the plant—an idea not so uncouth as it sounds. Anyway it is a most grotesque growth, the little black fungus finger above and the shrivelled brown skin, retaining the shape of the dead caterpillar, below. It well deserves its honoured place in the Chinese pharmacopœia, entry into which is obtained only by intrinsic merit in the realm of natural curiosity.

There was a species of Apollo butterfly on the ridge, at this season just emerging from the larval state, and it is possible that the pupa of this insect, burying itself in the ground on attaining its full growth, is attacked by the lurking mycelium ; these fungus threads, feeding on the entrails, then give rise to the spore-bearing club above ground, leaving only the caterpillar's skin as a sort of root below ground.

[1] I am informed by Mr. F. T. Brooks of Cambridge, to whom I sent specimens, that the fungus is a species of *Cordiceps*.

F

On July 24th we started down, reached Silong in time for lunch, and crossed the glacier torrent to Milong the same afternoon. It is a rather remarkable fact, as showing how small must be the amount of abrasion caused by these ice-falls, that the water of this stream is scarcely turbid, so pure indeed, that it would, I think, never be taken for glacier water at all until seen actually issuing from the ice-foot.

Instead of crossing the Mekong next morning and returning to A-tun-tzu, I decided to pay a second visit to the temple glacier, and setting out in good time we reached the upper temple by midday.

That evening we had another thunder-storm, or rather the very fringe of one, for though the sky looked stormy only a few big drops of rain fell, and the lightning was never near us ; the echo of the thunder amongst the mountains was most weird, a shrill metallic sound like that caused by shaking a piece of sheet tin. A-tun-tzu got most of the rain, and, indeed, it was curious how, day after day, the wind blew from the north-east instead of, as ordinarily, from the south-west ; even the few storms we had coming from the former direction, though this wind as a rule heralded fine weather.

A couple of days later we made another attempt to climb the spur above the temple, and this time success crowned our efforts ; we had, indeed, previously exaggerated the difficulties by trying to find a route too high up the valley.

Now we ascended by a dry gulley below the temple, though we found it extraordinarily steep, and in one place had to climb up a chimney. At last we reached the crest of the spur close to the tree line ; then, turning westwards up the ridge, we presently came out into the open and had the satisfaction of looking straight across the smaller glacier north of us to the camping ground we had just quitted. The herdsmen had already returned to their pastures, and the opposite slope, where we had picked flowers and hunted for Chung-ts'ao three days ago, was speckled with yak, enjoying their brief sojourn amongst these highest meadows.

Southwards quaint little glaciers could be seen hanging over the big valley, and the snow peaks above us rose abruptly out of a frozen sea.

We found several new plants on this excursion, including a purple Meconopsis, evidently a rare plant. Lower down, the rocks in the gulley were blotched with the dull crimson flowers of a small Rhododendron. The chief difficulty encountered in the ascent had been the steepness of the gulley, and the danger of falling rocks. Where the gulley was fairly broad the three of us had kept abreast, but higher up, amongst the precipices, it was necessary to move one at a time ; those below crouching into any cranny they could find till the climber, safely ensconced above, had stopped. Descending, we tried yet another route, still following a gulley of course, as the cliffs of vertically tilted slate, standing off the mountain side like bulkheads, were quite unscaleable.

The forest below the temple was as open as an English park, so far apart did the trees grow on the steep slope, and here, scattered amongst the dead leaves, grew a beautiful little Vaccinium,[1] and a ground orchid (Spir-anthes) with a rosette of variegated leaves.

On July 28th the vanguard of the annual army of pilgrims arrived, and spent the afternoon walking round and round the temple twirling their prayer drums and

[1] *V. modestum* sp. nov.

telling their beads ; so the solemn march went on to the repetition of prayers, sometimes interrupted by a smothered laugh as quite lay matters were slyly alluded to. The temple is, as a matter of fact, off the route of the main stream of pilgrims who make the circuit of Ka-kar-po, and is visited only by comparatively few people from the surrounding districts who do not care to make the big pilgrimage.

With a minimum temperature of 51° F. and a maximum of 69° F. on the day we arrived, the temple seemed very hot after the coolness in our last camp but a little rain each day soon brought the temperature down, the average maximum for the next three days, during which 0·60 in. of rain fell, being 63·8° F. It was not till we were returning across the Mekong that the heat became a discomfort, the thermometer registering 91° F. in the shade at Pu, at two o'clock on the afternoon of July 29th. Here the vegetation, accustomed though it was to arid conditions, was actually shrivelling up for lack of water. Yet so dry was the climate that one was not seriously inconvenienced.

We did not stop at Pu, however, but setting out again late in the afternoon camped by the stream high up on the road to A-tun-tzu in the shade of some big conifer trees. Here for the first time in this country mosquitos found me out ; I was tired that night too, as I had been energetically pursuing some splendid butterflies in the valley.

The fine weather continued, and the sky was cloudless again on the morning of July 30th. The snow range, from which much of the snow had gone, presented quite a different appearance to what it did when I was first enchanted by it in June after three months of winter storms, and was marvellously silhouetted against the dawn sky which slowly darkened to deep blue as the day broke.

We reached A-tun-tzu at midday after a fortnight's absence, and the first news I heard was that the *kuan-tai* Lin had been dismissed. I was not surprised.

VI

Plant Hunting on the Sierra

LITTLE rain had fallen in A-tun-tzu during our absence and the peasant population were beginning to murmur. Surely the crops would fail this year, and then I thought of the hundred soldiers, who so rarely received any wages, and wondered. Nevertheless on the night of the great storm, already described, a mud stream had slunk down the mountain and we found it plastered over the valley to a depth of nearly two feet, and still soft, though the sun was fast baking a crust over it. The average minimum temperature for the next five days was 50·6° F. and the maximum generally touched 70°; on August 1st more rain fell, 0·11 in. being registered in the twenty-four hours; but August 2nd made up for it again with glorious weather, and I climbed to the summit of A-tun-tzu mountain, 3486 feet above the village.

In the west a grand panorama now unfolded itself, about sixty miles of the Mekong-Salween divide from Wei-hsi-t'ing in the extreme south to Tsa-kha-hlo in the north being visible. Far away in the south, beyond the gaping breach in the range where two passes lead from the village of Londre—the Londre-la south-west, and the Do-kar-la north-west to the Salween—I caught sight of a snowy peak, though except for an extensive snow-field on its eastern flank, no details were visible. North-

wards from this strange peak the mountains grow lower
and lower till the nadir is reached in the gap above Londre,
which gives the impression of a chunk bitten out of the
range. Immediately afterwards the grandest heights are
attained by the Ka-kar-po group, a succession of glittering pyramidal peaks.

The first, a graceful delicate-looking, triple-peaked
mountain, is the highest, though one at the northern
end is a good second. Next comes a nameless peak,
followed by that above the temple which gives rise to
the largest or temple glacier as I have called it. There
must, I think, be a group of peaks hidden behind this
last, otherwise it is difficult to account for the size of
the glacier, which stretches a mile further down its
valley than any of the others. The fourth peak is nameless, and the fifth is the aiguille, above our Ka-kar-po
camp. The sixth peak, a very high one, is also nameless.
Behind it another peak is just visible.

I cannot, with certainty, identify the peaks which, as
seen from Tsa-rong further north dominate the pilgrims'
road all the way down the Wi-chu valley. But I think
they lie towards the northern end of the range. Their
calm peaceful grandeur must urge on the foot-sore
pilgrims both in the long hush of the moonlight winter
night, when they gleam blue like bergs in the pallid
Arctic, or in the brilliant orange light of day.

North of Ka-kar-po, the central peaks of which were
opposite me as I stood on A-tun-tzu mountain, the range
again becomes lower, the rocks very bare, and of a red
colour. Here the Shu-la crosses the range, which presently rises again, in a group of about six craggy peaks,
with several dead glaciers flowing towards the Mekong.
These, however are not to be compared with the ice

cataracts of Ka-kar-po, though the peaks themselves may be nearly as high ; for the snow-line itself is now raised. Lastly, following on another broad gap [1] a fine snow peak is visible, rising clear above the surrounding mountains. This is Damyon, a range I caught sight of from above the Mekong, between Samba-dhuka and Garthok, in 1911.

Great rolling masses of cloud, which rubbed against each other and continuously altered their form, hung over this magnificent rampart throughout its length, or rested lightly as thistledown on the tips of the mountains. A breeze fluttered the pages of my notebook and carried a loose one eddying into space. Reluctantly I turned my back on the threshold of a land flowing with milk and honey, and descended through the fir forests to the village.

Next day, August 5th, we set out once more with porters and riding ponies, our destination being the Yangtze-Mekong divide right above A-tun-tzu ; thus we needed to travel only one day's march before finding a good camping ground in one of the numerous alpine valleys. At the same time I sent two of my Tibetan collectors back to the Do-kar-la to see what they could find and report on what seeds were ripe, telling them to be back in ten days.

The weather was fine and hot as usual, but no sooner had we climbed out of the valley than we saw behind us the Salween divide smudged over with falling snow. The main stream of the A-tun-tzu torrent comes down this valley and debouches just below the village, after leaping over the spur in a fine cascade. Crossing the torrent by

[1] This is where the Pi-tu-la and the Di-la cross the Mekong-Salween divide ; both passes lead to the Yü-chu

a plank bridge, we walked through patches of meadow, golden with globe flower (*Trollius patulus*) beneath banks on which grew dwarf raspberry bushes with giant fruits, under fir trees, and amongst thickets of myriad-berried barberry. Such shrubs, whether packed together in the valley or scattered on the mountain side, are a feature of the drier mountains east of A-tun-tzu. Passing a hanging valley on our right, we entered a larger valley, its mouth blocked with knee-deep Rhododendron scrub, where progress was so difficult that we were glad to ascend the hill-side a little and keep to the more open fir forest till the trees failed. Across the valley was a flat, grassy knoll by the stream side, where some time previously from A-tun-tzu mountain I had caught sight of black tents and herds of yak scattered up the slope. Towards this spot, therefore, we directed our steps, arriving at four o'clock in the afternoon.

It was a jolly alp for a camp, the mountain rising steeply above us, dotted with juniper trees, dwarfed and gnarled, the source of our firewood, flowers all round us, and the stream rattling over its bed amongst the bushes below. The men soon had the tents up, and began laying in a stock of firewood, for though the altitude was only 13,681 feet it felt colder here than at Ka-kar-po camp, and I was glad of a fire outside my tent all the time. The average minimum for nine days (August 6th–14th) was 39·6° F., and the continual showers and clammy mists sweeping up the valley sufficed to keep down the day temperature, which never rose above 62° F. The average maximum for the same time was 58·8° F. and the rainfall 1·62 in. Most of the rain, however, fell in forty-eight hours, though we had showers every day, at least on the heights.

Next day we ascended the valley which is dominated by the highest peak on this part of the range, a ponderous blunt-headed buttress of dark rock, where snow lies in the gullies all the year round, though the glaciers have long since disappeared.

At first we followed the flower-girt stream which now wandered with divided waters over a flat sandy channel, starred with red and white saxifrage, and anon rushed noisily between bush-clad gravel banks where tall yellow poppies nodded to us as we passed. Presently, leaving the stream and ploughing knee-deep through Rhododendron we began to climb more steeply over very uneven hummocky country, interrupted here and there by grassy alps, where numbers of yak were browsing. The black tents of the herdsmen were visible at the foot of the slope just across the stream.

It was rather dangerous work climbing over the enormous piles of lichen-fretted boulders which here encumber the valley, for they were partly covered by a loose growth of small shrubs concealing holes and crannies in which one was liable to trip. Amongst these boulders grew tall hollow-stemmed herbs, such as *Meconopsis Prattii*, the yellow gentian with its hanging bells, and a stately Umbellifer, bearing aloft plate-shaped inflorescences arranged in meticulous order. On our left bare screes stretched up to the splintered cliffs of the ridge, a thousand feet over our heads.

Presently shrubs grew more scattered and finally died out. Masses of pale-grey rock lay in disordered heaps. Small level pockets of sand occurred here and there along the stream, and before us the stony ground rose steeply in every direction, barren and forbidding. We were again in the land of *the* blue poppy.

Of this magnificent plant (*Meconopsis speciosa*) I will give some details. One specimen I noted was 20 inches high, crowned with 29 flowers and 14 ripening capsules above, with 5 buds below—48 flowers in all. Indeed the plant seems to go on throughout the summer unfurling flower after flower out of nowhere—like a Japanese pith blossom thrown into water—for the stem is hollow and the root shallow. Another bore 8 fruits, 15 flowers and 5 buds, and a third, only 15 inches high, had 6 flowers, each 3½ inches across, besides 14 buds. But for a certain perkiness of the stiff prickly stem, which refuses any gracefulness of arrangement to the crowded raceme, and the absence of foliage amongst the blooms, these great azure-blue flowers, massed with gold in the centre, would be the most beautiful I have ever seen. The Cambridge blue poppy is, moreover, unique amongst the dozen species[1] of poppy-wort known to me from this region, in being sweetly scented. On one scree I counted no less than forty of these magnificent plants within a space of a few square yards, but, scattered as they were amongst big boulders, they only peeped up here and there and did not look so numerous.

The natural history of this Meconopsis is also interesting. It is a plant which produces an enormous number of seeds, very few of which ever germinate, for the capsules are attacked by a small grub before the seeds ripen, and cruelly decimated. Of those which survive till October or November to be shaken out amongst the

---

[1] *Meconopsis speciosa*, M. *integrifolia*, M. *pseudointegrifolia*, M. *rudis*, M. *Delavayi*, M. *Prattii*, M. *impedita*, M. *Wallichii*, M. *lancifolia*, M. *Henrici*. M. *speciosa* was discovered by Mr. George Forrest some years ago; but so far has resisted all attempts to introduce it into this country.

hard, cold rocks, standing like tombstones, witnesses
to the slaughter on every hand, how many are fertile ?
How many perish before spring comes again ?   How
many grow into seedlings, only to form food for some
hungry creature awakening from its long winter sleep ?
Alas, few, very few, hidden away snugly deep down in
some dark crevice amongst the snow-roofed boulders,
will survive through all these dangers, and live to flower
in the second summer ! Think what it means, the forty
plants counted above, bearing say twenty-five flowers
each, with five hundred seeds per capsule, i.e. half a
million embryos to be scattered amongst the boulders,
for the seeds are not shaken far afield ; yet will there be
fifty plants here next year where forty are now ?   I
doubt it.   Yet if there are, the sacrifice was not vain.

But such extravagant reproduction is not peculiar to
this plant ; it is, on the contrary, typical of the highest
alpine plants, and a terrible wastage naturally follows.
Besides two other species of Meconopsis (*M. rudis* and
M. integrifolia) both of which produce a large number
of seeds—though neither will compare with *M. speciosa*
in this respect—there are the saxifrages, gentians, the
cushion plants (*Diapensia himalaica, Arenaria polytrichoides, Potentilla sp.*) and the Rhododendrons. Even
the Compositae which flourish on the highest cliffs
and screes—species of Saussurea and Crepis, show
reckless seed production. Thus, in one plant of *Saussurea
gossypiphora* I counted 828 seeds, a large number, considering the care that is bestowed on each ; and a plant
of *Crepis rosularis*, forming a flat rosette on the ground,
produced 728, most of them probably fertile.

Evidently in places where the vegetative season is so
brief, a plant has no time to produce elaborate fruits

containing a few seeds—consider, for example, the time
it takes to ripen the large fruits of *Podophyllum Emodi* :
not less than four months. Hence less food material
is packed in the seeds, which consequently ripen more
rapidly, and in order to compensate for the hasty workmanship, these inferior seeds are produced in as large
numbers as possible. It follows, therefore, that all these
plants, necessarily having small dry seeds, will also have
capsular fruits which scatter their contents on the wind,
it being impossible to provide for any other method
of dispersal with the material, and in the time available.
This consideration limits the number of species which are
able to follow a retreating snow line and establish
themselves at higher altitudes, since those plants which
are not already provided with capsular fruits will not
be able to establish themselves, however excellent their
methods of seed dispersal may be.

Pursuing another line of enquiry one may ask what
effect, if any, has this mortality amongst the unripe seeds
(in the above case due to a grub) on the plant ? If it has
no effect, then Nature has provided a tremendous surplus
of embyros, whether fertile or not, for a side issue,
namely the feeding of a grub ; the common dangers to
be faced are not such as would otherwise warrant this
extravagant reproductive effort. But does Nature work
on these lines ? Is it not much more likely that the
increased seed production is in part an *effect*, not entirely
a cause, of the grub's presence ?

True, it is a condition of their survival, as shown
above, that all these high alpine plants should, in the
first instance, produce plenty of seed. But it is probable
that if the plant concentrates effort in one direction
the result of that effort will tend to be magnified in the

next generation, and for that very reason expose the plant to new risks by upsetting a certain balance of forces ; in fact, the intensification of a character useful in one direction may easily be carried to such an extreme that it eventually becomes a positive menace to the plant in another.

For example, species of Bombax and of Eriocaulon have so increased the development of the cottony covering on the seed coat, that the fruits now contain more cotton than seed, most of which never reach maturity, probably owing to faulty nutrition set up by too great specialisation in one direction.

To return, then, to *Meconopsis speciosa*, it seems to me very probable that the plant, adapting itself as rapidly as possible to surroundings which impose as a first necessity of existence the production of seeds small and numerous rather than large and few, presently found itself exposed to attack from a new quarter, and met it by a still greater increase of seed production. One might naturally ask how ?—and I reply that the nutrition of the ripening capsule being disorganised by the presence of the grub, the surviving seeds receive a larger share of food and give rise to more vigorous plants, which again attempt to evade the fate of extinction which threatens the species by increased seed production in the next generation.

But, owing to its peculiar situation, the species as a whole cannot continue indefinitely to disturb the balance of nutrition in this way ; if it goes on from genera- tion to generation taxing the resources of the reproduc- tive organs more heavily each year, then, the amount of available food remaining the same, malnutrition of the vegetative organs must inevitably bring about some change in the plant, be it in the colour of the flower, size of the leaves, length of root, or height of stem, and such a change must again react in the life history of the plant, which becomes plastic within, and henceforth in a condition of unstable equilibrium in relation to the forces acting on it from without. In short, the species changes its character.

There are other plants besides those of *Meconopsis speciosa* whose seeds are similarly attacked and decimated; for instance, the wild cherry (small boring beetle), several species of Pedicularis (grub) and of Rhododendron, Primula, Caragana sp. (grub) and *Pinguicula alpina*—whose fruits are bitten off entire, apparently by a small bird; while a large proportion of the seeds of *Lilium giganteum*, *Primula minor* and others abort, for no assigned reason. Here then is no struggle for existence amongst the offspring of one species, for few survive to face any struggle at all.

To return to the ascent of the valley.

A stiff climb, made more difficult by the irregular blocks of stone over which we had to clamber, brought us presently to the usual small lake at a bend in the valley. Scattered plants clothed the lower slopes on our right, up to the base of the high cliffs on the main divide, and steep earth screes completely bare of vegetation, rose on our left, but the valley was filled with the same grey piles of angular rocks as hitherto. Masses of cloud came sweeping up on the wind, bringing cold stinging rain, and blotting out the view.

I saw nothing new by the lake, which was very shallow, its basin being almost filled with sand; along the edge of the water grew the curious semi-aquatic *Cochlearia scapiflora, Oxygraphis glacialis,* and several species of Oxytropis with yellow, purple and lilac flowers, all prostrate on the wet sand. A last climb of several hundred feet from the lake, still over boulders, piled in the greatest confusion, brought us to a pass at an altitude of 15,685 feet, not, however, on the main divide; just ahead, but separated from us by a deep valley, was a second pass, evidently on the watershed.

There were still quite a number of plants about, woolly Saussureas, cushions of *Androsace chamaejasme* and *Arenaria polytrichoides,* warm and soft to sit down on, tufts of Sedum and scattered poppies, but from a distance the ground looked bleak and bare, though the blue poppy and the woolly white *Saussurea gossypiphora* are visible a hundred yards off. Patches of snow lay about in sheltered nooks, and the ground was covered in places with moss, and the white threads of a lichen known to the Chinese as *shueh-cha,* that is, snow tea, from which a beverage is prepared. The temperature of the soil on the pass was 44° F., that of the air out of the wind 42° F.

We were in an old glaciated valley, mounting terrace by terrace. Piles of boulders mark the old moraines; this lake basin, too, was ploughed out by ice, which has so over-deepened the main valley that all the lateral valleys are left high in the air.

Comparing this valley with the glacier valleys of Ka-kar-po one could see how they resembled each other in their contours, and the great depths to which they have been eroded, whether by water or ice. There is here the same steep pitch at the foot of the cirque, where, in the case of Ka-kar-po, the ice comes staggering down in fantastic pillars torn off the glacier; but the valley outlines are now softened by screes, the accumulation of centuries of weathering, and only the crest of the ridge sticks up above the all-engulfing debris. The absence of perched blocks, or any indication of lateral moraines no longer causes surprise now that I have seen the Ka-kar-po glacier, for the small amount of material which falls from the cliffs is very quickly swallowed up in the crevasses of the ice-fall, or in the yawning gap between the ice and the cliff. Allowing, then, for the subsequent effects of frost and running water in reducing the greater inequalities, and redistributing the moraine material at the glacier foot, and for the work of the alpine vegetation in softening many hard outlines, these valleys now present very much the appearance that I should expect the hanging valleys of Ka-kar-po to present, were the ice removed; the upper valley at the Do-kar-la camp, has yet this appearance.

We got back to camp drenched, and towards evening masses of cloud came rolling up from the A-tun-tzu valley, and settled over us like a wet blanket; it drizzled steadily all night, and on the following day with the wind at last in the south-west we were treated to heavy showers with only brief intervals of sunshine. This day I discovered a Pedicularis, with curiously bearded flowers, and the enormous sulphur-yellow flowers of *Meconopsis integrifolia* on the high jagged ridge above. The latter plant is thickly clad with soft golden-brown hairs.

When I awoke on the following morning I could see from my tent the highest peak of Ka-kar-po clearly framed between the forested sides of the valley; space was annihilated, the intervening Mekong did not exist in the picture.

After breakfast I went up our valley to the Tibetan

G

tents and called on the herdsmen, three saplings to which
as many big black watch dogs were tied, bending almost
to breaking point as the fierce animals strained every
muscle to get at the intruder and tear him to pieces.
It was a noisy welcome. Then I lay up amongst the
boulders and had shots at the giant pica-hares which
flashed in and out of the crevices like streaks of light,
but they were too quick for me. I also saw a couple of
wicked little weasels (*Mustela sibirica*) moving furtively
across the open, no doubt in pursuit of the woolly grey
hares.

It poured all that night, and we could not see across
our valley till ten o'clock on the following morning,
when the wind began to break up the clouds. I was not
feeling well, perhaps as the result of drinking too much
Tibetan beer, and spent the morning in my tent, but
in the afternoon I went up the main valley, following
the path which leads towards the Run-tzu-la, and so
to Mo-ting on the Yangtze. Just after I started a
heavy thunder-storm swept up the valley, thoroughly
drenching me, but a couple of hours later it cleared again
and the sun shone out ; A-tun-tzu, only two miles distant,
took the brunt of this storm.

People told me afterwards that from two o'clock
till five it poured, and the water, having no time to sink
into the soil, rolled down the mountain side cutting
great grooves in the steep barley fields, and washing away
what little soil there is in rivers of mud. Terrific claps
of thunder burst like harmless shells over the village,
while the frightened people huddled together and watched
the havoc wrought amongst their crops. Nearly two
inches of rain must have fallen in the three hours the
storm lasted, and though this may not seem anything

wonderful in a heavy tropical downpour, yet when it rains like that in a dry mountainous region such as the A-tun-tzu district, things happen.

Turning aside from the main valley at the first lake— a triangular pool of water surrounded by high boulder banks, I ascended abruptly to the more level of a small hanging valley which leads to an interior pass west of the Run-tzu-la.

At the lakelet the main valley, which here turns through a right angle, has been tremendously over-deepened, and the climb up over the boulders, where marmots scamper amongst the bushes and whistle shrilly to each other, is very steep. I may note here, in passing, that these lakes occur wherever the valley makes a knee-bend, both in the main valley and in the lateral hanging valleys. A little higher up we found ourselves on a steep-sided ridge occupying the middle of the narrow valley, with a shallow trough covered with alpine turf and dwarf bushes on the left, and a similar trough filled with big boulders, amongst which the blue poppy blooms in considerable numbers, on the right. This central ridge is, in fact, an old moraine, and extends up the valley as far as the flat at the foot of the cirque, which is not occupied by a lake only because it has been filled up with sand, though it is always marshy after heavy rain. Just above is the pass (15,408 feet) over which a cattle track leads down a narrow sterile valley to A-dong, a village only a short day's march north of A-tun-tzu on the Ba-t'ang road.

On our right, a couple of hundred feet above the narrow pass, which is hemmed in by rock slides several isolated and curiously sculptured cliffs jut up from the steep slope, and on the opposite side, facing north, lay a big patch of melting snow. Soaked as I was, the raw wind which nipped through the narrow opening made it feel much colder than the 43° F. registered by the sheltered thermometer.

Eastwards I had a good view of the high peak on the divide at the head of our valley-buttress peak, but standing up as it does well above the surrounding mountains, I could see no prospect of ever climbing its vertical cliffs. There was fresh snow on its northern face but no glacier, so that it cannot be more than nineteen or twenty thousand feet.

On the way down from the pass I met two little half-naked Tibetan boys, who were looking for some yak which had strayed over the pass from the A-dong side. It made me shiver to look at them. Feet, legs and arms were bare, and a single goat-skin, its tatters fluttering on the breeze, partly covered the body. They were cheerful urchins with pinched faces and hands thrust up into the sleeves of their hairy garment for warmth. What a grand, lonely life they led throughout the short summer, cattle ranging in these high valleys !

On the way back to camp I presently came upon a clump of *Spiraea laevigata*, looking radiant after its bath, for its thin reedy stems now shone ebony black and the rain-drops hung like silver beads from its glaucous leaves borne on red twigs.

August 10th was a wretched day, drizzling all the morning after a regular deluge in the night, which brought the fresh snow down to within 1500 feet of our camp. Whitish-grey clouds hung like smoke over the mountains, and I was confined to my tent with an attack of sickness. Just before dark the whole range of snow peaks across the Mekong shone out clearly for a moment, but was almost immediately hidden again behind masses of cloud which boiled up from the deep valley, like steam from a cauldron. On three consecutive nights this happened, each time just before dark. I have since noticed the same thing on the north-east frontier of Burma.

On August 11th the weather improved greatly and we made another long excursion, this time following the path up the main valley to the summit of the Run-tzu-la, 16,504 feet. As far as the first lake, the triangular one just referred to, there is an excellent path by the stream, and the going is easy. Then one climbs to a second pool, and another fairly level bit in the stream bed, where low willows strain their branches towards the pass as though they had been stretched on the rack; but it is only the wind that has done this. After passing a wide-mouthed hanging valley, from which a stream cascades into the big valley, a very steep ascent over a cliff three or four hundred feet high brings us to the third lake.

This is obviously a true rock basin which has not been silted up at all, and the water shelves rapidly to considerable depths; on a fine autumn day it is beautiful to see the rocky snow-bound crest of the divide reflected in the placid heart of the little lake, every spire and peak from the Run-tzu-la to the buttress mountain looking as though it had a real existence below the clear surface. The altitude was 15,107 feet and the temperature of the water 41° F. The water flowing from this lake to the valley below has cut a channel through the cliffs which hem it in on the south-west side, whence it tumbles in a series of cascades to the valley below, so that the water must once have stood at a higher level, and eventually, no doubt, the lake will be drained.

On Pai-ma-shan I subsequently found another exactly similar rock basin and cliff, and that in a valley where higher up a glacier still existed. It will be recalled that above our camp in the Do-kar-la valley a cliff, cut through by a stream, stretched across the valley.

Above the lake, boulders again make the going difficult though the ascent is gradual. Here are yellow-flowered Senecio and Cremanthodium, whose massed leaves choke the stream which wanders abroad over the stones, forming shallow pools. I was surprised to see such big leaves on any plant, for we were approaching the limit of flowering plants. No shrubs grew here, and away from the stream only scattered plants of strange aspect.

Perhaps the most remarkable of all was *Saussurea gossypiphora*, which is in the form of a blunt cone, six or eight inches high, encased in a woolly coat of overlapping scales; it looks more like some weird Arctic animal dressed in a blanket than a plant.

And now the Run-tzu-la is right above us. Leaving the main valley and the stream which flows down from the northern face of our buttress peak, we ascend the steep face of the ridge for nearly a thousand feet by a zigzag path, and finally stand in the very notch which we had seen so clearly from Ka-kar-po camp.

The most striking peculiarites of the Yangtze-Mekong divide are, first the steep and narrow passes, as though a segment had been split out of the precipitous ridge with an axe ; secondly the tremendous amount of erosion which has taken place in the valleys ; and thirdly the hewing out of isolated towers, pinnacles, and small needle peaks. Such features are generally of limestone.

The snow was not yet all melted. Except a few tufts of moss and lichen there are no plants on the pass itself, which forms a regular funnel for the wind to shriek through, but higher up on the cliffs are a few saxifrages and Saussureas.

No description of the Yangtze-Mekong divide would be complete without some reference to the scree plants which are so important a feature in the vegetation between 15,000 and 17,000 feet. Practically all slopes facing south on this range are screes, but there are, as a matter of fact, three types of scree, each characterised by its own peculiar flora.

(i) Boulder screes, filling up the cirques at the foot of the range, and giving rise to all the hummocky country which forms the transitional step between the lower shrub-clad levels and the sandy flats and rock-basins above; their most characteristic plant is, of course, the Cambridge blue poppy, and there is little else. (ii) Gravel screes formed by fragments shattered off the cliffs accumulating on slopes, characterised by a number of brightly coloured flowers (e.g. *Aconitum Hookeri*) or plants rendered otherwise conspicuous by their foliage or massed inflorescences. Here and there, under the lee of a friendly cliff occur darker bands of dwarf shrubs, including *Lonicera Wardii*, in fruit one of the most attractive of all the dwarf honeysuckles. However, it does badly here, no doubt lacking water. (iii) Earth screes in the highest part of the valley under the shadow of the divide, formed like the last, but usually from slaty rocks instead of schist or limestone, and practically devoid of plants. It is, therefore, only about the plants of the gravel screes, which exhibit several interesting structural features fitting them to their rather extraordinary mode of life, that I need say anything.

Looking at these screes, which slope at an average

angle of about 45°, and seeing how quickly they dry after rain, one would think that the greatest difficulty with which the plants have to contend is lack of water. No doubt this is partly true, though not to the extent it appears, for after digging through the gravel to a depth of 18 inches I found the soil finer and of more uniform composition ; and this subsoil was quite moist. In fact, it appeared that the gravel scree closely resembled the earth scree. Consequently the great length to which the root-systems of these plants grow is designed more with a view to meet the shifting of the scree material than because of any serious difficulty in obtaining water, though the poverty of the soil may also be a reason. For instance, a Saussurea 105 mm. (4¼ in.) high had a root system penetrating to a depth of over 770 mm. or 2¼ feet, to which depth I had dug when it broke off short ; this would mean an aggregate length of many yards if all the roots were joined up. As a rule the main root divides first into a X or L shaped bracing piece before forking repeatedly into a number of nearly parallel rootlets, or, in the case of a L root, ramifying widely right and left parallel to the surface of the scree.

The erect Saussurea above referred to (*S. gossypiphora*) is the most interesting of all the scree plants, for its leaves are crowded in such close overlapping spirals that no part of the stem is visible, and they go through a series of remarkable changes. When young they are oval in outline, stand upright on long stalks, and are fringed with reddish crimson hairs. As they grow older they become more and more deeply incised, passing through elliptical to strap-shaped, with long pointed teeth ; meanwhile the red fringe has gradually disappeared, its place being taken by a thick white tomentum like cotton-wool, covering the entire leaf. By this time the leaves are no longer upright, but curl back or hang down limply, giving the plant a pineapple appearance.

A more typical habit is for the stem to be so weak that it lies along the surface of the scree, growing up hill ; then as the scree shifts the stem is simply carried along towards its point of origin without being damaged. Still a third type is furnished by *Lactuca Souliei* and *Crepis rosularis,* whose stems rise less than an inch above the surface, bearing a rosette of leaves which lie flat on the ground. One specimen of the latter possessed 80 leaves in three overlapping tiers radiating from the central hollow stem, with 182 capitula, each bearing four flowers ; and all this on a convex receptacle only an inch in diameter and half an inch above the ground ! Such compactness, of course, considerably enhances the conspicuousness of the plant, and hence its chance of being picked out by bees or other insects.

The hemispherical cushions of *Arenaria polytrichoides* —which grow amongst boulders with the blue poppy, and on cliffs, are absent from these screes. This is probably because they would be specially exposed and liable to suffer damage more than most other plants from three of the greatest dangers in scree life—namely, bombardment from the cliffs, being torn out of the soil and stranded owing to shifting of the scree, or buried by material slowly slipping down from above. To these last two dangers they would not readily be able to accommodate themselves.

Another beautiful plant found here is a Labiate, with woolly white arched leaves overlapping like the scales of a fish so as completely to hide the stem, while here and there clusters of shell-pink flowers peep out from beneath their warm armour. Some years later I brought seed of this species to England under the number KW 4644.

August 14th was our last day in camp, and on the 15th, in better weather than we had yet experienced, we hired seven yak from the herdsmen up the valley and returned to A-tun-tzu with our spoil.

VII

By the Turquoise Lake

AT the end of August I received a telegram from an Englishman in Li-kiang telling me to expect him and a friend in A-tun-tzu about mid-September ; to which I replied that I would meet him at a certain village in the Mekong valley, on my way back from the Do-kar-la, and return with him. An approximate date was therefore arranged, and the meeting eventually contrived within a day of that calculated.

Instead of going direct to the Do-kar-la, however, straight down the Mekong as heretofore, I now proposed to cross the snow mountains of the Pai-ma-shan group, descend to the Mekong valley, and from there follow the usual road via Londre.

When I enquired in A-tun-tzu whether a route across Pai-ma-shan existed or not, I received contradictory replies, most of those questioned saying it was impossible to cross the range, while one or two said that there was a path. Clearly, therefore, if there was a route—and one old Tibetan persisted in saying that the hunters knew of one, though he had never traversed it himself—it was evidently little used, hence little known.

Being eager to find a route I naturally clung to the

belief of its existence, and though my informer could not direct me, I had myself climbed on the fringe of this range in 1911, and knew where to seek a pass.

Here I will digress for a moment to point out what an excellent centre A-tun-tzu would be for a party contemplating climbs on the Pai-ma-shan group, though these peaks do not compare with the Himalayan giants. However, its curious hanging glaciers, and the extent to which they have retreated within recent geological time, besides its wonderful flora, would afford matter for endless study.

Considering that a party starting from A-tun-tzu could camp at the foot of one of the Pai-ma-shan glaciers on the third day, in a delightful grassy valley, with water and firewood to hand, at an altitude of about 16,000 feet, an ascent in fine weather should present no difficulty; and from an altitude of 20,000 feet in that pure, dry atmosphere, poised over the Mekong river on the one hand, with the Yangtze valley on the other, the climber would have such a view as would well repay the long journey to A-tun-tzu.

To north and east, he would look deep into the heart of the Tibetan country, eastwards over a range of desolate mountains, here and there gladdened by a snow peak—nay, it is autumn, so perhaps all those miles of mountains will be white crested, as breaking waves ; and north, down dim, unlit corridors of awful depth, growing smaller and narrower as they converge, till it seems they must at last unite where the cloud-puffs clasp heaven and earth in one embrace.

Due west, the great snow range of Ka-kar-po towers before him, but northwards, where the peaks are lower, he will look into the dry valleys of Tsa-rong, and further south will peep through the Londre gap and looking across the Salween valley, see beyond into Burma itself.

To return to my plans.

I had hoped to start on September 1st, but though the Tibetans came with their animals, they straightway declared they had not sufficient food for the journey; hence that they could not start until next day. This day, September 1st, flags were flown in honour of the inauguration of the Republic, though the new regime was by no means popular amongst the merchants, probably because they hated the official. Meanwhile there were almost daily rumours of trouble in different parts of China.

Next morning the Tibetans again demurred—they did not want to cross Pai-ma-shan at all, in fact. We argued the matter out at some length, and finally they agreed to accompany me as far as the Pai-ma-shan pass, leave me there, and return by the main road; I was to join them two days later in the Mekong valley. And this matter being satisfactorily settled, we set out to seek our pass.

We made only a short march that day, camping at about 12,000 feet; it was by no means cold yet, the temperature only falling to 39° F., and on the following night, 2000 feet higher, only to 37° F.

Throughout the day a few clouds writhed, melted and reformed in the upper eddies, a few light masses brushed the mountain tops; but this never hindered the brilliant sunshine, and a glorious evening succeeded, the clouds finally dying out of the sky as the sun set.

Then there shot up from behind the snow range in the west a fan of pink rays, while overhead a few bright stars twinkled; but presently the fan flickered and went out, leaving a warm glow long after the heavens elsewhere glittered with stars. Later, flashes of lambent flame might be seen running across the southern sky. Everything promised well for the morrow—it seemed that at last the snow peaks would be clear—and I had crossed the pass seven times previously with no more than an occasional glimpse of them !

At noon next day we stood on the pass, at an altitude of 14,800 feet. The snow range is invisible from here, but in the north-west the view of the Salween divide and of the Tibetan mountains was sublime, though a faint haze rendered the most distant peaks indistinct. At the summit is a sort of glaciated plateau, furrowed by streams flowing south to join the main glacier river. On the west side, hummocky country covered with a carpet of alpine flowers, hides the snowy range. Immediately east of the pass a line of limestone cliffs conceals a region of lofty downs and spongy green valleys, a beautiful, clean, spacious country, where graze thousands of yak.

I now sent one of the Tibetans up to a tent we saw to question the herdsmen about this mysterious path we were seeking. He came back saying they knew nothing of such a route. This was discouraging ; but presently a caravan came along from Tung-ch'u-ling, and I made further enquiries.

At first the men denied the existence of a path, but afterwards they admitted they had heard of one, but hastened to add that neither animals nor porters could cross the range ; which indeed was not to be expected.

After lunch I sent my caravan on ahead, instructing the men to pitch camp by a little stream a mile or so distant and a few hundred feet below the pass. We were on a broad gently sloping plateau covered with dwarf Rhododendrons, growing like heather ; the spot chosen for our camp was protected on the north by the limestone range already referred to, which, rising to a height of about 17,000 feet, and facing due south, is almost bare of vegetation. The snowy range on the other side of the shallow valley is composed of porphyry ; and there are some striking differences in the flora in consequence.

My Tibetan guide and I now set out up the slope towards the snowy range to reconnoitre the suspected pass, and gather what information we could from some more yak herders, said to be encamped in the valleys immediately below the highest peak.

After crossing one of the intervening ridges we descended into a hollow and sure enough found the herdsmen, who told us that there really was a path across the range. However, they did not know where it lay and said that it was very dangerous, a man having been killed there by falling stones in the previous year ; nor could I prevail upon any of them to accompany me. Instead, they directed us to another valley in which were yet more herdsmen, who, they said, would be able to give us the necessary information for reaching a village called Hoa, on the other side. No one on this side of the range ever went across, it seemed.

Continuing south-westwards, in the direction of the snow mountains, across undulating ground, we presently reached the summit of another ridge, and looking across several narrow, stony valleys, beheld a grand sight. For the first time I saw, perfectly clear against a China blue sky and quite close to us, the northernmost of the snow peaks, the black buttress of Tsa-ya, a massive tower down whose near wall there crawled, its blunt arms outthrust aimlessly, like a gigantic amœba, all that was left of what must once have been a big glacier.

It was the oddest sight imaginable, that white fungus-like growth, clinging to the face of the cliff, its blunt-nosed pseudopodia protruding stiffly from its much scratched body ; with icy grip enfeebled by approaching death, it now hugged the rock it had so mauled and gashed ; its tentacles clawed weakly at the face of the tower they had so wounded. And as it hung there dying, dying in the stillness, I stood spellbound.

The highest peak of the range, called by the Tibetans Tsa-ya, is this one at the north end, overlooking the pass. Its height I should estimate at about 20,000 feet. On its northern and eastern flanks are two glaciers, which rise from a snow-filled depression occupying the summit ridge ; but on the Mekong side not one glacier is visible. The main glacier is of what may be called the amœboid type, that is to say, it is an independent glacier, being cut off during the summer from the snow-field above.

The southern buttress of Tsa-ya runs out in a lofty ridge, which also separates two deep valleys, one of them embracing Tsa-ya itself, and collecting water from its two glaciers, while the other drains the next peak to the south, called Omagu. Both streams, after flowing almost due east, turn south, and unite to flow under the eastern flank of the snowy range, collecting water from all its glaciers. It is this river which I think is the head-stream of the Kari river.

North of the Tsa-ya the peaks are lower, and it appears that there are no more glaciers. But climbing in this direction, I saw a small glacier tucked away out of sight in one of the lofty valleys. This clearly is a " dead " glacier—that is to say, one which is not fed from any existing snow-field, and must soon become extinct. Such dead glaciers are not uncommon on the Yangtze-Mekong divide. North of the Ka-kar-po range, there are quite a number on the Mekong-Salween divide also.

One cannot but be struck by the tremendous retreat of the ice on this range. Formerly the glaciers came far down the valley towards A-tun-tzu, and the plateau-like summit of the divide, which is now a paradise of flowers, must have been a huge ice sheet.

The main glacier valley is tremendously overdeepened ; curiously, the glacier stream evades the lakelet at the corner, which might filter it. Hence the small lateral valleys, which also have lakes at their heads, are all hanging valleys.

On either side of the tower the range was notched. These passes seemed to present no particular difficulty, that at the northern end being the lower and apparently easier, and I suggested to my Tibetan that here lay probably our route for the morrow ; but on descending into the valley below, another herdsman pointed to the southern pass as the one we should have to cross.

Having obtained this much information, we started back for camp, and leaving the bare stony ridges behind us plunged down the slope knee deep through Rhodo-dendron scrub, and so into the beginnings of the fir forest ; away down in the green valley below us the sun was shining its last on the tents, and dark shadows were creeping up the cliff.

There followed a cloudless night with scarcely a breath of wind ; behind Pai-ma-shan the lightning danced

H

with the meteors in the star-strewn sky, and after making final preparations I turned in early, telling the men to be up before sunrise.

At half-past five, in the bare light of dawn I rose, and after making a hearty breakfast, we prepared to start. Meanwhile my men were breaking camp, and having loaded the animals, they turned back towards the A-tun-tzu valley by the way we had come.

Besides my Tibetan interpreter I was accompanied by one of the porters, who carried my blanket, cooking pot, and enough food for two days at a pinch, though we expected to reach the Mekong on the following day. I myself carried a camera, prismatic compass, and a mountain aneroid and thermometer, as I wished to make a rough traverse of the route ; and thus lightly laden we set out long before the sun had kissed the night dew from the reeking valley.

Presently we reached the last of the fir trees, crippled and twisted by the wind before they finally succumbed ; and losing the track, we struggled nearly waist deep through wet Rhododendron scrub, the tightly laced branches of which are as resistant as thin steel.

In time we got out of that too, and walking easily over the carpet of dwarf Rhododendron, at last found ourselves on the screes at 16,000 feet, amongst scattered cushions of *Arenaria polytrichoides* and clumps of golden saxifrage and blue gentians. *Myosotis Hookeri* also grows here, though I never saw it in any condition to flower ; and several species of Meconopsis, such as *M. rudis* (Oxford blue flowers) and *M. speciosa* (Cambridge blue flowers). But these of course were over. So far we had kept straight up the slope towards the snow peaks which, after an hour's climbing, rose into view ; and now throwing ourselves down on the stony ridge, we gazed at the curiously creased glacier, all shrunk up on the black cliff face, as though wrinkled with age, and the milk-white stream winding through the deep flower-carpeted valley at our feet.

Behind us the tops of the fir trees were already touched by the sunbeams, their trunks throwing long shadows against the grass where one half of the valley was gilded with the splendour of the morning. It was a glorious sight, everything just waking, as it seemed, in the first bath of sunshine; what little snow remained on the ridge where we lay was crisp as candy, and the air was deliciously cool.

The ascent to the pass at the southern end of the buttress looked very steep, though the slope was grassy and dotted with grazing yak. At one point I observed that we would have to pass right beneath an overhanging cornice of the glacier which had already piled up a heap of fragments below; over these it would be necessary to scramble, but it did not look difficult, though there might be some danger of falling ice later in the day.

On the other hand it was now obvious that there was another equally easy pass at the north end, rather closer, though we were separated from both by the deeply scoured glacier valley—or rather what had once been a glacier valley—and one or two smaller valleys which opened into it.

Far away to the north-north-east I caught sight of a very high peak thrusting its snowy pyramid through a thin belt of cloud above the surrounding mountains, and had we crossed by the southern pass I might have had a good view of it; as it was we did not see it again. Evidently it was across the Yangtze in Ssu-ch'uan;

anyhow, the next climber on Pai-ma-shan should keep
a look out for it.

In the bare valley at our feet a black speck indicated
a herdsman's tent from where we hoped to receive final
instruction. At the head of this same valley was one of
those little turquoise-blue lakes which are such a feature
of these glaciated mountains.

Reluctantly leaving our view point, we scrambled and
slid down the scree towards the tent, the bare slope
gradually becoming more and more gay with flowers
as we descended. Patches of a lovely pale blue Aconitum
and the dark blue *Aconitum Hookeri*, both charming
dwarfs, were conspicuous. Long before we reached
the tent the big black shaggy dogs had sighted us, and
were making the valley ring with proclamations of our
arrival, as the saplings to which they were tied bent like
bows to their struggles ; nor dared my men approach
till the herdsmen had come out of the tent and held the
beasts by their collars. These fierce, alert animals are
kept chiefly for the purpose of giving warning of the
approach of leopards or bears, since strangers hardly
ever visit these remote valleys, least of all for the purpose
of robbery.

These men, as expected, pointed to the southern pass,
telling us to cross the main valley, where we should find
still another encampment, and climb up beneath the
cornice we had seen from the ridge, hugging the side of
the cliff.

We now stepped abruptly over the lip of our valley,
and dropping down to the main glacier valley 1500 feet
below, came upon the last tent, only to learn from the
herdsmen that the northern pass was the better of the
two, and that if we persisted in crossing the range south

of the tower, we should not reach the Mekong next day ; there was another deeply scoured valley beyond the ridge to cross.

I will say a few words here about these yak herdsmen so frequently mentioned.

From the time the snow disappears in the high valleys about the end of June, till the early morning frosts whiten the grass with rime, at the end of September, the Tibetans send their herds of yak in charge of two or three men to graze on the alpine pastures.

Here they pitch their camps in grassy dells by the stream side, moving higher from month to month as the snow melts and the yak stray further in search of food. At night the animals are brought back to camp and picketed in rows close to the tent, guarded by fierce dogs, but by day they wander at will far up the mountain slopes. It is a hard, lonely life these men lead for the brief summer months, in their dark, smoke-dimmed shelters, half tent, half hut. But the air is keen and fresh up here just below the snows, where the gentians and saxifrages and blue poppies flourish for a space amongst the grey stones ere they fall asleep, and the inconstant clouds reshape themselves with every whim of the breezes which eddy amongst the hills.

These shelters consist of a rude stone wall, rather oblong in plan and about two feet high, over which is spread, by means of a ridge pole, the coarse brown tent cloth. The open space above the black wall, against which stands the poor little altar with its daily offerings of *tsamba* and its row of crude clay figures, is blocked up with branches. Inside all is darkness, dirt, and disarray. A couple of hard boards and a pile of thin hempen blankets and goat-skins indicate the bed ; in one corner stand the tall wooden cylinders for churning tea, and against the wall several tubs of yak milk which is fast curdling. A few hide bags of *tsamba*, a couple of long, lean guns with pronged supports, and a fire blazing in a shallow pit in the middle of the earthen floor, complete the furnishing of the tent.

Yet when the wind whirls down from the passes, flinging the cold rain this way and that, the cosiest place I know is a corner by the fire inside such a shelter, having my wooden bowl filled again and again by the hospitable herdsman with hot buttered tea frothing from the churn.

At night when white mists roll up the valley wrapping the mountains in ghostly garments, the herdsmen fall to prayer. Their voices rise and fall in monotonous droning chorus, as they chant the oft-repeated words never omitted because they live thus hermit-like away from their village ; and presently the muffled notes from iron-throated yak bells ring solemnly through the darkness.

To return to the shade and smoke and smell of the tent on Pai-ma-shan where we rested for half an hour, drinking rich but sour yak milk, and eating our lunch.

We now took leave of our friends and started up the main valley. It was very hot now, and I found the steep climb up the little flat, not far from the lake we had looked down upon four hours previously, rather tiring.

In spite of the lonesomeness of these stony troughs, the scenery always appealed irresistibly to me. The barren valleys through which the now atrophied glaciers once ploughed a way, separated by stark ridges, here and there hemming in a jewel of water ; the different coloured rocks, and especially the manganese-red limestone com-

mon on this range which, reflecting the yellow afternoon
sunshine, throws a rich crimson light into the valley;
and watching over all the frowning bulk of Tsa-ya, its
remnant of glacier pushing forth long arms as though
feeling its way carefully down the precipice and then
suddenly finding, too late to draw back, that it is steeper
than it looked.

At the bend of the valley we reached a deep lakelet,
from which the water escaped under the boulders. The
lakelet, however, did not receive the main glacier stream,
being cut off from it by a low mound; it received just
sufficient to tint it a wonderful clouded blue, but I
called it the milky lake. The glacier stream had cut
a passage for itself through the cliff which held up the
lake, independently.

The valley turned at right angles here, and immediately
above the lakelet we found ourselves on a broad, sandy
flat at the foot of the cirque—probably a silted-up rock
basin. Glaciers had done this work.

We had seen exactly the same features on this range
further north, whence the glaciers have long since
disappeared.

Here matted bunches of *Cochlearia scapiflora* flourished
amongst pools of icy water and a network of crystal
streams.

After crossing this flat the going became very bad, as
we had to scramble amongst boulders of all sizes. Higher
up, a glacier from the north face of the mountain swept
across the narrow valley, blocking it, but had so far
retreated that it scarcely turned down the valley at all.
However, it had piled up a considerable moraine on what
was formerly its flank (now actually its foot). This
moraine stretched some way down the middle of the

valley, thus showing how far the ice had quite recently extended. On our right was a wall, at the summit of which opened several hanging valleys. These had once poured small overflow glaciers into the main valley, but the ice here had retreated till only the main glacier, flowing north, remained; and that was hidden from view.

We had now to climb up on to the glacier, and a difficult business it was. For whereas no one was anxious to venture out on to the glacier itself, the moraine bore in many places only a thin veneer of rock debris, and was too steep and loose-knit to afford convenient foothold; while following a middle course along the glacier edge was risky, as stones occasionally came clattering down the slope on to the glacier, much to our embarrassment. However, we were soon across the worst bit, following a track in the snow which led to the pass itself.

Meanwhile clouds had gathered round Tsa-ya. There was a fine view westwards nevertheless, across the blue shadowy gorge at the bottom of which, 8000 feet below us, flowed the Mekong, to the Salween divide and so, through the big gap of the Londre-la, far away to the snow peaks of the Salween-Irrawaddy divide, floating in the clouds as it seemed. Eastwards, a high spur completely shut out the view, even the little blue lake, and the sandy flat hemmed in by rough screes, and the herdsman's tents below, being invisible.

As usual, a cold wind ripped through the notch, which was our pass, over 16,000 feet above sea-level; but there were a few scattered plants amongst the boulders, all wrapped in skeep-skins, so to speak, as a protection against the hostile conditions. Foremost amongst these were some intensely woolly Saussureas.

It is interesting to note that different species of Saussurea occur on the limestone and the porphyry.

Presently we prepared to descend, and matters now became more difficult. There was no path at all, and it was evident that not even the sure-footed yak could cross the range here, since we had to leap from boulder to boulder, a matter more befitting the agile mountain goat. However, the easiest route across this confusion of boulders was indicated by little cairns set up on the bigger rocks, placed there by hunters who come up into these mountains in pursuit of deer and sheep. Sometimes the cairns were so far apart that we lost the way for a time, but patient search always revealed another cairn ahead.

Below us, the valley grew rapidly narrower, and a wilderness of tumbled boulders became jammed between precipitous cliffs as far down as the fringe of spruce which clung to them like fur. We began to traverse along the spur on our right, leaving the valley to its fate ; the noise of the swelling torrent grew fainter and fainter ; gradually the trail became plainer, but still it was a sheer climb up and down the cliffs, round gullies and over small spurs, till at last, one of the men sang out that Hoa monastery was in sight. Scrambling up on to a rock, I saw far below, white against the trees, a little gleaming speck, without doubt the monastery.

Here, amongst scrub and boulders, a lovely lavender-blue Codonopsis hangs its shy head. The inside is streaked with purple—seen through the corolla these streaks look like blood vessels.

Quite suddenly we found ourselves on a good path traversing the hill-side, and half an hour later threw ourselves down on a clear grassy space at the summit

of the spur which stretched unbroken below us and dipped
to the Mekong. Directly in front rose the Ka-kar-po
range, half in cloud; but the southernmost pyramid
stood clear, with a band of cloud across its loins, so that
its steep glaciers tumbled unexpectedly out of a misty
ocean. It looked near enough to toss a biscuit across
the invisible Mekong.

For miles and miles to north and south we could
follow every twist and turn of the valley, and count scores
of spurs like that on which we lay, colossal ribs, between
which pulsed the Mekong aorta, now at diastole, arching
down from the enclosing divides; not far to the north
A-tun-tzu mountain, though presenting a novel appearance from this angle, was easily recognisable. Behind us
Pai-ma-shan was already swallowed up in the murk.

Immediately below began the dry elfin forest of gnarled
holly leaved oak, and into this we presently plunged,
following a good path so that we got down at a great
pace. It was nearly dark when we at last reached a
second grassy platform on a lower shoulder of the spur
and saw before us a herdsman's hut. What a relief,
I thought, throwing myself down on the sward, but alas !
the hut was unoccupied and my men could not find
the water supply—indeed, it did not appear that there
was any water now, so dry and burnt up were the surroundings : it had been an extraordinarily dry summer.
There was no alternative therefore but to continue the
descent of the ridge, where forest presently gave place
to open scrub and allowed us glimpses into the valley.

I was past tiredness now—in the course of a prolonged
day's climbing one seems to get over the first feelings
of weariness, and go on almost mechanically without
even laying by future discomfort in revenge ; particularly

is this the case when the effort is prolonged over two or three days, as I have noticed once or twice when lost in the mountains. Bodily weariness is humbled in the presence of mental concentration.

Night had fallen before we reached the valley, and it was pitch dark when at last we heard the barking of dogs and lights began to show up in Hoa village.

Guided by a fearful din, we approached the first house ; and saw, in the ruddy glare of pine torches, a crowd of priests and others engaged with drums, cymbals, trumpets and oft-repeated prayers in exorcising the devil from a sick man. The noise alone would have been enough to drag any but a helpless invalid very quickly from his bed.

At our unexpected appearance out of the darkness the noise ceased, and the fact that the crowd was by this time hilariously merry, in spite of the solemn occasion which had brought them together, added to the usual warmth of a Tibetan greeting. We were now escorted to another house and made comfortable by the fire. Food and drink were set before us and my guides were very soon as drunk as our hosts ; but personally, being hungry after twelve hours' marching, I only sipped the raw spirit.

So we sat round the fire while my two men talked as long as they could of the day's adventures, and I cooked myself a meal ; it was all very enjoyable and homely— the young wife with a baby at her breast baking flap-jacks on an iron pan, our tall unkempt loose-limbed host, the dark room with the circle of faces lit up by the glow of the fire, fading into darkness where outlines became suggested rather than seen, and my two tired men sprawling anyhow on the floor.

Afterwards I went up on to the roof and lay down as I was, in a pile of straw, and covering myself up with a blanket, soon fell fast asleep under the stars; while a warm breeze floated up out of the Mekong valley and rustled through the trees, and at intervals the summer lightning flashed out palely.

Daylight showed Hoa to be an extensive but disjointed village, built on a series of terraces above the stream. The monastery, small but dignified, boasting a hundred priests, brooded over all at the junction of two streams, one from either pass already referred to.

Like Londre and many another village, Hoa is not only invisible, but its existence would be quite unsuspected from the Mekong valley road, and I think that the population of the valley is at least twice as great as it appears to anyone travelling by the river side.

Before I left next morning, the woman of the house asked me for some medicine for her baby, who, by the way, was scarcely two years old.

" What's the matter with him ? " I asked.

" He's got a stomach ache," was the reply !

Goitre is certainly one of the commonest diseases amongst the eastern Tibetans, but a stomach ache is the one most commonly complained of. Once, coming down the Mekong valley, a woman held up my entire caravan to ask " Bimbo Chimbo " ¹ for some medicine.

" What does she want ? " I asked my Tibetan guide, expecting to see her drop dead from heart failure any moment.

" She complains of having a stomach ache," he replied !

¹ དཔོན་པོ་ཆེན་པོ (Pöm-po Chhem-po) = Great Chief; a common form of polite address in this part. In Eastern Tibet it is pronounced as above.

People would go miles out of their way to find me
and ask for medicine to give their silk relatives, and sometimes I managed to visit them. Then I would feel the
patient's pulse, tap his chest, examine his tongue, ask
his age, and turning round to the expectant crowd who
stood hanging on my words, staring round-eyed with
astonishment into the little black box filled with bottles :
" I know what's the matter with him," I would say
impressively—" he's got a stomach ache " : and at that
they would all applaud. Still, I had a great reputation
all through this country, so I think I must have cured
some of my patients ; at least there were always plenty
more willing to take the risk.

We reached Ko-niang by the Mekong, at ten o'clock
in the morning, after an hour's ride, and found it op-
pressively hot till the afternoon breeze sprang up ;
the mules did not arrive till late in the afternoon. The
minimum only sank to 70·5° F. that night, but even
down here there were unmistakable signs of autumn
in the air. Already the winter crop of buckwheat was
coming up, the millet and maize were nearly ripe, the
pears had been sliced and spread out on the flat roofs
to dry, and the walnuts piled in heaps. The local people
of the valley, who did not wish to make so long a journey
as the complete circuit of Ka-kar-po, were plodding
northwards, dressed in their gayest clothes, to visit the
temples in the glacier valleys, while bands of regular
pilgrims from Tsa-rong were daily wending their way
down the valley towards the Do-kar-la.

VIII

With the Pilgrims to Do-kar-la

ON September 6th we ourselves marched through the Mekong gorge to Londre. The only bits of colour between the emerald-green oases now was afforded by patches of gamboge " dodder " (*Cuscuta sp.*) enveloping bush after bush in fatal embrace. Then up through the forest to our old camping ground in the meadow, reached on the 8th.

Many fruits were already ripe in the forest. It is a remarkable fact that scarlet berries are generally pendent, while black ones stand erect, at least in these forests. Thus the fruits of cherry, Podophyllum, Euonymus, Oligobotrya and *Ribes moupinense* are all pendent, as they are likewise in many species of rose, Rubus, Cotoneaster and Lonicera. The erect fruits of *Panax ginseng*, Clintonia, *Ribes glaciale* and some species of rose, Rubus and Lonicera are on the other hand black. The pendent habit is typical of the wetter forest and meadow plants, whose flowers, concealed beneath the leaves, are thus protected from rain ; and red berries are conspicuous in the forest where black ones would be invisible.

The meadow was now past its best, but a good many plants were still in flower, amongst them the following : *Meconopsis integrifolia, Primula brevifolia, Primula pseudoikkimensis, Gentiana detonsa, Aster fuscescens, Cardamine macrophylla ;* species of Pedicularis, Allium, Impatiens, Adenophora, Acontium, Polygonum, Salvia, Corydalis, Saxifraga and Codonopsis. Later in the season I collected seed of *Aster fuscescens* and introduced a pretty plant into England.

The boulder screes were gorgeous with fruiting shrubs. There were large golden-red raspberries, profuse amongst sea-green foliage and waxen stems, the scarlet berries of a Lonicera, translucent in the sunlight, and bunches of red-winged samaras, hanging from the maple trees.

One morning we climbed to the pass. For the last few hundred feet of the ascent the rocks are covered with tiny stone altars on which offerings to the spirit of the mountain are laid ; some slices of dried pear, a few walnuts, or a little bowl of *tsamba*, it may be. Several bands of pilgrims passed our camp, men and women twirling their prayer drums and muttering the everlasting prayer ; even small children trudged bravely along with their parents. Thus do the poor Tibetans acquire merit, walking for eight or ten days through the river gorges and over the passes with the sacred snow peaks ever on their right-hand side.

It rained nearly every day while we were at the Do-kar-la, more than half an inch falling on the 13th. Yet the total rainfall for the six days was only 1·09 in. The average minimum temperature over the same period was 42·1° F., the lowest recorded being 40° F. on a clear morning, when a heavy dew was deposited. During the daytime the thermometer never rose much above 50° F.

On the last night of our stay I went across to the boulder beneath which the Tibetans were camped. In the purple dusk the younger ones went forth to collect firewood and herbs for the evening meal. Presently someone climbed up on to the rock and sang out : " Come, friends, supper is ready." One by one they wandered back, some carrying bundles of faggots, others with lily bulbs, garlic and toadstools, and all hungry. A large iron pot bubbled over the fire, and into this were thrown various leaves, a pinch of coarse salt, and lumps of butter. Then the wooden bowls were brought out and each received a portion of soup. Meanwhile, buttered tea was being churned in the tall wooden cylinders till it frothed, skin bags of barley flour were untied, butter boxes opened, and the Tibetans now set about their meal in earnest.

The night was fine. Through the trees one could see the constellations rolling majestically across the swarthy sky. Someone began to twang a little bamboo jews' harp, to which was presently added the mournful wail of a reed whistle. Outside the night wind blew softly, making the trees scrape against each other as though whispering secrets ; an owl hooted plaintively, and the torrent grated over the gravel. Suddenly the silence was rent by a clatter and roar as an avalanche of rock emptied itself down one of the gullies.

My companions were a strange lot of scarecrows. One girl with a huge goitre was deaf and dumb, and one of the men, similarly burdened with two goitres which dangled in a pouch of his neck, was blind in one eye and stone deaf. There was an oldish man who was nearly bald, and an undersized thick-set little man with a pock-marked face. One old woman had but two teeth in her head, and immense eyes like a fish. Finally, there was a tall man with thick curly hair and a prominent nose, a very good fellow ; and a pretty little girl, slightly disfigured by goitre, who was the life and soul of the party, always singing, laughing or dancing. She kept everyone in good spirits—but indeed all were merry and cheerful. The deaf and dumb carried on a spirited language by signs, from which I at any rate learnt that hooking the two little fingers together signified firm friendship.

Meanwhile those swains who were the fortunate possessors of lady loves, pillowed their heads on their mistresses' laps, and had their hair donc. The sham queue (made of blue wool, carefully plaited) was first unwound and detached, the hair combed out, buttered and plaited ; and the false queue, with its section of elephant's tusk threaded on it, hooked into position. Finally the whole was rebound on top of the head.

The Caucasian strain which is found running through some of these people is hard to account for. Whether it results from some remote Græco-Bactrian invasion of western China ; or whether some of Alexander's soldiers succeeded in making their way across Asia via Gilgit and Turkestan, let others decide. The fact remains that Caucasian features and characteristics are continually cropping up amongst the medley of peoples along the border.

On September 14th we moved down again. On reaching the Mekong I received a note from Mr. Widler saying that he would join me next day ; and on the 16th we met and went on to A-tun-tzu together. Travelling with Widler was a youth named Tom Roberts, who had been a pupil of mine at the Shanghai Public School some years previously.

It was still roasting hot in the Mekong gorge, 81° F. in the shade at five o'clock in the afternoon ! The minimum on the previous night had been 66° F. No wonder the shrub vegetation on the sunny slopes was scorched, even

I

high up in the A-tun-tzu valley ; for no rain had fallen. During the next week, however, the weather was showery, though less than half an inch of rain fell ; the average minimum temperature (September 18th–24th) in A-tun-tzu was 50·8° F., the maximum rarely exceeding 60° F.

On September 24th Widler and Roberts left for Ba-t'ang. I walked up with them to the top of the pass at the head of the A-tun-tzu valley, whence a long winding descent through a delightful country of crags and forest and spouting torrents, takes one down to A-dong. The slopes were a maze of vivid colour, the gorgeous scarlets of Pyrus and barberry mingling with the limpid yellows of birch, poplar and willow. Above, sombre conifers were preparing for the stern fight against winter.

It remained now to go the round of our summer camps and collect seed of the flowers we had discovered ; so on September 26th we moved out of A-tun-tzu and camped in the old glaciated valley on the Yangtze-Mekong divide. The sun did not reach us till nearly ten o'clock, and after a frosty night we would moodily watch the shadows shortening across the valley, and the sunshine gnawing slowly into the white crust which flashed into sparkling light at its touch. Close by was a yak herder's tent whence I obtained fresh milk every day. Towards nightfall we would hear the monotonous droning of prayers, interrupted by the *woof woof* of the big dogs if we dared to make a sound ourselves.

On September 29th, after six degrees of frost, it snowed all day on the heights, a bitter wind blowing. Everything was shrouded in a pall of mist ; frozen-looking flowers shivered and huddled amongst the grey boulders—the delicate and refined *Gantiana heptaphylla* was still in bloom, so were *G. Georgii, Aconitum Hookeri,* and other late alpines. It is amazing how these delicate looking plants survive the cold, and ripen their seeds under snow. The streams were hushed, or slunk gurgling out of sight under the boulders; the shallower lakelets were dry, and the wind, nosing through the hollows, found there only sand which it flung angrily aside. The snow continued; the herdsmen descended to warmer levels; and on October 1st we packed up and followed them. The fine weather now set in, sunny days and keen nights, with boisterous winds blowing up the valley.

On October 6th we set out for Ka-kar-po camp—none too soon, for the seeds were now falling from their capsules in the crisp air. In the forest, ropes of red-winged fruit swing from the maple trees, and the lacquered-silver leaves of *Pyrus,* flushed with orange, shone out amongst the black trunks of the conifers. We pitched camp on the open spur above the forest, and lit huge fires, for the wind blew cold off the glacier. After another fall of snow in the night my breath hung like fog in the tent and we spent a cold day collecting seeds. At dusk a heavy dew came down and drenched the grass. The distant peaks of Pai-ma-shan glittered in the lingering glow long after the valley was wrapped in darkness; and while the shadows crept slowly out of the tremendous gulf and quenched the last twilight, I sat by the leaping fire and dreamed of the mysteries beyond the mountains.

On October 11th we were hurrying down again. As we approached the village two children ran out to greet their parents who were returning with us after a few days' absence. The little girl clasped her mother's hand, the boy manfully shouldered his father's long gun, and together they walked back to their home. In the evening

I brought out my gramophone and delighted the people ; only one baby boy, being suddenly frightened, turned away from the magic box and cried, whereupon his father picked him up in his arms and comforted him as tenderly as any woman might. Finally, the tall Tibetan kissed him — or rather licked him, and set him down comforted.

In the East children are more dependent on their parents than are European children. Babies cannot bear to be left alone for a moment, and so we see Eastern women who work in the fields all day, carrying their babies about with them, tied on their backs and half smothered in a goat's-skin or a large cloth. The pleasure-loving Europeans employ foster-mothers or nurses.

We now paid a flying visit to the Ka-kar-po temple above the glacier in the next valley to the south, on the same range. The glacier had speeded up during our absence, and ice pillars crashed over the cliff with greater frequency. Pilgrims visited the temple daily, and would spend hours walking solemnly round and round the tiny platform, turning the heavy leather prayer drums as they passed.

On October 16th we made a long march down the warm Mekong valley, changing our transport animals three times so that it was an hour after dark when we reached our destination. Next day we proceeded through the gorge in the teeth of a howling gale. It was necessary to go with caution up and down the steep flights of steps, and round the projecting cliffs, where one was exposed to the full blast. The men held on to the ponies' tails, shouting " go slow ! go slow ! "—a warning they did not require since it was impossible to go fast ; sometimes they were almost stopped dead by the terrific

gusts which, with legs outspread and heads turned side-
ways, they withstood as best they might, though balanced
on the edge of this wonderful cliff road, 300 feet above
the raging Mekong.

On the following day we reached Londre, passing
between cliffs hung with ferns, orchids and waxen-
flowered Asclepiads.

On October 19th we pitched camp at the old spot
below the Do-kar-la, now transformed; the meadow
flowers had died down, the river which flowed knee deep
in September had shrunk to a shallow stream, and seeds
rattled round us as we brushed through the dying undergrowth.

The first night in camp was cloudy, and the temperature only fell to 32·5° F., but on October 20th it cleared
up, and after a brilliant night the sheltered thermometer
registered six degrees of frost; we got up to find the
meadow stiff with rime.

Hardly any flowers remained now, though the screes
actually yielded a couple of small orchids and a few yellow
saxifrages, besides the hardy little *Gentiana heptaphylla*,
one of the Ornata series ; and having collected our seeds,
we started back through the forest. Brightly coloured
leaves were falling with gentle rustle.

We passed some men from the distant province of
Pomed at the bend of the Brahmaputra, this day—tall,
wild-looking fellows with long unkempt hair falling over
their shoulders. They had been to A-tun-tzu to sell
musk, and had invested the proceeds in iron pots which
they were now taking back with them. They travelled
slowly, for their loads were immensely heavy, and said
they would be two months on the road.

Arrived at the little monastery of Ho-pa, or Yangsta,

on the Mekong, I found a lama from the big monastery of Drayü on a visit there ; he had heard from the local people of my wonderful singing-box, and nothing would satisfy him but that I should at once bring it out. Though it was late in the evening I complied, and all my porters, girls as well as men, in spite of their heavy day's march, sat round in a ring to listen ; while from ten o'clock till midnight I held the company entranced. The lama from Drayü was spellbound, but all he remarked as he shook his head slowly was " *yak po !* " (good).

Next morning as we were starting, he requested me to take his photograph. He was dressed in a sort of black silk cassock, and his long hair hung straight down. He was well educated too, and wrote some Tibetan in a book for me, an accomplishment of which the Ho-pa priest was incapable.

By means of a forced march we reached a village in the A-tun-tzu valley after dark that night. It was a tight squeeze in the small room placed at our disposal, but we were up and away the earlier for the discomfort, reaching A-tun-tzu on October 23rd. Thus ended our autumn journey.

IX

The Start for Tibet

MY seed collection was now nearly complete, and the next five days were spent in drying and packing seeds, and in preparation for a winter journey through eastern Tibet. Having made arrangements with my Tibetan interpreter (known as the " Monkey ") to accompany me, and with my Chinese servants to take my collection down to Tali-fu, I packed everything and only waited till the last seeds were brought in, dried, and safely wrapped up.

The start was fixed for October 30th.

A Tibetan friend of mine in the village had five ponies, and I arranged with him to take me as far as the Mekong by the little road over the mountain to Pu, whence we could cross the Mekong at Silong, and follow the right bank northwards.

The ponies were to come at 3 a.m., and that night I packed everything—instruments, thermometers, collecting things, cameras and plates, gramophone, warm winter clothing, bedding, tea, soup and chocolate—(the only stores I was carrying as we could do ourselves well in Tibet)—a couple of cooking pots, rifle and gun ammunition, a few necessary books, and about a thousand rupees in silver.

After making my last observations, and giving final instructions to my Chinese boys, who were to leave for

Tali-fu later on the same day, I turned in at midnight, and fell asleep almost immediately.

At the first sound of men moving in the kitchen I awoke with a start and sprang out of bed into the cold and darkness ; presently I heard a footstep on the cobbles outside and a faint tinkling of bells.

" All is well, the ponies have come," I thought, and quietly opened the door. Meanwhile the " Monkey " was preparing breakfast, which we ate by the fire at five o'clock.

At last everything is ready, the boxes are tied on to the ponies, I say good-bye to my Chinese servants who are leaving for their homes a couple of hours later, and we set out on the journey.

It is just six o'clock, and a faint grey light is appearing in the sky, but the street is deserted, not a soul witnesses our departure. Half an hour later we are in the forest. Dead white clouds hang like smoke over the eastern mountains, but soon they are tinged with pink as the light grows ; in the west the clouds are slate blue, and before we reach the first pass a drizzle of fine snow is falling ; but the air braces us like a tonic. In places the path is slippery with ice.

At the pass (11,984 feet) where we find ourselves in sunshine for the first time, the shade temperature is 29° F.

After crossing the second pass (12,554 feet) we went down the steep path to the Mekong as quickly as possible, halting at nine for a hasty breakfast. Then on o Pu by the river-side, where ripe crab apples were seen, and the villagers were threshing the millet.

From Pu the ponies started back. After collecting the necessary eight porters with as little delay as possible, we continued up the left bank of the river as far as the rope bridge, and crossed to Silong.

It was four o'clock when we reached Silong, and five before we had changed porters and were ready to go on again ; I therefore suggested we should halt for the night ; but the " Monkey " would not hear of it, so on we went.

In the headman's house at Silong there was a long stick, marked by cuts into twelve sections, representing the months of the year. In each section a number of notches indicated the number of porters supplied to travellers during the month. Thus no false claims for payment could be made by people who had not done any carrying, all the wages being paid to the village headman for distribution, as the custom is.

It was dusk when we started and pitch dark before we entered a deep gorge. Following a very bad path which presently dipped steeply to a torrent, we crossed by a narrow plank bridge ; the ponies were led slowly forward for we could not see five yards ahead. However, there was a village opposite us which the Tibetans hailed, and having ascended the cliff we were met by the people of Jong carrying torches, and crowded in a body into a great gloomy room half lit up by a ragged fire. An old man from time to time set spinning a small eight-sided wooden cylinder fixed in a stand which stood on the hob ; this was a miniature prayer drum.

We had been travelling for thirteen hours, and after a hasty supper I turned in but did not sleep easily. I dreamed that at the next pass on the frontier we were stopped and turned back. Consequently I was anxious to be off on the following morning, and after a breakfast of boiled rice and fresh yak milk with eggs and cream

cheese, we set out, still following the right bank of the
Mekong.

The people of these villages scattered along the valley
on emerald oases perched high up on the buff-coloured
cliffs, or in little bays lower down, are quite well off; yet
they look poor, by reason of their dirty dress and unkempt
persons. Crops of golden maize, millet and buckwheat
have just been cut in the fields, and herds of yak, goat
and cattle are now wandering over the stubble which in
three months will be green again with the spring wheat.
Big square houses, their white walls gleaming in the sunshine, dot the slope, half hidden beneath heavy shaded
walnut trees, and tinkling streams of water keep sweet
the narrow lanes, hedged with pomegranate. Then the
streams splash on from terrace to terrace, over high
banks which in spring are smothered with flowers.

Sometimes, however, the appearance of the villagers
is quite different; we might be in a new land altogether.

A couple of miles above Jong the valley becomes more
arid—not a tree is in sight, the mud-coloured houses,
no longer white, huddle together for warmth. A couple
of twisted lanes—half blocked by grunting pigs searching
for a meal—thread their way from house to house, and
we tramp ankle deep through black mud to a wooden
gate in the wall; passing through a small cattle yard into
the stable we mount through a square hole in the roof
by means of a notched log.

Upstairs is the family room—kitchen, dining-room,
bedroom, sitting-room, and large enough for all. But
it is not the only room. On the other side of the gallery
which runs round the square opening are small store rooms
or cupboards, and the family chapel, and it was in one
of these snug retreats that I slept the night.

Such a village was Hotring, where we changed porters again. Just below is a rope bridge, called by the Chinese Lu-t'ou-chiao, where a guard used to be stationed. Opposite us opens the A-dong gorge, where the main road from Yen-ching,[1] on the left bank of the Mekong, leaves the river to ascend to A-tun-tzu. Once there was a village here—some walls still mark the site—but it was razed to the ground during the fight for A-tun-tzu in 1906.

While we were changing porters I took photographs of the valley and of a group of almost naked children who were eyeing me from a doorway.

The scenery here is more varied than is usual in the Mekong valley. After all there is something grand about these stark cliffs with the river pounding its way through them. Just before reaching Hotring we had crossed a high rocky spur, and on the opposite side of the river, which is here closely confined, a big gable-shaped cliff blocks the mouth of the A-dong gorge, forcing the torrent aside. On the spur stood a *mani* pyramid. From this point there was a fine view northwards, the toy-like village of Hotring being in the foreground at our feet, and beyond it dun-coloured spurs dipping down into the blue river flowing beneath a turquoise sky and clasped by the mountains on either hand. A single mare's tail cloud drawn out into wisps nebulous as a comet, floated across the valley and disappeared before it reached the opposite mountains.

Above Hotring are gravel cliffs carved into fantastic pillars by furious cloud-bursts or torrents which have

[1] Tsa-kha-hlo. ཚ་ཁ་ལྷོ་ . This is the generic name for the seven villages situated round the brine wells, by the Mekong. Each village has a name of its own.

swelled up and died away again almost before the echo of their brief passage can have been flung back across the river. The path winds up the cliff, ascending steeply till it is 600 or 800 feet above the river, and presently enters another gorge where the river makes a remarkable S bend ; here the path is carved out of the cliff face.

At five o'clock we reached Meri-shu, which is approached across a level terrace lying between the mountain foot and the high river bank. Not a tree anywhere, not even a stick, or a blade of grass, merely a smooth grey gravel plain ; but just before entering the village we came suddenly on a dry watercourse, fissuring the plain like a trench ; it was 50 feet deep and only 20 feet wide.

The people here, as all up the Mekong valley, are rather goitrous, even quite tiny children carrying unsightly lumps of flesh in their necks. The Chinese of A-tun-tzu say it is due to their eating the dirty red salt of the Tsa-kha-hlo brine wells; they themselves buy Chinese salt from Tali-fu. The only difference, however, is in the method of preparation.

We were now amongst the Tsa-rong people who are even more prosperous than the Tibetans further down the valley ; though there is not a stick of firewood to be had without going far into the mountains for it, and water is only obtainable by means of a flume which draws it off from the torrent in the nearest ravine, half a mile away.

The women dress in dark blue pleated skirts, and wear a thin silver plaque, studded in the centre with coral, stuck jauntily on one side of the head. The same style of pleated skirt is worn by the Tibetans of Pang-tzu-la on the Yangtze, and further south by the Mosos of

Li-kiang. Considering how conservative in dress people really are, this is evidence in favour of the Tibetan origin of the latter tribe.

The minimum temperature that night fell to 45·5° F., and on November 1st we left the Mekong and started up a side valley with four yak and four men who were to see us safely to the Wi-chu, a big tributary of the Salween. We were now following the main road into the heart of Tsa-rong, by which all the pilgrims, musk traders, and caravans come into China from southern and eastern Tibet. M. Bacot, the French traveller who crossed Tsa-rong in 1909, had followed this road before me, but I hoped in a few days to leave his route.

The path was very rough at first, ascending steeply over great piles of boulders between limestone cliffs. Presently vegetation began to appear, at first only bushes covered with festoons of silvery Clematis fruits ; but higher up, where the gorge widened out into a more open valley, mixed forest. Here grew lime trees, maples, birch, poplar, oak, pine, and still higher, Rhododendron and fir trees. From a platform some way up the gorge we looked back for the last time and saw the great mountain range which rises like a wall on the other side of the Mekong, itself no longer visible. The main road to Tsa-kha-hlo on the left bank, 2000 feet above the river, was just a zigzag line and a white speck of a village now came into view. Then as we turned the corner and entered the forest, we saw the Mekong gorge no more.

Presently a party of pilgrims on their way round the snow mountains came along singing, with their worldly belongings on their backs, tightly packed in bamboo frames. This road, as I have said, is used a great deal,

especially in the spring and autumn, by the Tibetan caravans coming to China or visiting Lhasa, and every cliff we
passed was black with the smoke of generations of camp
fires, every fir tree charred and chipped for torchwood.

Early in the afternoon we reached a broad open glade
where the valley divided into two, and following the
right-hand branch, camped an hour later under the
trees. Snow was lying about in patches here, and every
rock and tree trunk in the stream was festooned with
icicles. The altitude was 12,984 feet. Towards morning
I felt so cold, when we had nine and a half degrees of
frost under the trees, that I was glad to turn out of bed
at six and get over by the fire. I had no tent, but had
brought a canvas sheet to rig up as a roof over my camp
cot.

At 8 a.m. we were on the road again, ascending
steadily through forests of Abies from which fluttered
long streamers of pale green lichen. These shone like
silver in the sunshine. Smaller and smaller grew the
stream, tighter and tighter the bonds of ice which
gripped it ; now the forest grew thinner, big junipers
appeared scattered amongst dwarf barberry bushes ;
then they in turn died out.

At the head of the valley we overtook a party of
Tibetans who had been to China and were carrying iron
pots back with them to Tsa-rong. They were still
encamped, two of their donkeys having died in the night.
The rest, with big sores rubbed through their pinched
backs, some of them lame, most of them looking as though
they would like to lie down and die, were standing with
bowed heads staring vacantly at the stony snow-covered
ground where a few patches of withered grass afforded
the only sustenance.

The vegetation and scenery of the Shu-la (Chu la on the latest map of Tibet published by the Survey of India) north of Ka-kar-po range is different to that of the Do-kar-la, being much poorer in shrubby species.

It is the Yangtze-Mekong divide over again—the same forest, the same shrub belt, the same piles of rock, bold bare cliffs, and stone-paved causeways over which the stream meanders at the head of the valley. That is to say, it has been glaciated. A few birds were still abroad in the forests below, but here all was silent ; once a pica-hare shot noiselessly out of a hole and disappeared again amongst the boulders.

Now we trudged through deep snow up the steep wall to the pass ; it was not melting in the brilliant sunshine but evaporating in the bitter wind. Near the summit I suddenly caught sight of a number of snow partridges huddled together under a rock squeaking plaintively and signalled to the Tibetan who was carrying my gun to hurry up. By the time he arrived the partridges had scattered somewhat, walking up the snow slope, but I bagged four with the first barrel and ought to have bagged some more only the second cartridge missed fire ; the remaining birds then went off with a surprised squawk and sailed down the mountain side. They were not the only surprised party at this success ; the Tibetans were dumbfounded. " Four ! " one of them kept repeating, " four at a time ! " and shook his head slowly, as the Tibetan always does when nonplussed, examining the birds, and the gun, and then the birds again as though he thought there must be some mysterious attraction between the two.

And now I was beginning to get excited, as one does when approaching a pass after travelling for hours through the dark forest, climbing steadily higher, to face at length a rock wall beyond which you feel is a great void. I begin to speculate on what we shall see. Mountains of course, but rivers ? lakes ? a great plateau, as further north, where the Mekong bends round towards the west, or these great parallel ranges again ? Now I struggle up the last few yards knee deep in snow, some way ahead of the snorting yak, and stand on the pass, 16,031 feet above sea-level ; it is eleven o'clock, the sun is overhead and I can take photographs to east or west.

A magnificent panorama is spread out below ; there is not a single spur to interrupt the view. Behind us is the Yangtze-Mekong divide and the Run-tzu-la black against the burnished sky ; in front an ocean of blue mountains, tinged along their summits with snow ; and northwards the twin pyramids of a glittering snow mountain called Orbor.

In spite of a chilly wind I sat for some time gazing at this colossal chaos of mountains flashing in the sunlight, the deep valley of the Wi-chu [1] at our feet, and then range beyond range to the Salween, and beyond that again more mountains. Why yes ! I must be looking at the very sources of the Irrawaddy itself, and there in the south-west, one, two, three, I know not how many ranges away must be the gorge of the Taron, and beyond that Burma. Wonderful ! I seem to hear the tinkle of temple bells away down in the golden pagodas of the hot south wafted up on the frozen wind. And yet, though I am actually looking into Burma, what a terrific journey it must be from here to Myitkyina and the

---

[1] Or Yü-chu, from the important monastery of Drayü on its bank. It is probable that Wi-chu is simply the local pronunciation. (See Mr. Eric Teichman's map of Kam.)

Irrawaddy confluence! longer than going back by the
main road to A-tun-tzu, across the Chung-tien plateau
to Li-kiang, and so across Yun-nan through Tali and
T'eng-yueh : that would take forty-two days ; well,
to toil up and down over these mountains across these
numberless rivers would not take more than fifty days
perhaps.

But the caravan is far down the opposite slope, which
is steep and stony ; I must get on with my work quickly,
so I take what photographs I can, and bearings to all
the peaks. The temperature out of the wind is 28° F.,
four degrees of frost. Half-way down the steep slope,
an unexpected sight came into view on our left. Quite
close to us rose the northernmost snow peak of Ka-kar-
po, like a crystal dome. What a splendid point from
which to climb it !

We now turned away to the right, that is, north,
leaving the stream and traversing along the side of the
spur. There were a few gentians and saxifrages in bloom
here and a little lower down I found small tufts of
Primula Henrici in fruit on some bare schistose rocks,
looking very withered in this arid place. Seeds of this
plant were sent home and flowered in 1915. Plants
and trees here, as well as the general aspect of the
mountains, were the same as on the Yangtze-Mekong
divide. The road, now running north-west, through
forests of larch and oak, though steep was good ; we
were gradually approaching the valley of the Wi-chu
which flowed 4000 feet below.

Across the valley, a high ridge blocks the view westwards and at its southern end two prominent sugar-loaf
peaks stand guard at the entrance to a gorge where the
Wi-chu turns suddenly at right angles to begin its

K

sensational series of wriggles before reaching the Salween. From a spur we caught sight of another snow peak further north.

Then came a terrific descent of 3000 feet through pine forest. This we accomplished in an hour and a half, and it brought us to a big stream coming down from the east. We pitched camp under some maple trees at an altitude of 10,365 feet ; and having built up a big fire against a rock I had supper and lay down to write my diary in the ruddy glow. The sky was again brilliant with stars which peeped between the trees, and the splashing torrent soon lulled me to sleep. The temperature in our sheltered nook only sank to 30° F. that night.

Next morning, following down the stream past dozens of blackened camping grounds, we soon emerged from the ravine, and climbing up to the shoulder of the spur stood right above the river. The Wi-chu is swift and green, twenty-five yards in breadth, here flowing south, but presently turning due west. Nowhere is it navigable, being shallow and frequently interrupted by rapids.

Our route lay due north up the left bank of the Wi-chu, and looking back down the valley through narrow gorges and across mountain chains, we had a perfect view of Ka-kar-po rearing its snowy peaks up into the blue vault of heaven. What a glorious sight for the pilgrims, marching down the valley, of whom we met two parties during the course of the day ! Immediately above us rose the tremendous cliff we had descended the previous evening. Across the river well-wooded mountains dipped steeply to the water, but the left bank was less abrupt, and very dry, with only scattered pines and oak trees. Below us, alongside the river patches of cultivated land began to appear, though the soil from these metamorphic rocks appeared thin, stony and poor. An excellent road wide enough for two pack animals to pass, wound along the mountain side round the gullies ; and after several miles of this we descended steeply to some cultivated fields close by the river-side, where stood two substantial houses.

Half a mile ahead of us on a low level platform overlooking the river was the village of Jalung, where we arrived at one o'clock, finding good quarters in the *bisi's* (chief's) house, though the " Monkey " had thought it advisable to go on ahead and prepare the way, as he felt that my reception might be cool.

The people of the Wi valley are evidently prosperous in spite of the apparent poverty of the soil. The houses, scattered amongst irrigated fields, in which crops of hemp and turnips were still standing, are large, the main walls built of stones plastered with mud and whitewashed, the superstructure generally of planks or of roughly hewn logs. The people are well dressed in the usual Tibetan style and have plenty of finery such as silver ear-rings, brooches and bead necklaces, besides considerable variety in the way of food.

So warm was it in the middle of the day that children went about naked, but in the afternoon a strong breeze blew up the valley, though we had only two degrees of frost in the night.

X

By the Yü River

JALUNG (10,069 feet) is a village of ten families,
but two or three houses on the opposite bank of
the river and two more a quarter of a mile back,
brings the total to fifteen. It is very difficult to
estimate the average number of a Tibetan family, owing
to polygamy and polyandry. In the *bisi's* house where
I stayed, the family numbered nine, six of them being
brothers and sisters, a large family for this country. But
they were not all present.

We were a very cheerful party round the family pot
that evening; the *bisi* gave me a solid lump of honey,
like glue, made by boiling and stirring the honey in an iron
pot, till it is quite thick, and then drying it; also the
scales of a Fritillaria bulb found in the mountains
(*F. Delavayi*) which, boiled and eaten with butter, has
an excellent flavour. I had out the gramophone and
the company were of course charmed.

We started late on November 4th, a bright warm day,
as usual in Tsa-rong at this season, and followed an
excellent road through a populous part of the valley,
climbing gradually. The mountains on the left bank
of the river here descend in broad flat terraces, on which
are built small villages and scattered houses shaded by
walnut and crab-apple trees; down below nearer the
river are cultivated fields.

From an isolated spur we had a good view northwards of broad river terraces dotted with clumps of trees, indicating villages, on the left bank, and looking south, we saw the two northern snow peaks of Ka-kar-po for the last time.

Now we descend again and travel easily across the flat cultivated land, past several *mani* pyramids, past an excellent cantilever bridge across the Wi-chu and beneath a wooden aqueduct raised high on trestles. Finally we climb sharply up to a ledge cut out of the limestone cliff, to find ourselves hanging over the river, which thunders through a narrow gorge several hundred feet below. Next minute we turn the corner. There, between the dark trunks of pine trees we see the chalk-white walls of a monastery bathed in the last rays of the setting sun. It is Pitu or, as the Chinese call it, T'sa-p'u-to.

That view of the village, when the mountains were casting long shadows aslant the dust-coloured terraces, gradually dulling the white walls of house and monastery with the cold touch of night, is unforgettable. As I stood on the narrow path looking down on the scene, some women passed carrying bundles of firewood ; my little caravan came along, the men singing, but still I stood and looked and looked. It was all so typically Tibetan, so big, so grand, so royal—the rampart of dry, brown mountains all round me, the green river whipped here and there into foam below, the big bluff houses clustered in a little bay where the sunshine lingers later than elsewhere, the turquoise sky overhead.

Beautiful country, how ill these narrow-minded superstitious folk fit in with the vast freedom your open gates seem to let in ! And yet is it not true that all the wide lonely spaces of the earth have been inhabited by bigots, slaves fettered by narrow custom ?

You, nomads of the wilderness, who have night by night watched the great constellations circle overhead, have turned your thoughts to the stars and invented systems of astronomy older than Chaldea! You have watched the loud rivers roll down their dreadful floods in summer from their mysterious origins in the white mountains and called them sacred, and have made pilgrimages to the holy places. You have marked the seasons, and watched your flocks dying because the rains were held back, and rejoiced when, with the bursting of the storm, the dun-coloured hills have shone green again. Your world, a world of big things, was full of mysteries which baulked you at every turn ; and in your search for truth you probed not deep. Presently iron custom shackled you ; a necessity of existence founded on obedience to the Law. And error grew up alongside the truth, like tares, and hardened, and choked the truth, reigning as superstition in its stead.

Is not this what happened to Inca and Arab, Mongol and Tibetan, overwhelmed by the spaciousness of earth and sky—a desert, lit by five thousand suns—heaven-kissing mountains? So the domination of the few could impose that cruellest of all burdens, custom, and petrify for ever the springs of originality !

But to the children of a happier northern clime, where the mountains are low and the seas beckon men, and the stars are not always visible—to us, who were uncouth and ignorant when you had invented writing and could count the months of the year across the starry belt of heaven, was left the carrying on of the torch you had lit.

Now we rode across the upper terrace towards the village, and saw a second terrace below, quite close to the river, with more houses scattered down a gentle slope. A big *chorten* stood close under the monastery wall, and round this and at the entrance stood numbers of yellow-robed priests, eyeing our approach.

However, they gave me a smiling welcome, albeit the smile was in some cases a trifle sour, as we rode round the monastery. Then we entered the courtyard of the *bisi's* house, which stood off a narrow lane behind a row of poplars.

News of our arrival flew like wild-fire through the village and presently the *bisi* came running up. He smiled broadly in greeting, and a crowd of twenty or thirty laymen and monks slowly collected in the courtyard. There was an important lama living in the house, a fellow with a bucolic nose and bleary eyes who was half drunk when we arrived at five in the afternoon; and while a room was being prepared, I satisfied the curiosity of the gaping crowd which pressed closely round, by showing them my shot-gun and field-glasses. Meanwhile the lama, speechless with liquor, having looked through the glasses, announced, in dumb show, his intention of keeping them, favouring me with the most idiotic smile imaginable. For a moment I was a little scared that he meant it; and the crowd, though they enjoyed the entertainment, were as picturesque a lot of blackguards as I had come across. They kept looking at me as though they did not know quite what to make of it, but were prepared for anything.

But the debauched old lama was only having a game and turned out to be quite a good fellow at heart, while the crowd were curious but harmless.

Picturesque blackguards they were! Tall, filthily
dirty, their faces almost black, each man wore only
a single sheepskin coat tied round the waist and reaching
to the knees. The wool, turned inside, was clotted
into a stiff mass, grey with grease; one shoulder was
thrust out exposing the powerful chest muscles and
biceps; leather-soled cloth boots covered the feet and
legs, and the coal-black hair was tangled over the
head or done up into a pig-tail. Large ear and finger
rings added a gipsy touch to these swarthy sons of Tsa-
rong.

The "Monkey" now came to me and said that the lama
being drunk we would have to wait till morning before
conferring with him. He did not seem very optimistic
of the result however, and had already expressed the
opinion that it would be best for us to follow the Wi-chu
and the road through Pemba and Shuopando—the route
followed by the pandit A. K.—instead of attempting to
cross Pomed. The latter province, he vowed, was full
of robbers and consequently very unsafe for so small
a party.

I sent a small present to the lama and the chief therefore, and settled down for the night, and next morning,
sent my man to interview the authorities. After half
an hour he came back and said the chiefs had told him
that the head lama of the monastery, a living Buddha
or reincarnated priest, who held supreme authority,
was away; we might therefore either wait here three
or four days till his return and then see him, or we
might go straight to Menkung and see the authorities
there. They themselves could not grant us permission
to continue by this road to Lhasa, which is five weeks'
march from Pitu.

I was anxious to avoid Menkung, having already been there in 1911. On the other hand, I chafed at the prospect of waiting four or five days in Pitu. But my guide pointed out that by going to Menkung we might be able to carry out the original plan of penetrating into Pomed, as that, and not the Pemba road we were now on, was the way thither. So after a little discussion we decided to accept the offer of conduct to Menkung and start that same afternoon.

Then we set out to look at the monastery and take photographs.

The monastery is a small compact building, nothing like so magnificent as the great monastery of Chung-tien which has the appearance of a village, nor so picturesque as that of Menkung or of Tung-ch'u-ling; it boasts indeed only sixty priests. Inside the stone-paved courtyard a number of monks lounged round or sat on the stone steps of the temple, twirling their prayer wheels. Black curtains drape the front of the building, which is high and imposing, with big wooden doors, and a roof decorated with the usual copper ornaments, like pepper castors.

But now one of the priests invites us inside, and we are taken up a flight of steps in semi-darkness to a gallery, and so to the apartments set aside for the living Buddha. This is a small plainly furnished room with a little chapel opening off it, where the priest prays.

A Lhasa rug with a silk cushion lay on the floor, and on the wall hung a beautiful piece of Chinese embroidery, presented to the priest by the previous rulers of Tsarong. Chased silver cups, a silver prayer wheel, and other belongings of the absent lama were also shown me (it was like the Wallace collection). Finally we descended to the kitchen where our guide regaled us with walnuts, buttered tea, currants and twisted rolls of crisp bread, fried in oil and very hard.

After leaving the monastery I walked a little way up the valley past a long row of prayer drums near which, beneath a grove of weeping willows, some very ragged-looking pilgrims were seated.

The valley appears more open to the north, and no very high peaks are visible; a little beyond Pitu is another pass over the eastern divide leading to Yen-ching on the Mekong. It was this pass, the Pitu-la, that Major Bailey and Mr. Edgar crossed in 1911.

Drayü-Gomba is reached in four easy marches, and from there a third pass crosses the snowy range of Damyon (a part of the Mekong-Salween divide). This leads to Samba-dhuka, a village on the Mekong which I reached from Ba-t'ang in 1911 ; this last was A. K.'s route. M. Bacot was at Pitu in 1909, and several Tibetans told me they remembered him.[1]

I now paid a farewell visit to the tipsy lama, who was sitting cross-legged in his sanctuary armed with Bible, bell and bottle. He was most friendly, pressed me warmly by the hand and begged me to drink with him. The ponies presently arriving, we resumed our journey at two o'clock.

Our route lay south through the gorge and so down the left bank of the river as far as the wooden bridge previously noted, by which we crossed to the right bank. From the bridge which is built in two spans, twenty-five yards in length, and unprotected by handrails, we

[1] Since this time several travellers have visited Pitu, notably the distinguished consular officer, Mr. E. Teichman. Vide *Travels of a Consular Officer in Eastern Tibet.*

had a good view down the Wi-chu. Its rocky banks are well covered with trees and shrubs, which displayed gorgeous autumn colours over the water. On the right bank the path ascends gradually through pine woods towards a low gap in the range. Now we look back for the last time and see the Wi-chu at our feet, flowing southwards. Across the valley are the sharp peaks of the Mekong divide.

A moment later we plunge into thicker forest, and climbing steadily soon reach a low pass, the La-Drang-Dang (or Tong-la) at an altitude of 11,795 feet; I race up the last few yards as it is growing dark, and I am anxious to see the view.

Wonderful! We have only just this minute turned our backs on the Wi-chu and certainly it was flowing due south; yet here it is at our feet again, this time flowing north! Surely I must be dreaming!

" What is the name of that river ? " I ask, pointing to the streak gleaming like a sword blade in the dusk.

" The Wi-chu," replies one of the Tibetans. We are standing in a notch of the high ridge which northwards separates the Wi-chu from the valley of the Salween. Round the base of this bluff the river races ; flowing on one side due south, on the other due north.

How this extraordinary loop has been formed an examination of the highly tilted rocks would perhaps inform us, but I suspect it is a case of what may be called a combination river, that is to say, a river made up of the fragments of two or three older rivers, which have been gradually forced into each other's embrace as the result of earth movement, or of cutting back by head erosion.

In the Wi-chu valley, limestones and schists are to

be seen dipping at a high angle, due *north*. This is unusual. Throughout this country, particularly in the river beds, the nearly vertical strata dip generally either west-south-west or east-north-east.

Here we have a hint of two distinct series of earth movements. First, a thrust from the north lifting the bed of the ancient Tethys above the waves and forming the foundation of the Himalayan ranges. These are, as it were, ruckles raised against the unyielding coast line of peninsular India, once, I believe, coterminous with the backbone of China, which separates the Yangtze and Yellow river basins. At this time the Himalayan flora must have spread far into China.

Secondly, a tremendous thrust from the west which has pinched all this border country, and almost obliterated the original main east and west ranges beneath a series of north and south ranges. This has separated the Himalayan ranges from those of Western China, and through the gap thus made pour the rivers of Tibet. The original geographical connection is easier to trace through the Sino-Himalayan flora than through the geological structure of the country, owing to the confusion of the border country.

Now it is possible that as a result of irresistible pressure acting along the axis of a mountain chain, shearing might take place, and the axis be actually slewed round, giving rise to a structure like the letter Z. This is what seems to have taken place, the result being the extra-ordinary courses of the Wi-chu, Yangtze, and Ya-lung rivers. Furthermore, after being pushed bodily east-wards up an inclined thrust plane, with the cessation of the pressure, the whole mass of country may have sagged back. The weight of the folds dragging on the synclines and breaking them, might thus have initiated the valleys of the Mekong and Salween.[1]

[1] In 1922, Professor J. W. Gregory and his son visited Yun-nan and came to certain general conclusions of great interest concerning this remarkable country. At the time of writing his work is not available (but see " The Alps of Chinese Tibet and their Geographical Relations," *Geographical Journal,* March, 1923). His main conclusions, in so far as they affect us are (i) That the main axis of the Himalaya is prolonged eastwards into China ; (ii) That Yun-nan is an area of subsidence.

XI

On the Road to the Salween

THE Wi-chu after flowing north for ten or twelve miles, again turns back on itself, and finally bends round to enter the Salween obliquely. From our vantage point we saw the whole valley coiled loop against loop like an intestine amongst the mountains ; the sun was setting behind the twin crystal peaks of Orbor, and black cliffs crowded up one behind the other from the Wi-chu to the Salween, their feet in the curdled mist, their heads amongst the brilliant stars. Darker and darker grew the shadows, the crimson faded from the sky, and indigo dusk curtained a scene of savage grandeur.

It was almost night when I left the pass and started down in the wake of the caravan. An excellent broad road wound towards the river, and shone white in the moonlight. Dust lay inches thick, and was kicked up in clouds by the animals.

Chu-mi-la-tung, where we spent the night, comprises four small houses scattered over a few acres of cultivated soil in the sleepy hollow.

In the house where we put up was a family of nine, the youngest not a year old, the eldest a granny of sixty-nine, though she looked ninety. To make room for us in the house, two small boys with shorn pates (they having been dedicated to a monastery) were turned

adrift, and slept on the roof in each other's arms, with
a couple of rugs thrown over them. I also slept in an
open passage, the rest of the family and my followers
occupying the warm kitchen. It did not quite freeze in
the⸲night, but it was surprising to see a small child step
naked out of the warm house into the raw morning air.

We had some difficulty in procuring the necessary
ponies and porters here, in spite of our modest require-
ments. While the "Monkey" was routing them out,
I went up towards the pass we had crossed the previous
evening to get a glimpse of Orbor.

When I returned to the house I found granny seated
by the fire twisting sheep's wool into twine, and roasting
barley in an open iron basin, stirring it from time to
time with a leather-covered mop, in order to brown it
evenly; but of transport not a sign, though I could
hear the "Monkey" expostulating with someone in
the next house.

After a good deal of talk, we procured five ponies,
and the necessary followers. Shortly after ten we set
out, continuing along the left-hand side of the shallow
valley. Some way ahead was a high cliff overlooking
the Wi-chu, where the river bends round a rocky prom-
ontory jutting out to the north. There I spied the
road again, which immediately in front of us was lost
to view, as it made a considerable detour to the east.

Half a mile down the road we passed a spring which
bubbled into a horse-trough, whence the village draws
its scanty water supply; its surface was now glazed with
ice. Lack of water is a serious menace in this arid country,
hence the numerous flumes.

The tops of the ridges are covered with pine woods
and oak scrub, but the slopes below us and the Wi valley

itself are quite bare of trees. Like the Mekong valley the Wi valley supports only a thin bush growth.

After traversing for some distance and crossing several deep gullies, all but one of them dry, we mounted steadily and soon found ourselves on a narrow path under the limestone cliff. From above the Wi-chu bend we had a good view of the neighbourhood.

The valley we had descended opens out on to a broad terrace, and a little beyond gapes the mouth of another still broader and flatter valley, with a snow peak in the background. This valley is quite thickly populated, a small monastery and two or three groups of houses being visible ; a second monastery is seen at the foot of the ridge on the other side of the Wi-chu, here spanned by a wooden cantilever bridge. Just opposite this second monastery is the village of Troshu, with about fifteen families. Thus there is seen to be a fair amount of cultivation at the river bend, though now all is brown and bare under the turquoise sky, no sound of flails falling on the house roofs, no voices singing in the fields.

Still mounting, we soon reached the highest point on the road (11,308 feet), and presently began the descent to what looked almost like a plain, a broad gently sloping cone of detritus washed down from a side valley, and spread out into an extensive platform. This platform had been carefully terraced by the people of Wábu, a village just gripped by the jaws of the valley.

On the way down we met a small caravan, but considering the excellence of this road across Tsa-rong, which is better than most roads in China, I was rather surprised at the paucity of traffic. Bands of pilgrims on foot we did sometimes meet it is true, and no doubt the road is more used in spring, when the Tibetans go

much to China : but at this season most of the big
caravans, whether of monks or traders, are on pilgrimage
to Lhasa.

Our arrival at Wábu in the middle of the afternoon
created something like a sensation. Dogs barked, people
poked heads out of windows high above the narrow
lanes, and one old woman actually barred the door, refusing us admittance. I expected that we should stop
the night there but the chief said that he would procure
us fresh transport at once, and we could reach Kábu
the same evening. Very nice of him I thought—little
dreaming that he was only desperately anxious to see
the last of us as soon as possible.

We therefore went into the house and had a meal,
while a number of old women were deputed to carry
the baggage.

The chief, like so many of these Tsa-rong men, was
a great traveller ; he had been as far east as Ta-tsien-lu
and spoke Chinese, which he enunciated very clearly.
His long black hair fell loose over his shoulders.

Soon after five we left Wábu, and it was evident that
we should not reach Kábu before dark.

The road, which is cut out of the mountain side a few
hundred feet above the river, maintains much the same
level for several miles and is surprisingly good.

We were now opposite the narrowest part of the
ridge which separates two loops of the Wi-chu, and at
one point where a depression occurs in the dividing
ridge and a path zigzags up to a low col, there must
be only a few hundred yards of rock between the two
channels. No doubt this will in course of time be worn
away by the constant attrition on both sides, and this
loop of the river disappear altogether.

L

Over the top of the ridge, only a few hundred feet high, we see huge portals framing the entrance to a wild rocky valley, lying south-west, and it is here that the river finally wriggles its way out of this mountain maze and turns bravely to meet the Salween. In the failing light, the view down the valley, girded by giant rock ribs, is wildly imposing. Terrific gusts of wind buffet us in the face as we continue down the river, and I find the greatest difficulty in taking compass bearings. Now the pink glow which for an hour has lingered, changes to silver as the moon rises into a sky of palest blue, illuminating bands of white road. I feel in the highest spirits, and sing as we march along in the warm darkness under the brilliant dome of night.

Soon I am far ahead of the porters—only my guide has gone on with the ponies, and except for the splash of the river down below and shrieking gusts of wind which whirl up thick clouds of dust, the night is very still. Presently I am standing on the summit of a high spur, a deep gully into which the moonlight can find no way, below. Looking back, a snow peak is seen glittering in the north, and the moonlight has turned the river to quicksilver.

The descent is steep and stony, I trip frequently, and have to go cautiously. At last I reach the bottom in safety, cross the gully, and ascend a little way up the opposite side. Silence everywhere. For some minutes I stand listening. Suddenly I hear dogs barking, and see lights, though it is too dark to make out the village. So I blow several blasts on my whistle, and along comes the " Monkey " with a torch, followed by two strangers. We are arrived at Kábu.

Now we are ushered into a house and almost immediately find ourselves the centre of a crowd. They come in one by one, big men with weather-beaten faces, wearing high boots and long cloaks, flint and steel and snuff horn rattling from their girdles as they swing along ; I am seated by the fire by this time, having supper, and as the giants enter, the heads of many almost touching the roof, they cross their legs and sink down on the floor, till there are twenty or thirty of them in the room.

" Welcome, Bimbo ! "

One of them speaks Chinese and I exchange a few remarks with him and hand round cigarettes.

They tell us that the grand lama of Pitu is here, and people are flocking from the surrounding country to see him, but I am satisfied with our arrangements and impatient to get on, so do not ask for an interview. Goitre is noticeable here, but it is neither so common nor so disfiguring as in the Mekong valley ; there were a few cases also at Wábu and at Pitu, mostly women, who concealed it by wearing stiff collars of blue beads.

Kábu is a village of about fifteen houses, all clumped together on a sloping platform which is terraced down to the river bank. The region is intensely arid, and bare rock is seen on every hand. No barley is grown, only maize and buckwheat.

Immediately after starting on November 7th, we descended to the river, and crossing to the left bank by a wooden cantilever bridge, kept close to the water the whole way to the next village, Rata, where we changed our transport again. Presently we left the Wi-chu which dashes out from a rocky gorge in the east, while we continued in a southerly direction ; we had in fact reached the end of the long spur crossed three days ago, round which the river coils itself.

From the top of the spur one can follow the Wi-chu eastwards, and see in the distance a fine snow peak, evidently on the Ka-kar-po range ; or, looking north, we obtain an extensive view down the valley and see the snow peak noticed yesterday, and the La-Drang-Dang. By the river bend is another small village, but we keep well above it and continue up a valley in front of us. After a very steep ascent for some hundreds of feet we enter the shade of pine woods, which is welcome, for it is hot in the valley. A little higher up we come to a clearing, where half a dozen rough log huts have been built.

At 2.30 when we halted for lunch at the clearing, the temperature in the sun was 73° F., but half an hour later, entering the mixed forest immediately above, frost crusted the ground. Here willow, poplar, birch, Picea and other conifers grew together, as at the Do-kar-la.

After climbing for half an hour through the forest, following a good, but steep path, we reached the pass called Tondu-la (12,550 feet), and an extraordinary view burst upon us.

We were looking almost due south over the roof of the pine forest, and down the Salween valley as though down a corridor. At the far end a fine snow peak appeared on the Salween–Irrawaddy divide above Saung-ta, pale against the incandescent sky. The winter sun was fast dropping down—it was four o'clock now—and a film of haze hung like a veil over the scene. Long shafts of light separated by the shadows of the spurs pierced between the western peaks and shot across the valley, giving a most wonderful effect. At first they looked like walls of pale fire, but as the sun sank they seemed to dissolve slowly in the thick atmosphere.

A steep descent through the pine forest soon brought us to still drier regions, where oak scrub replaced the pine trees, and at one place we passed twenty or thirty pilgrims resting in the shade.

Lower down the path is much torn up by running water, though it was dry enough now, and after descending about 4000 feet we reached the valley. Following down a small stream between high bush-covered banks to the village of Lumpu, we passed under a wooden gateway with no gate, the top of which consists simply of a board on which is carved an inscription in Tibetan— for a wonder it is not the sacred prayer this time. Large houses are scattered amongst cultivated fields in the triangular-shaped valley bottom, and we halted at the chief's house for the night. I did not get to bed till nearly midnight, after a seventeen hours' day.

Early in the morning the *bisi* came to us with a long face and said he could not give us transport to go on to Menkung without orders, as there was trouble brewing, and he had therefore despatched a messenger with the news of our arrival. However, we persuaded him to let us go down to Jana, on the right bank of the Salween, and thither we set out, continuing down the valley which opens out suddenly from the mountain foot. Above, the semicircle of mountains is merely trenched by several converging streams, but after they join up, the valley expands into a narrow isosceles triangle, like a half cone. It is in fact nothing but the usual alluvial fan overgrown with scrub and in places cultivated.

This is the typical form of valley amongst the lower spurs of the mountains, which are subjected to a brief deluge of water when the snow melts in spring, or the summer rains break, but run almost dry for the rest of the year.

It took us less than two hours to reach Jana. Just above stands a *chorten* and long rows of *mani* pyramids, the sacred characters of the oft-repeated prayer deeply incised in slabs of slaty rock, and beautifully coloured.

Beyond the *chorten* we found ourselves by the Salween, and turned down the river for a quarter of a mile to the village.

The good people of Jana remembered my coming in 1911, and were very friendly, promising to find me transport for the half day's journey to Menkung. But an hour later they began to procrastinate, saying that their ponies were all out feeding and could not be brought in till the morning; they promised faithfully to take us on to Menkung next day, if we did not mind waiting just for the afternoon.

But I did mind, and said so, and told them to collect porters, and not trouble about the ponies; but they would not do that either, and looked blankly at one another.

" Bimbo," they said at last, " we cannot take you to Menkung, we dare not ! we shall lose our heads if we do ! "

Then I said, " If you will not take us, because you are afraid, I and my interpreter will go early to-morrow and interview the great chiefs ourselves."

But at that the Tibetans threw off all reserve and begged us not to go, promising me presents, and beseeching me on their knees to desist from my project. This was serious; and in the evening an event took place which rendered my proposed excursion unnecessary.

Jana is another of those villages where the houses are all bunched up together under the cliffs, with a little tortuous lane threading its way between them. The walls are built almost entirely of irregular-shaped stones plastered together with mud, with narrow wooden window frames, obviously because stone is here plentiful, while the forests are some distance away. The platform on which it stands is terraced below and irrigated in the usual way, maize being the principal crop.

The river flows in a deep trench, and a similar gravel platform occurs on the left bank a little lower down ; both are ancient river terraces, and other smaller terraces can be seen here and there. The one on which Jana stands is nearly 500 feet above the river. Just behind the village is a narrow gash in the mountains through which the tip of one of the Ka-kar-po peaks becomes visible at sunset, when the snows burn like fire.

A wild nigger-looking man with woolly hair, carrying a long muzzle-loader arrived at our house in the afternoon ; he was one of the soldiers from Menkung, but he had no news to tell us except to assure me that there were no Chinese troops at Menkung now.

The women of Jana are very interesting and I shall have more to say about them later. For the present I wanted to get some photographs of them, but as they were shy, I brought my gramophone down into the street. A crowd slowly collected to see what this mysterious machine could be, not however going too close, lest it might explode or bite. When all was ready, I played the part of the prologue, bidding the people come and hear the wonderful singing box and not be afraid ; let the children and girls sit down in front—and suiting the action to the word I grabbed some of them and sat them down—and the men stand up behind in a semicircle, so that all could see. There must have been an audience of thirty by this time.

Then I turned on the band, and dumb applause following, no sooner had I got them thoroughly wrought upon, than I whipped out my camera and took several photographs of the enchanted crowd. When the banjo tinkled the children laughed with glee. How they did enjoy that wonderful box to be sure, and I had to play every tune before they were satisfied.

But to return to the people. They call themselves Tibetans, and speak Tibetan. Yet the dress and appearance of the girls is quite different from that met with in other parts of Tsa-rong, and to find its parallel we shall have to go further down the Salween, or cross the mountain to the west. Indeed I shall presently show good reason for believing that these people are not pure Tibetans at all, though they have Tibetan blood in them. The girls dress in skirts of coarse puttoo, neither pleated nor ornamented ; the hair is worn in a pig-tail, and cut in a short fringe round the forehead, the pig-tail never being artificially enlarged and bound round the head or ornamented with tassels as is commonly seen in Tsa-rong. They have small cane baskets of Nung[1] workmanship slung across the left shoulder, in which food and a bobbin of wool are carried, and as they carry their loads by means of a head strap, the contrivance of the jungle folk, instead of the usual Tibetan method of shoulder straps, they have their hands free, and walk along twisting thread like any Kachin. Bead necklaces and ordinary Tibetan ear-rings are the only adornments, though the people of the Salween valley do not seem badly off.

[1] The Nungs, or as the Shans of Hkamti call them, Hkunungs (i.e. slave-Nungs), inhabit most of the country to the north and east of the Hkamti plain, and especially the Taron valley. The Chinese call them Kiutzu. (See next chapter.)

I puzzled over these peculiarities for a long time, and it was not till I had made my second journey amongst the Lutzu tribe, and had seen something of the Kiutzu that I could offer any explanation.

I was seated at supper in the evening when there was a diversion, and the " Monkey " came to me in a perturbed state, saying that the *bisi* had arrived from Menkung to see me, and would I come. I hurried through my meal, therefore, and came into the big kitchen lighted only by the leaping fire ; cushions had been spread for the chief on one side of the cauldron, and he was already seated, cross-legged, but rose as I entered. I then took my seat on some more cushions placed on the opposite side of the square fire-place, my interpreter and the people of the household arranging themselves in a ring between us.

The chief spoke first, addressing himself to the " Monkey," while all listened attentively, the two men who were with the chief scarcely opening their mouths except to corroborate some statement with a " *Ri, Ri.*"

At last he stopped and my man in turn made a speech, interrupted by no sound save the bubbling of water in the pot, and the fall of a log in the fire. He pointed out that I was an Englishman, that the Tibetans and English had been good friends since the Dalai Lama returned from Calcutta, that I only wished to travel in the country, and paid the inhabitants well for everything ; that I wanted to see the country and people, and that I was collecting plants. My hopes rose and fell as I watched the almost expressionless faces by the light of the flickering flames. How the scene comes back to me now as though it were yesterday !

Now the envoys from Menkung rose and came over

to me, while the "Monkey" translated their reply into Chinese.

"There is great trouble in Tibet this year," he said. "The Chinese are trying to get into Tibet, and there is much fighting. The main roads through Pomed and Zayul are crowded with soldiers; at Menkung itself there is a military official from Lhasa collecting soldiers, and Sanga-chu-tzong is an armed camp. These raw levies are much out of hand; they have killed the Chinese garrisons at Menkung and Rima, and the chief is really afraid to let you travel in the country under such conditions. Moreover, he has received strict orders from the Devashung (the Lhasa government) to allow no one to proceed without a passport." Of course I had no such thing.

Then the envoy unwrapped a parcel and spread out before me a striped blanket, hand-woven in Tibet, finishing up his harangue by going on his knees and saying : " Bimbo, please, *please*, don't go on to Menkung," at the same time laying his present at my feet.

So the interview ended, and having sent presents to the envoys I sat down to consider things ; but being unable to arrive at any satisfactory plan, I went to bed, though it was long before sleep came.

Laying aside his official air the Menkung envoy paid me a visit on the following morning, and to my surprise addressed me in Chinese, so I seized the opportunity to make one last appeal to him.

In vain !

"I dare not ! Bimbo," he said, "I dare not ! I shall lose my head if I disobey."

Then he asked me for some trifling presents—a pencil and a pen-knife it was he wanted—and I gave them to him, and promised him some more things when I came again.

" Come back next year, Bimbo ; when the trouble with China is settled, we shall give you as many men and ponies as you like, and let you go everywhere."

Before starting I photographed the old man and his two satellites, and having bid them all farewell, we turned southwards.

The Tibetans had said that we might go down the Salween and return to the Mekong over the Do-kar-la on the pilgrims' road ; or continue southwards till we reached Chinese territory at Tra-mu-tang. Very well, then, we would go down the Salween and try to reach the Taron, and so across the hinterland to Burma or Assam.

Prince Henry had crossed this region from east to west in 1895. Captain Pritchard had lost his life on the Taron only eight months previously, due west of where we now stood, but neither his report nor those of the British exploration columns which were operating between Hkamti Long and the Taron when I left Myitkyina in April, were yet available.

However, now that our proposed journey across Tibet had come to an abrupt end, I decided to try and cross the headwaters of the Irrawaddy, travelling due west from Tra-mu-tang.

XII

Dwarfs & Slaves

NOVEMBER 9th was a blazing hot day, and the march down the arid valley was most trying.

After a couple of hours across stony terraces, in places burst open by deep narrow ravines where not a drop of water trickled, the porters halloed to a village on the right bank to send over a relief. A reply having been obtained, we went on slowly, leaving the relief to catch us up, as soon as they had crossed the river by canoe. However, they were unable to bring ponies with them, so when they arrived I insisted on keeping the animals from Jana. Thereupon a dispute arose, a Jana man trying forcibly to unload a pony which was as valiantly defended by one of the new-comers, at my behest.

Meanwhile, to my astonishment, one of the Jana girls who had supplied a pony, thinking I suppose that we were going to annex her animal altogether, and being pushed roughly aside when she attempted to lead it home, burst into a flood of tears and went off stamping and sobbing, to sulk like a child.

In order to settle the matter as amicably as possible, and not promote a fight between the opposing factions, I hit the interfering Tibetan from Jana gently on the nose, so that he lay down and bled freely ; harmony was immediately restored, and everybody smiled again. Promising to send the animals back from Lakora, we continued on our way.

The Salween valley here presents a remarkable sight, terrific gorges alternating with more open reaches backed by gigantic screes of pale rock. The river twists like a serpent between dry lifeless cliffs ; big gravelly terraces scantily dotted over with a growth of low bushes, occupy the concave bends.

The Salween is evidently a much bigger river than the Mekong, but it was now 20 feet below summer level. It is frequently interrupted by rapids, with deep olive-green pools at the bends, quiet backwaters, and sometimes gravel bars over which the water chatters merrily.

Considering the nature of the country, the road, where it is necessary to cut one at all, is excellent, in spite of the scanty population ; indeed we did not pass through a village all day, though there are several on the right bank.

Not far from Lakora, situated in one of the big bends, are some hot springs, the water gushing up from amongst grey limestone rocks surrounded by green trees. It is a real oasis in the desert. Close to the river a bath has been built amongst the boulders, and hundreds of inscriptions, with pictures of Buddhas, snakes and birds, are scratched on the smooth grey rocks above. At the hottest spring the water wells up at a temperature of 82° F., but the others are not as warm as this ; the river was 46° F. Masses of green algæ and a brittle-stemmed Chara float on the water, but I saw none of the jelly-like blue-green algæ commonly met with in hot springs elsewhere. In January, on the return journey, I found a

Veronica in flower in the water, also a Luzula, two species of Compositae, and two ferns. The last formed patches of emerald verdure wherever the water flowed, advertising the spot from afar.

A wonderful bit of road consisting of slabs of schist or slate, insecurely supported on long poles, carries us through the last gorge. Then, after passing a big village across the river, connected with the left bank by a rope bridge, we pass beneath a high, fluted, gravel cliff, and reach Lakora temple after dark. There is a white *chorten* here, pierced by two passages at right angles to one another, and surrounded by prayer cylinders let in to the outer walls ; also a single hut.

Next morning there was considerable delay in starting, as porters had to be called from a distance. While waiting I crossed the big glacier torrent from Ka-kar-po, which here rolls out of a gorge, and went a little way up the pilgrims' road towards the Do-kar-la. The smooth limestone rocks are covered with inscriptions, traced by the heaven-guided hands of saints and holy men on their pilgrimage.

At Lakora we met some Chinese merchants from the Mekong, returning thither by the Do-kar-la. They had intended to go to Zayul to trade, and had half a dozen mule loads of goods with them, but like ourselves had been stopped and turned back at Menkung by the authorities.

From Lakora the road ascends gradually to the summit of a high spur, from where a good but limited view of the river is obtained, and descends again to another difficult piece through a gorge, where the narrow overhanging road is composed of big flat slabs laid in steps, steep and slippery ; I watch with dread lest a pony slip, and precipitate some precious boxes into the river.

However, all negotiate it safely. A short march along the sandy river-bank brings us to the ferry at Trenge, a small village by the stream on the far side. From Trenge a road goes over the mountains to the Taron.

Here we charter a canoe for the voyage through the gorges to the first Lutzu village; and presently I am lying comfortably back on my boxes as we float down the river.

There was a flood mark on the cliffs of the gorge about 15 feet above the present water level. By January, when the water must be derived entirely from glaciers and melting snow, the temperature had fallen no less than six degrees, being only 40° F. The proportion of rain water is highest in August or September, depending, of course, not only on the season of heaviest rainfall in the mountains, but also on the time when all temporary snow is disappearing; but the difference between summer and winter temperatures can hardly be more than 12° or 15° F., which is certainly very little. Hence it is evident that the Salween derives much of its bulk from glaciers.

We reached Laungpa, the first Lutzu village, in an hour. After a short halt we boarded another canoe and slipped easily down the river to Saung-ta, reached at dusk. Now the men banged their paddles against the side of the canoe to attract the attention of the villagers, who presently came down and carried the boxes up to the chief's house.

There is nothing to distinguish these Lutzu huts from the Tibetan houses of Jana; the rooms may be a little smaller, the furniture less ; but the flat mud roof reached through a square hole by means of a notched log, the open shed for storing grain and corn on the top, the tiny window-frames and other details are all Tibetan. The houses are crowded together as at Jana. The valley is still arid, but at Laungpa, below the gorge, trees begin to appear, and Saung-ta is the last village in the arid region. Stick insects and alarming centipedes of great size, sure signs of the coming climatic change, were crawling about the house.

Here the river is broader, divided by a shingle bank only covered in summer, and navigable for canoes. But immediately below the village it plunges through a granite gorge ; when it emerges a few miles lower down it flows placidly through a new country. Here the climate is quite different. Orchids and birds'-nest ferns clothe the trees, and rice grows green on the terraced hill-sides. In summer these gorges are impassable, and are turned by a path which crosses the mountains ; in winter the latter is snow-bound, and the river route is used, not without some danger. However, I leave a description of it till later.

The Lutzu of Saung-ta—black Lutzu[1]—who recalled my journey up the Salween to Menkung in 1911, and were very friendly in consequence, are as wild-looking and dirty a people as one could find. The men dress in the long Tibetan cloak (*chu-pa*) but wear no boots, and

---

[1] The Chinese speak of " *he* " Lisu and " *pai* " Lisu, " black " and " white " Lisu respectively, having regard to their degrees of uncouthness, though they are as a matter of fact clans of one tribe. I have followed the same nomenclature in order to distinguish the Lutzu of the arid region with Tibetan characteristics (black Lutzu) from those of the Chinese Salween, influenced by the Chinese.

do not plait their hair, which is left in a tangled mop. Only the chief had a thin pig-tail, hanging down behind. The women, however, instead of dressing like the Tibetan women of Jana, follow the tribal fashion and dress more like their sisters lower down the river, the " white " Lutzu. That is to say, they wear a white hempen skirt, with narrow blue stripes and fringed ends, wrapped round the waist and reaching half-way to the ankles, and a short loose-sleeved jacket of ample width. To this is added a hempen towel thrown over the shoulders if the weather is cold, and used as a blanket at night. Most of the children and younger girls, however, dress in goat-skins sewn together, hair inside—a warm and cheap garment—for large flocks of goats are kept here. I counted five hundred on the hill-side in one place.

Amongst the " black " Lutzu two quite distinct types are recognisable—a Tibetan type, seen in the tall men and good-looking women, and a tribal type, represented by the ugly dwarfs of both sexes, met with in every Lutzu village.

Who then are these Lutzu, a tribe occupying some fifteen or twenty miles of the Salween valley, and the valleys to the east, from the arid regions of the Tsa-rong Tibetans to the rain-drenched forests of the " black " Lisu ?

We have already noted that in this part of the Salween their houses and dress are practically Tibetan. Further south they have been more influenced, within recent years, by the Chinese, though it is evident from their language that they are of Tibeto-Burman origin.

Now Lutzu is practically Kiutzu, or, as we say, Nung, the language spoken on the Taron, which again is related

M

to Maru. Hence it is certain that the Lutzu are, if not Nungs, at any rate closely related to them.

But if so, how, when, and why did they emigrate from the Taron to the Salween?

The answer to that question is, I think, to be found in the slave dealing of the Tsa-rong Tibetans.

It was not, however, till January, on my return journey, that I first saw the dwarf Nung slaves kept by the Salween Tibetans. I will merely remark here that I believe the Lutzu to be partly pure Nung and partly a cross between Tibetan and Nung.

Children most readily learn the language of their mothers, though they soon pick up another language if surrounded by people who speak it. As the slaves obtained their freedom, they would move down the Salween valley to the jungle region, where there were no Tibetans, and a knowledge of the Tibetan tongue would grow scantier, which was exactly what we found to be the case. Eventually they would be stopped from extending further south by the Lisus.

Here then is a little colony of Nung and half-Nung wedged in the Salween valley.

I have already drawn attention to the similarity between the Tibetan women of Jana and the people from the west, and, on the other hand, their dissimilarity from the other Tibetans of Tsa-rong. They too are of Lutzu origin, perhaps released slaves married to Tibetans, influenced in matter of dress and personal adornment by the Tibetans. Though by no means dwarf, occasionally indeed not strikingly short, they have neither the build nor the features of the Tsa-rong women, and the most likely explanation is that they too are a cross, derived from the slave population.

As regards the "black" and "white" Lutzu, the former are simply those who remained in the arid region in contact with the Tibetans, the latter those who pushed south into the monsoon region, and have recently been influenced by the Chinese. It is also evident that the Tibetans themselves once spread further south, at least as far as Tra-mu-tang. Indeed there are distinct traces of Tibetan influence as far south as Yuragan.

If the Lutzu are not a cross between Tibetan and Nung, then they must be pure Nung—there is no other way of accounting for the practical identity of the two languages.

But what then can have driven them into the Salween valley? Certainly not any pressure from the west, for their country is most sparsely populated. Or did they emigrate of their own accord?

Dwarf Nung are to be found in the arid Salween valley, both at Menkung and further south, but only as slaves; and since we know that the Tibetans do go over and capture them, this seems a perfectly satisfactory explanation of their presence.

I heard a curious story of the Taron people from the Tibetans before ever I saw a dwarf Nung. Somewhere, not many days' journey from Menkung, they said, was found a people who lived in trees with the monkeys, as their country was a swamp full of snakes and tigers! They had no clothes, because they could not sew, and the Tibetans were only able to trade with them twice a year!

It was a most romantic story, though I did not believe it all—not the snakes and the tigers, anyway. But there is no doubt that such a tribe does exist near the sources of the Irrawaddy, and is none other than the Hkunung or Nung tribe.

The late Captain Pritchard mentions seeing a single Hkunung hut in a tree sixty feet from the ground, and though no mention is made of snakes and tigers by three travellers[1] who might have come across them, there is sufficient evidence to show that the story is certainly not a myth. Personally I suspect these arboreal people inhabit chiefly the unexplored regions lying immediately south-west of Menkung.

There is yet another interesting point about the Nung themselves.

I have already stated that the Chinese call the people of the Taron Kiutzu, that is the people of the Kiu-kiang— the Kiu river, or Taron. This name is used indiscriminately for the Nung who come over to Sukin further down the Salween, and for those who are found on the Tibetan Salween to the north.

But these people are not quite the same. While living amongst the Lisu at Sukin, I saw several dozen Kiutzu, who had come over the Yuragan pass to trade in the Salween valley. These people were essentially the same as those I subsequently met with in the 'Nmai hka valley further south—the black Maru, or Naingvaw.[2] True they were much worse off for clothes than the southern Marus, and were altogether more uncouth ; nevertheless they were Naingvaw. But these people are not the same as the *dwarf* Nung met with on the Tibetan Salween,

[1] M. Bacot, 1909; Captain F. M. Bailey, 1911 ; Captain B. E. A. Pritchard, 1913.
[2] The Naingvaw occupy the valley of the 'Nmai hka north of the Mekh confluence. Mr. F. V. Clerk says they are of mixed Kachin and Chinese descent.

for to begin with they are of normal height ; neither do they tattoo the face between the eyes and down the bridge of the nose, as do the dwarf Nung, or speak the same language. They belong to the Maru family, using the term Maru in its generic sense ; but are not Lawng Vaw. Their language is more akin to Chingpaw.

In trying to classify the tribes west of the Salween one is met further by the difficulty that in almost every valley, as I am informed by Mr. Barnard,[1] the people call themselves by a distinct name, after the name of the river on whose banks they live. Thus we have the Mut-wang, the inhabitants of the Mekh (Mut) river, the Seinku-wang, inhabitants of the Seinku river, and so on. This is not uncommon, however, amongst the primitive people of a mountainous country where communications are bad.

In December, 1914, when travelling in the Burmese hinterland, I engaged porters from Hkamti Long to Myitkyina. These were Hkunung (i.e. slave-Nung) hired from the Shan sawbwas, and came from the region to the north-east of Hkamti Long. They were small people, very similar to the Kiutzu, or Naingvaw, I had seen at Sukin.

They were, I think, without exception the hardiest, the most indifferent to discomfort, or rather what we would call downright misery, the most cheerful and resourceful of any people I have ever met with. With two threadbare garments apiece, after carrying a sixty-pound load for ten or fifteen miles, over mountains, in stony river beds, across wide rivers, waist deep, and through dense jungle ; on two meals of rice, eked out

[1] Mr. J. T. O. Barnard, C.I.E., of the Frontier Service.

with roots dug up on the march ; they would lie down
on the ground to rest, sheltered from the chill wind by
a few leaves of the fan palm stuck in the ground, or a
rampart of shingle thrown up in the river bed, caring
nothing for the dank mists and raw cold.

These slave Nung were a most merry-looking crowd,
with thick mops of hair, round faces, broad, flattened
noses, and rather large eyes. They were not, however,
particularly well developed—indeed many of them,
contrary to the general belief that coolies are always
powerful men, looked weakly. But their tremendous
powers of endurance, in spite of such paltry food, is not
a question of physical strength, but of some other quality
developed by carrying weights from childhood. Samson
himself would have been outmarched and outstayed by
those Hkunung coolies.

I believe the Hkunungs are so far uncivilised, that they
do not even have regular meals, but, like the beasts, eat
when they feel hungry. Thus they grub up edible roots
while on the march, a peculiarity of savages and young
children.

It is interesting to note that the Lutzu trap and eat a
small mountain vole (*Microtus Wardi*). The Hkunung
also eats rats, mice, snakes, lizards or anything else they
can catch. Maru and Naingvaw are also said to eat dogs
—as do the Naga of Assam—though the dogs are not
obtained for that very purpose, but for certain religious
festivals.

To sum up, then. The Lutzu are probably a cross
between Tibetan and Nung, and the Nung themselves,
of which there are several sub-tribes, are nearly related
to the Maru. We see evidence in the religion of the
Lutzu, which is a mixture of primitive *nat* worship and

lamaism, of a previous southern extension of the
Tibetans in the Salween valley, but this is of little
importance, except in so far as it probably accounts
for the fact that the Lisu have not extended north to
Tra-mu-tang.

I saw no goitre amongst the Lutzu, nor amongst the
Tibetans from Jana southwards, though all get their salt
from Tsa-ka-lo which is popularly supposed to be the
cause of it. Nor is goitre common amongst the Lisu
further south, though I saw occasional traces of it.
Small-pox, however, seems to be prevalent, and faces
pitted with this disease are frequently met with amongst
the tribes.

I bought some maize flour at Saung-ta, and had a supply
of bread, or rather biscuits, made before leaving.

The process is simple enough. The meal is first mixed
with water in a wooden bowl, and thoroughly stirred into
a paste. It is then smeared over a circular slab of stone,
which has previously been rubbed clean with wood ashes,
and strongly heated. In about five minutes the side in
contact with the stone is crisp and brown, and the
biscuit is then turned over ; when done outside it is still
rather moist inside, but as it easily splits in half, this is
soon remedied by standing it up on edge in the ashes,
and toasting. Eaten with fresh yak butter it is excellent.

It was noon on November 11th before we started,
the porters, mostly old women, being busy all the
morning collecting food. The mountain road turns up
a gully just below the village, crosses the stream and
ascends steeply through pine woods ; we did not get
far, and camped at dusk, having reached water at an
altitude of 10,500 feet.

I spread my bedding on the ground and slept warmly in spite of a slight frost; the moonlight through the pine trees was beautiful, and it was jolly to lie on one's back on the steep mountain side looking straight across an open valley, and watch the great constellations wheeling majestically overhead. I pointed out Aldebaran, the Pleiades and Venus to the " Monkey," who had said the Tibetans have names for the biggest stars, and asked what he called them. In the case of the Pleiades, known in country districts at home as the " seven sisters," there is not much room for mistaken identity, and when the " Monkey " said the Tibetans called them " seven eyes " I believed him; but when it came to Aldebaran, Venus and others, I am not at all sure that he knew which stars were which, and Venus at any rate he probably mixed up with Sirius, besides making the old mistake of giving Venus two names.

The temperature was 33° F. when we started at eight o'clock next morning. A little higher up, out of the forest, the ground was white with frost, which, however, quickly disappeared in the sunshine. From a ridge above we had a fine view of the Salween both to north and south where it flows between sheer granite cliffs. At one point, after narrowing to half its usual breadth, it drops down several feet, and becomes a flurry of white foam for a quarter of a mile. Although it looked absurdly small from here, we must have been at least 3000 feet above it, and yet could plainly hear the roar of the water.

After following a ridge for some distance, we reached the stream side and began to ascend through Rhododendron forest. The stream was draped with icicles, and we soon got into the snow. A little below the summit we halted for lunch in a very cold wind, amidst bushes half buried in snow. The last part of the ascent is very steep, and impossible for mules.

From the pass, picturesque views to north and south are obtained, though they are limited in extent, a range of mountains west of the Salween shutting out the country behind. Northwards, a snow peak called Jug-kur-jan-tso overlooks Menkung, and in the west is the Tra-mu-tang snow peak.[1] Southwards we obtained a glimpse of the Salween valley and the Mekong-Salween divide, with snow on it in many places, but no snowy ranges.

While I rested there taking photographs, bearings and notes, several parties of Lutzu came up carrying corn, which they intended to sell in Tibet, buying salt in exchange.

There is a considerable traffic backwards and forwards in these commodities, during the winter months, for there is no salt west of the Mekong, while, on the other hand, the arid regions of Tsa-rong do not produce enough grain for the population.

The descent on the south side was terrifically steep, involving actual climbing in some places. Soon we came upon larch trees, Enkianthus, and vegetation similar to that seen at the Do-kar-la ; a tree Rhododendron with enormous leaves covered beneath with thick rufus-coloured woolly hair also attracted my attention.

After descending several thousand feet by a ridge, we reached the stream bed, where vertically tilted slate rocks crop out and render the going very bad, especially as the stream flows as a rule parallel to the strike, causing small waterfalls the whole way. The stream is swaddled

---

[1] Gompa-la.

in dense forest which becomes more luxuriant at every step, ferns especially being abundant and in great variety.

At last we halt, and camp under a cliff by the torrent, and I write my diary by the light of the blazing logs. In the gloaming the old women sitting in a circle round the fire, legs bare to the knees and drawn up under their chins, skirts pulled tightly round them, wraps thrown over their shoulders, look like witches. I am reminded of the three grey sisters in the frozen cave visited by Perseus in the home of the north wind, who had but one eye between them and passed it round by hand from one to the other. Look, these people too are handing something round !—but it is only a pipe passing from mouth to mouth ; whiff here, and it goes to the next person, who in turn takes a whiff and passes it on. For now we are in the land of the tobacco plant, which does not grow in Tibet. In Tsa-rong I offered cigarettes to men who looked at them and asked what they were !

The Tibetans do not smoke—they take snuff. But with the introduction of cheap cigarettes into Yun-nan, they are gradually finding their way thither.

Here, however, everybody smokes—men, women, even children ; the pipe is universal amongst Lutzu and Lisu. In the west, too, everybody smokes : Nung, Maru, Kachin, Lashi.

We reached Kieunatong before midday after a difficult march, at first down the left bank of the stream, then crossing to the right bank, and so back again. On the way we met more parties of Lutzu carrying maize flour into Tibet.

No sooner does the stream emerge from the forested

gorge than it splays out a wide cone of rubble. The sides are terraced and the stream, wandering whimsically, now occupies only a fraction of the cone. Down below the sun shines on the white walls of the French mission house.

XIII

Amongst the Lutzu

AT Kieunatong I called on Père Genestier whose acquaintance I had made in 1911. Half an hour after my arrival a second unexpected guest was announced, none other than the military official from Tra-mu-tang.

After a talk with Père Genestier, I continued down the valley between high grass and tree-clad spurs, in the wake of the porters, reaching the Salween again at dusk. From across the river I heard the shouts of the men in answer to my whistle, but missing the steep path down to the water, it was half an hour before two children with pine torches came across and showed me the way. The crackling wood shot a lurid glare over the still water, and out of the darkness below came the roar of distant rapids ; then we skimmed rapidly across in the canoe, while the torches fizzled and spluttered and finally went out, and I found quarters in the hut where my party had already ensconced themselves—eighteen in one small room.

In the night the first snow fell on the mountains. Next day we continued along the right bank of the river, at first over boulders in the river bed, then up and down by a steep narrow path through the jungle. Just above a large scattered village on the left bank is a rope bridge, but it is scarcely used in the winter, the river then being navigable for canoes.

Arrived opposite this village, however, the Lutzu porters wished to obtain a relief, but as this would have implied a considerable delay, I refused, and having taken possession of the only slider for crossing by the rope bridge, threatened to throw it into the river if they would not go on to the next village. Perseus, when he stole the peevish sisters' eye, had not his victims more completely in his power, and consequently the next village, called Num-chi, was soon reached. Here we did take on a fresh lot of porters.

Passing through a fine gorge of crystalline limestone, the trees festooned with orchids and ferns, we presently emerged into the broad valley at Tra-mu-tang. While resting by a couple of *mani obos* the military official we had met at Kieunatong overtook us. He exchanged a few polite words with me, offered me the loan of a sleek little pony he was riding, and when I refused, went ahead and announced our approach to the civil authority.

Arrived on the outskirts of the widely scattered village, I sent my man up to the officials with presents and greetings, while we kept on across a deep gully which trenches the sloping platform. Up this gully the snow peak called Gompa-la is just visible. Thither lies the road to India.

It was pretty to watch my procession of Lutzu girls on the march. Supporting their loads by means of a head strap, thus having their hands free, they usually walk alone twisting hemp fibre, held between the teeth ; a supply of hemp, together with food, being carried, not in a basket such as the Tibetan girls of Jana sling over the shoulder, but in a cloth bag like that carried by the Kachin and Maru. When the girls are not so employed, however, they clasp their hands behind the head, elbows straight out and heads thrown back the better to balance themselves : and so they marched now, their bare feet pattering down the steep path.

We took shelter in the house of a prosperous Chinese immigrant who had married a Lutzu wife. Like many of the Chinese in Burma who marry native wives, he spent his time lamenting the uncouthness of the barbarian, ridiculing her customs, reviling her manners, and regretting her lack of refinement. Few people are more prejudiced than the Chinese, and woman being a mere chattel, the emigrant Chinaman grumbles at the women of his adopted country as we might grumble at the food.

The iron bond which holds the Chinese together is not patriotism, nor even tradition—the past idealised, cleansed of its dross and used as a guide and stimulant for the present ; but custom, rigid law imposed once and for all, from which the people dare not depart a hair's breadth. Their authority for this extends back to Confucius.

A Chinese doctor I knew in Moulmein, who had married a Burmese wife and lived with her for years, had never been able to get over the disgust he felt at seeing the Burmese eat with their fingers.

" They are like savages," he said. " Why don't they use chop-sticks ! " I remarked that the Burmese are as civilised as the Chinese, that they eat clean food, build fine temples, and wear pretty clothes, but he scoffed the more at their clothes ; " they wear nothing ! " was his comment. " The English are very clever," he

said, " but the Burmese ! "—here he made a grimace,
and noises of disgust. Some Burmese youths were
playing *chin-lone*, in the street outside, and he drew my
attention to them. " They sleep and eat and play games,"
he said, " but they don't do any work."

The more communications are opened up in China,
the more will the people, despite the tyrannical imposi-
tion of custom which makes them all do the same things
outwardly, recognise their racial distinctions, and the
less likely is any great organisation or co-operation
between them. Simultaneously with the dawn of
consciousness of the Empire in the minds of the Chinese,
will come its dissolution.

To resume the story. The son and daughter of my
host had as usual taken after their mother in dress, and
spoke Lutzu and Tibetan, but not Chinese.

The Lutzu women are small and slim with merry
round faces, and regular features. They wear a loose
long-sleeved jacket of blue cotton cloth, and a short
skirt of the same material, or sometimes of white hemp,
tied round the waist ; to this is added a white hempen
blanket with striped ends, extending diagonally across
the chest from the right shoulder to the left armpit.
Similar blankets with fringed ends are worn by the Nung
of the Taron, whose dress differs from that of the Lutzu
only in its scantiness. And this is owing to the absence
of Chinese garments. In cold weather a goat-skin waistcoat is added, hair inside. Hardly any jewellery is worn,
what there is being of Tibetan workmanship—clumsy
finger rings, or brooches in the form of collar buckles.
No natural ornamentaion such as the rattan leg rings
of the Kachin or the cowry belt of the Maru is met with,

and the pig-tail, though bound on top of the head, is never artificially lengthened and tasseled, like that of the Tibetan matron.

The men dress very similarly, only, like the Lisu, they wear a long gabardine of white hemp cloth, trimmed round the collar and cuffs with pale blue very effectively. Beneath, they wear loose cotton breeches, like those of the Yunnanese. The pig-tail when present, is not bound on top of the head, and the hair is cut in a fringe over the forehead, an almost universal custom west of the Salween. Strips of cloth, like puttees, are wound round the legs, a very necessary precaution against the torment of insects. Maru and Lisu west of the Salween also wear these cloth gaiters, kept in place by rattan rings above the calf. The men, who use the cross-bow, generally carry an arrow case of black bear skin, the woman always a cloth bag, embroidered with hard grey " seeds," [1] but of plain workmanship.

Next day all efforts to obtain porters for the journey to the Taron proved futile, for the evident reason that the Chinese authorities did not wish me to go, and consequently had forbidden the villagers to carry for me. That of course was not the reason the latter gave, alleging that the snow was too deep, and that they were busy with their crops.

We spent the next day trying to get porters, calling upon the Lutzu chief, and promising his people fabulous sums to carry for us. The chief brought me a fowl as peace offering and was vastly polite, but he dared not disobey the orders he had evidently received from the

---

[1] *Coix Lachryma.* It is cultivated on the Hkamti Long plain and elsewhere. The so-called seeds are part of the inflorescence and contain the flowers.

Chinese; and not a soul would stir. He, however, promised us porters to continue down the Salween and said that we might go to the Taron by the big road from Sukin, that is, by the route Prince Henry of Orleans traversed in 1895. But as a matter of fact the season was far too advanced. Had we gone the porters would never have got back to their homes.

It was evident that we should not be able to cross the snow mountains without assistance, and every day's delay now added the risk of fresh snow on the divide—though the weather in the valley itself was still perfect. I therefore acquiesced in this proposal, and reluctantly gave up the idea of crossing the Tra-mu-tang pass and gaining some insight into the flora of the snowy range.

A few words will suffice to describe Tra-mu-tang.[1] The Salween has just emerged from the gorges, and the valley now opens out into a big bay backed by sheer limestone cliffs. The ground slopes rather steeply to the river, and is cut in two by a deep gully. North of the gully are terraced rice-fields, and close up under the cliffs a grove of poplars through which may be seen the old monastery, now the *yamen* and barracks for a dozen soldiers. On the south side there is grazing and cultivation. The left bank of the river is more exposed, and the slopes are covered with bracken and scattered pine trees, and higher up with forest. Including the houses on both sides of the gully, Tra-mu-tang has a population of forty families.

---

[1] " The flat plain on the (river) bank." Spelt Chamutong on the maps. The Chinese cannot pronounce the "ra" sound, and call it " cha " or " tsa "; but strictly speaking it is a Tibetan regional name. The Chinese came to the Salween after the Lutzu had established themselves and after the Tibetans.

N

An excellent mule path follows the right bank of the river as far as Choton, but after that it begins to deteriorate, though as a matter of fact it would be quite easy to build a good mule road to Sukin. At present it is necessary at one point to cross to the left bank, and then recross at Sukin itself. The river is navigable for canoes between Tra-mu-tang and Choton, where there is a big rapid, and for about a mile below that rapids become frequent. Except for ferries between villages there is no more navigation till Sukin itself is reached; and though rope bridges occur at frequent intervals they are evidently not much used south of Kieunatong; most of them seemed to be abandoned. Wherever the river is navigable fishing is carried on, sometimes with nets, sometimes with lines. The Lisu, Maru and Kachin throughout the Burmese hinterland all catch fish. On the Taron, I was told, the Nung spear their fish, like the Andaman islanders, but the usual Kachin and Maru methods are to trap them, or else to divert a torrent and net them in the rock pools, left behind in the former bed.

To return then to our journey from Tra-mu-tang. At the entrance to the next village one passes under a rude gateway, consisting simply of two upright saplings and a cross piece, from which are suspended wooden daggers inscribed with charms, stones and dummy spears. It is a religious structure, I was told, and its object is to scare away evil spirits from the village; in fact it is our old friend the booby trap, any evil spirit rash enough to pass through it on a visit to the village, receiving a stone on his head or a wooden dagger through the gizzard.

At Choton there is a ferry to Chiora on the left

bank, connected in turn with two roads over the
mountains to the Mekong. Here we changed porters ;
below this point the valley contracts again, and the
path is not good. In the evening we reached the scattered village of Bibili, half on the right bank and half
on the left. The huts are small and the people poor :
only buckwheat and maize are grown, besides a little
mountain rice.

There was only one room in the hut where we slept ;
and round the fire, or rather *in* it, for they sat amongst
the ashes and played there with each other, with some
small pigs, a cat and two puppies, were five naked children.
They seemed very fond of one another and very happy.
One of them though three years old, was still unweaned :
however, in the intervals between a legitimate milk
diet, he ate maize porridge from the family pot with the
rest.

There is a small path from Bibili to the Taron, but
it is said to be very difficult ; also another from Choton.
But the best " road " is that which follows up the big
glacier torrent from Su-chi-tung, a village just above the
" marble gorge," near Tra-mu-tang.

We did a good stage next day, for this country ;
though the Tibetans would have smiled at it. Just below
Bibili, the river turns at right angles and flows due west
through a narrow gorge ; the right bank is clothed with
dense forest, where ferns, orchids and climbing Aroids
abound ; but the left bank, which is steep and rocky,
is thinly clothed with pines. The path hugs the river,
passing through crops of buckwheat and along open
bracken and pine-clad slopes, too steep for cultivation.
The soil is fairly good, but the mountains are not cultivated to any height above the river and the population

is scanty, though small villages are built wherever a
torrent debouches into the main valley.

Our chief difficulty was to get food : we could buy
neither milk nor butter, meat nor tea, and rarely
eggs. The people seem to live entirely on buckwheat
cakes and maize meal porridge, though there are plenty
of cattle, pigs and fowls. These, however, are kept for
religious festivals.

Another difficulty which now threatened to become
acute was that of language. As far south as Tra-mu-tang
the people had all spoken Tibetan, but beyond Pang-ta,
a big village across the river, opposite which we halted at
midday, we rarely met anyone who spoke anything but
Lisu or Lutzu, that is Nung, the language of the Taron.

Pang-ta, like Tra-mu-tang, is one of those villages which
covers a considerable area owing to the scattering of the
huts. It is only in those Lisu villages we shall presently
meet with that the huts are closely crowded. It will
be remembered that in the very arid regions of both
the Salween and Mekong the Lutzu and Tibetan huts
are crowded together, unless built on an alluvial cone,
when they are scattered down the fan-shaped slope
instead of being jammed into the mouth of the ravine,
a distinction which seems to be a mere matter of convenience. But in the rainy Salween valley we do not
find the villages sheltered by the same tree growth
usually associated with the Tibetan oases on the arid
Mekong. Here we find only a few scattered pear trees
and orange bushes, or an occasional weeping-willow.
Further south there are big clumps of bamboo sheltering
the Lisu huts, typical of the monsoon forest, on the
extreme edge of which we now stand. But where all
is verdant these are not specially conspicuous.

Pang-ta, too, has an almost Tibetan air about it, for
at one end of the high narrow bank on which it stands
is a white *chorten*, and several *mani obo* are scattered along
the path. One does not meet many Tibetans as far south
as this. Occasionally in the winter, salt traders go to
Sukin, and I saw one or two priests at Pang-ta, as well
as an old man incising and painting the sacred invoca-
tion, "*O mani padme hum*" on a slab of slate. However,
Tibetan Buddhism is now practically the adopted religion
of the Lutzu, nor need it surprise us to see them still
dabbling in *nat* propitiation as well. They have not been
able entirely to eradicate their primitive animism, and
still cling to some of the old rites ; though these have
been to some extent incorporated into the new religion.

It is rather surprising that the Lisu have not driven
the peaceful Lutzu out of the best portion of the rain
valley—that is between Pang-ta and Kieunatong. The
explanation is probably to be found in the origin of the
Lutzu tribe from a cross between Tibetan and Nung,
the Lutzu gradually replacing the pure Tibetan element
who once occupied this unhealthy valley. The Lisu
would hardly be a match for the Tibetans. On the other
hand it is certain, not only that the Lisu are comparatively recent immigrants, but that they *are* encroaching
northwards.

It must not be forgotten that the Tibetans once
spread much further south into the Irrawaddy jungles
than they do at present, even as far as Hkamti Long,
whence they were driven out by the Shan invaders. The
Tibetan race still occupy low-lying country in the
provinces of Zayul and Pomed, besides a few villages at
the headwaters of the Irrawaddy. These provinces are
subject to a heavy rainfall, and more closely resemble

Assam, or the Burmese hinterland, than Tibet as generally understood. It is probably in this forest region of S.E. Tibet, so widely different, either to the arid trenches and snow peaks of Tsa-rong, or to the rain-swept grassy plateaus and valleys further north, that we must look for the cradle of these tribes who have gradually spread southwards over Burma, Assam and along the Yun-nan frontier.

We slept that night in a small Lutzu hut at the village of U-wa, close by the river.

I awoke to see the sunlight streaming in between the chinks of the log walls, reflected from the dust and smoke in a hundred brilliant pencils of light ; this is the only source of light available in a Lutzu hut, which boasts but one door and no windows, nor even a chimney. The smoke percolates between the logs or through the slab roof. Consequently the hut, which usually consists of two very small rooms, is always full of smoke, not a bad idea really as it neutralises the smell of pigs rising up from the cattle-byre beneath the floor. Down here I noticed proper tiled roofs, slabs of slate being used instead of the wooden shingles used further north. On the whole, then, the Lutzu hut is a nondescript structure with no claims to any peculiarity of architecture ; in the arid region it is simply a small Tibetan house, and from Kieunatong southwards it is just a log hut on stilts, such as one meets with all the way down the Mekong valley.

There had been quite a sharp frost in the night, and the dew dripped like rain from the dense vegetation of the gullies long after it had been lapped up in the open. On November 18th we progressed only about two miles down the river ; we ought to have crossed to the left bank here, but omitted to do so, and consequently were compelled to make a detour on the right bank, climbing high to avoid some cliffs which rise sheer from the river. Our path lay up a gully where in the deep shade grew giant thistles twelve feet high, alders, tree of heaven, and bushes of Hydrangea. Here and there hurdles designed to keep the village cattle within limits blocked the path, for presently we came upon a Lisu village. Up this valley Prince Henry of Orleans had climbed to the Yuragan pass eighteen years before. Now we turned back to the river over a high spur, from the summit of which we saw the terraced rice-fields of Yuragan on the left bank, the winter sunshine gleaming brightly on the yellow stubble ; there is a rope bridge below, besides several small fishing canoes. Two dark objects floating motionless on the blue water turned out to be mergansers, and not, as I hoped, duck.

At the foot of a very steep descent we continued over big boulders in the river bed for a time, beneath a fringe of evergreen jungle from which hung garlands of golden-flowered Senecio, here growing to a great size. Everywhere the rocks, of slate or schist, are vertical, the river flowing now parallel to, now across the strike. Many long-tailed magpies fly from tree to tree, and the ever-watchful hawk sails majestically overhead in widening circles, peering pitilessly into the depths below.

Climbing the steep river bank once more we brush through fields of red buckwheat, to the small village of Ma-shih-ta on the next spur ; beyond appears a high mountain covered with fresh snow, standing over a broad gap in the western range. This mountain overlooks Sukin, and through the gap lies the main path to the Taron. In spite of frosts at night the days are quite warm, and in every village we pass through are to be seen pot-bellied babies running about stark naked, as in Tsa-rong. Several people were collected outside the chief's house at Ma-shih-ta, and on our arrival the crowd quickly increased.

XIV

Lisu & Nung

ONE of the first persons to rush forward and
select from the loads which my Lutzu porters
had set down in a row, was a girl. Round her
head she wore a tiara of small white buttons,
sewn to a band, from the front of which dangled a fringe
of beads and dummy brass bells. Her white hempen
skirt reached just below the waist, and she wore a loose
jacket of similar material. Necklaces of beads and cowrie
shells hung almost to her waist, on her wrists were
numerous small bracelets of finely plaited cane, and her
feet were bare.

Here then was a person quite different from anyone
we had yet come across; she was none other than a
" black " Lisu,[1] and we had indeed entered the territory
of that redoubtable tribe.

Of medium height, well proportioned, with a merry
round face, jet black hair, and well-bridged nose, the
tout ensemble was rather pretty; on the other hand, her
almond-shaped eyes set too far apart, sallow complexion,
and small mouth with rather full lips, were features of a
distinctly Mongolian type. Thus was I introduced to
the *hê* Lisu who monopolise the Salween valley from here

---

[1] *Hê* Lisu, or " black " Lisu, so called by the Chinese to distinguish
them from the *hua* or " flowery " Lisus (Yawyins) of the Burma-Yun-nan
frontier. Both speak the same language.

southwards for two degrees of latitude, and have spread westwards into the Irrawaddy jungles.

The head-dress, as well as the flowing skirt of thin white cotton cloth with narrow pale blue stripes, is characteristic. Very occasionally cowrie shells replace the buttons in the head-dress described above, and evidently this was really the original form, only the supply of cowrie shells ran short, or else buttons were found to be much cheaper, more easily procured, and quite as effective.

While, however, ornamentation of a sort is not lacking on the Lisu maidens, they have practically no other jewellery ; large silver ear-rings are, however, sometimes seen, though the ears are not pierced as is the case with the Irrawaddy tribes. They make up for poverty in this direction by wearing iron or bamboo hoops round the neck and little bracelets of plaited bamboo, often to the number of a dozen round either wrist ; sometimes several dozen varnished rings of fine rattan are worn round the leg just below the knee, looking like black cotton ; but this latter device is far more characteristic of the Burmese hinterland where the rattan, or climbing palm grows, from which these fibres are stripped.

The men wear long thin cotton gowns of similar material to that described above, reaching to the knees and tied round the waist ; this garment is cut down each side from hip to knee, like a skirt, but beneath this a pair of blue cotton Chinese breeches are often added. The head is left bare, unless a Chinese skullcap has been acquired, but the hair instead of being a tangled mop, as with the Nung, is plaited into a short pig-tail hanging down behind, like that of the Lutzu. Small plain metal ear-rings are sometimes worn, besides finger rings, with perhaps a worthless stone such as coral or turquoise, evidently of Tibetan origin. Every man carries a *dâh* in a wooden sheath, and a bag, usually of hemp cloth, unadorned except for the band by which it is slung across the shoulder, embroidered with grey " seeds." The chief men of the village, however, generally carry bags of leather, with a fringe like a horse's mane hanging down in front.

Not less characteristic are the Lisu huts which are the same everywhere, and quite different from the log shanties built by the Lutzu. They are, of course, raised on stilts—all huts in the monsoon jungles have this in common, with a cattle byre beneath—with walls of bamboo matting, or, in the mountains, of upright boards, and thatched roof ; the floor is nearly always of bamboo matting, delightfully yielding to sleep on, like a spring mattress. They are larger than the Lutzu huts, divided into two rooms, and quite dark. All the advantage of height is, however, sacrificed owing to the habit of stretching bamboos across from wall to wall, so as to make a partial loft beneath the gabled roof, thus reducing the height to less than six feet. From these, bamboo racks are suspended over the earthen hearths, on which are placed cooking pots, maize cobs in process of drying, and other articles in daily use. These racks are, of course, bearded with long feathers of soot which blow about one's food when sitting by the fire. Nothing is more exasperating when so seated, than to jump up in a hurry and knock one's head against this wretched rack, filling one's hair with soot and sending a shower of smuts in every direction.

Though it was scarcely two o'clock yet we did not get beyond Ma-shih-ta that day, for there was a festival on, and the people asked me to stop and drink with them ; they would give me porters next day, they said, but begged to be excused now. They were vastly polite, and I did not insist ; nor should I have got any porters if I had.

I found a crowd of people in the chief's house, though he himself was not at home ; all were sitting round the open hearth drinking thick white maize liquor and talking at the tops of their voices. Several men, including two Chinese pedlars who came in, were drunk, and the " black " Lisu, who are much addicted to liquor, get very quarrelsome in their cups. A row soon started, and before long the protagonists were on their feet, the argument waxing furious, till one man made a movement as though to unsheath his *dâh*. The row subsided before any damage was done, as I suspect most of such drunken brawls do, for the " black " Lisu, though a bit of a swashbuckler, has no great stomach for fighting.

We had no difficulty in securing our eight or nine porters on the following morning, in spite of the carouse the night before ; I conceived quite a liking for the much maligned " black " Lisu.

Our march of November 19th was a varied one, sometimes over sand and rocks in the river bed, beneath forest-clad precipices where a few orchids and masses of Senecio were still in flower, sometimes buried in tall grass and bamboo thickets, or again in waving fields of maize or buckwheat. Mountain rice[1] is grown in many parts of the valley up to about 9000 feet, besides Sorghum,

---

[1] Mountain rice is grown on dry hill-sides, requiring no irrigation, in contrast to the ordinary rice of the plains, which is grown in water. The former gives a red grain, and is considered inferior to ordinary rice, as no doubt it is.

the stems of which contain a good deal of sugar and are
chewed by the natives like sugar cane. Two other crops
are commonly met with, one a crimson-flowered millet,
called *gna-su*, used for making bread. Peach trees grow
in some of the villages, though the fruit is poor stuff,
and there are splendid golden oranges full of juice.
Another fruit I noticed in some villages was a quince,
but hard and sour. The Chinese call it *ma-kuo*. Cotton
is not cultivated here, though it grows in the Salween
valley further south. A kind of yam is also extensively
cultivated on the steep hill slopes, often being grown
indiscriminately with crops of buckwheat or Sorghum.
It has large sagittate leaves, and small tubers which, when
baked in hot ashes and skinned, are excellent eating,
being very farinaceous. Thus we find exactly the same
crops on the Salween as are met with in the valley of the
'Nmai hka to the west, the country of the Naingvaw,
and the forest vegetation is also very similar, though the
former valley is poorer in tropical species. Still we know
enough to realise that both in its crops, plants, and
insects, especially butterflies, the Salween valley shows
strong relationship with the Burmese hinterland, and
marks the eastern limit of the Indo-Malayan flora.

Finding this close connection between them as regards
the geographical distribution of both plants and animals,
we might reasonably expect to find a similar correspond-
ence between the peoples inhabiting these valleys ; and
so we do, as I have already pointed out.

Lo-pa-ta was the next village ; the people did not
waste ten minutes changing porters, and while we were
waiting the chief brought me out boiled maize cobs and
a bamboo tankard of liquor. A little later we again
changed porters, at a village close beside the river, which

then flows up against some cliffs rising from deep water ; the climb up through the jungle for about a thousand feet over these cliffs, and the descent on the other side, are very difficult. In places we had to haul ourselves up the rocks by means of roots, creepers, or tree trunks, and cross gaps and ravines by crazy logs. In an hour, however, we found ourselves by the river again, where it bends to the east, and perhaps three hundred yards further down stream ; just above us was a village, where a big stream, flowing in a wide valley, enters the Salween, and half a mile below on a long shelving platform quite like that at Tra-mu-tang was the village of Sukin.

It was now necessary for us to procure an interpreter, for no one down here spoke Tibetan, and very few Chinese. This we could have done by going on to Sukin ; but as our route to the Taron lay westwards up the side valley, and I did not wish to waste time, I decided to turn off here to the next village, and trust to luck in the matter of an interpreter.

So we continued up the left bank of the broad, swiftly flowing stream, spanned by an excellent plank bridge passable for mules, and climbing high up the cultivated hill-side, descended again to the stream and reached the village of Tzu-li, where the stream forks into two, and the valley closes in.

Tzu-li comprises eight huts clustered together on the left bank of the stream, and half a dozen scattered along the other side. We found here a party of Chinese pedlars from the Mekong ; they had crossed from Ailoa to Latsa, and so up the Salween valley, selling salt, cotton-yarn and Chinese clothes as they went. One of them, hearing that we were in difficulties, came across to our hut and offered his services as an interpreter, and learning that he spoke Tibetan, Moso, Lisu and Lutzu (or Kiutzu) and had spent several years wandering about this country, my man came to an arrangement with him to take us as far as Mu-wang, which is the Chinese name for the plain of Hkamti Long, thirty days' journey hence.

Near the village of Tzu-li I noticed some Lisu graves on the hill-side, low mounds roofed over with sticks laid like rafters against a central beam running the length of the grave. Sometimes the roof is made complete with slates. The first was a woman's grave, and at the head stood the property her spirit would require in the next world—pipe, basket, bamboo drinking vessel, and stone wine jar. A little further on was another with hat, arrow case, sword and crossbow hung at the head, protected from rain by a wooden shield, and a cooking pot and wine jar on the ground. Suspended from a bamboo stick a paper bird with wings outspread hovered over the grave. It is interesting to note that a bird was always figured on the elaborate Kachin and Maru graves I subsequently saw in the Burmese hinterland.

In English mythology, on the other hand, the bird is symbolical not of death, but of birth, for the stork is popularly supposed to usher the new life into this world. But while Lisu graves often have the flying bird depicted, no doubt representing the soul soaring away from the body, and analogous to the Kachin birds (which, however, are usually carved in wood), the beliefs of the Lisu are more closely akin to those of the Chinese. For the placing of the deceased's property on the grave not only implies a belief in a future life—which is common to all these tribes—but also that the soul will revisit this earth and use his things once more ; that is, return in the form of a *man*. It is, in fact, very much the same custom as that of the Chinese who visit the ancestral graves twice a month, at new and full moon, and place meat and wine there, and burn silver paper made up to imitate silver ingots; for spirits are remittance-men, and require to buy commodities in the next world.

That the Chinese believe in a material spirit with earth wants is proved by the fact that one sometimes comes across a grave with a number of little paper flags set up at intervals, leading to the deceased's house, so that the spirit can find its way back to the family hearth. All this is, of course, ancestor worship, the philosophy of the continuity of life. It differs from the fundamental philosophy of Buddha—all life is one—in manner, that is ritual, rather than fact, for both show the same belief in the interdependence of cause and effect—the doctrine of the continuity of effect, or Kamma.

As regards language, it seems to be established that the Lisu belong to the Tibeto-Burman sub-family, not to the Siamese-Chinese group. Physically, on the other hand, the Lisu bear no resemblance to any of the tribes west of the Salween, but resemble rather some of the Tibetan tribes of far western China. If then they originally came from the same country whence sprang the Kachins and Burmans, they must have branched off from those people at a very early period of their history, keeping more to the east, and hence free of the jungles. Thus they came more into contact with the Chinese.

Consequently there is reason to believe that their overflowing westwards into the Burmese hinterland, and perhaps even their occupation of the Salween valley, is comparatively modern.

There is, however, one argument in favour of a western or southern origin for the Lisu, to which I am inclined to attach importance. I noticed when travelling in the monsoon Salween valley that in December the weather is uncommonly cold; the days when fine are warm enough, but on clear nights there is always a sharp frost, and in wet weather a damp penetrating cold seems to chill one more thoroughly than the frosts. Even in December the snow lay only about 1200 feet above the river, and in January and February it must descend still lower. In spite of this the Lisu live in draughty bamboo huts, and what is still more important, have hardly any clothes, the single thin hempen cloak already described being their only garment.

Now, cold as the Salween valley is in winter, the mountains and valleys further east are colder still, and it is inconceivable that a people inhabiting such a country should not have invented adequate clothing; and once invented, they would not discard it, or forget how to make it. The inference is that the Lisu have emigrated from a warmer to a colder climate, conservatism and indifference, or laziness engendered by a most relaxing climate having prevented them from adapting their dress to the new climatic conditions.

This argument suggests that the Lisu reached the Salween valley from the south or west, not from the east.

It is, of course, very difficult to obtain reliable information from the tribesmen themselves as to their original homes. Most of the Lisu I questioned on the subject said they did not know; a few have told me their ancestors came from Li-kiang, and it is worthy of note that Prince Henry of Orleans was told by the " black " Lisu of the Salween that their ancestors possessed elephants. This, if true, can only indicate that their

o

home was either in the west, or in the far south, though
the Chinese have a tradition that Pu-hsien, who brought
Buddhism to China from India in the seventh century,
came riding on an elephant ; still the Lisu tradition is
not likely to have been confused with the mythical story
of Pu-hsien.

So far as their recent movements give any indication
of their origin, the Lisu may quite well have come from
the south, for the " *hua* " Lisu of Yun-nan are moving
gradually northwards and westwards into British territory, and the " *hê* " Lisu of the upper Salween are
spreading gradually westwards down the Ahkyang valley
even to the 'Nmai hka, where they are now found in some
numbers north of the Naingvaw. Eventually, no doubt,
the Lisu will become as powerful a tribe as the Kachins
—they are already almost as widely spread, though their
distribution is discontinuous.

No less strongly in favour of a non-eastern origin for
the Lisu is the undoubted similarity between their huts
and household goods and those of the tribes to the west ;
thatched bamboo huts raised on piles, bamboo drinking
vessels, gourd pitchers, the cross-bow and poisoned
arrows are all reminiscent of the jungle, not of the cold
Yun-nan mountains. Similarly the crops grown by
the " *hê* " Lisu, their hand-looms, and the plainly striped
cloth they weave, their thick liquor, their habits of
drinking and smoking, and their food all point in the
same direction. The origin of the cross-bowmen of the
Salween still remains a mystery, and at present we can
only say that their nearest living relatives are to be
found amongst the tribes of the Tibetan marches,
Lolo, Moso, Hsifan and others, though unlike the
Lolo and Moso, they have no written language ; here

again they resemble the Tibeto-Burman tribes west of the Salween.

As to their marriage customs, they are essentially those of the East, that is to say marriage by purchase, in other words, dowry, but there is a definite marriage ceremony. Polygamy is perhaps countenanced, but, as amongst the Chinese rural population, rarely practised, on the ground of expense, and the Kachin equivalent is not tolerated, at least not publicly, in the best Lisu circles.

It is, however, noteworthy that the " *hê* " Lisu are amongst the dirtiest of all the tribes ; and while we must not expect the same intimate association of cleanliness and licence here that in classic times caused so objectionable (but intelligible) a reaction against physical cleanliness by the early Christians, it is nevertheless significant that the cleanest of these trans-Salween peoples, the Shan and Maru, are what we should call rather lax in morals. But, as already indicated, so many factors must be taken into consideration to account for local morals, that to draw the hard and fast parallel is both misleading and unfair ; and the Tibetans themselves, than whom none are dirtier, are not the more moral on that account.

Next morning, November 20th, a party of Kiutzu arrived at Tzu-li from the Taron. They were an uncouth crowd. Their hair hung matted over their dirty faces, giving the men a girlish appearance. They possessed only two garments apiece, a sort of hempen blanket worn round the waist like a skirt, and another thrown over the shoulders and tied across the chest. They were very similar, both in dress and appearance, to the Nung slaves described in Chapter XVI.

They carried light loads in bamboo baskets, long spears,

big Shan *dâhs* in open wooden sheaths, and war-bows, with a span of four or five feet. The arrow case is usually made from the skin of a silver-grey monkey, with long soft fur, the legs making the shoulder strap, and the two little paws crossed rather pathetically over the lid. These monkeys are the sweetest little animals, with long tails and black faces—later I saw one alive which a Kiutzu had brought over with him.

The Kiutzu come to the Salween for salt, Chinese cotton yarn, and sometimes Chinese garments, breeches and jackets. Cloth is of no use to them as they do not know how to sew.

They bring in exchange huang-lien,[1] skins (monkey and black bear), musk, and gold dust. I am of opinion that trade between the Chinese and tribesmen, which is at present insignificant, will increase rapidly now that the Indian Government has brought Hkamti Long under direct administration.

Our best policy will be to facilitate it by all means in our power, but at the same time it will be very much in the interests of Burma to extend the road northwards from Hkamti Long, as well as eastwards to the Taron, in order to encourage our own trade with the tribesmen, which should be able to compete very successfully with any efforts from Yun-nan ; for communications on our side of the frontier are now better.

---

[1] Huang-lien is the root of *Coptis teeta*, which grows in the temperate forests of the Burmese hinterland, and in some parts of China. It is a valuable drug in the Chinese pharmacopœia.

XV

The Road to the Taron

STARTING from Tzu-li on November 20th, where the broad stream immediately divides into two boisterous torrents flowing in well-wooded gorges, we crossed the right-hand stream by means of a plank, and ascended the steep spur for several hundred feet. Reaching some cliffs, progress in this direction was presently checked, and we turned up the bigger of the two streams, following a very difficult path up and down the mountain side, here covered with scattered pines, alders, and oaks, and overgrown with bracken and tall anemones ; masses of tuberous orchids hung over the rocks, and the gullies were filled with a jungly growth of trees, ferns, bananas, small palms and many climbing plants. It is remarkable what a lot of the mountainous region of Yun-nan and the Burmese hinterland consists of this steep open park-like country, with bracken, grass and scattered trees. From the Mekong to the 'Nmai hka, between 6000 and 8000 feet, all south slopes facing due north are, at this altitude, covered with forest.

After a tiring traverse along the mountain side, crossing several deep gullies, the torrent far below us, we reached a group of Lisu huts. From here we turned north, following the main stream. Across the valley, we caught sight of the village of Ho-wa-ti.

For a few hundred yards our path now lay over large boulders in the stream bed, the banks of which were thickly overgrown. Here a fine purple-flowered Crawfurdia dangled its tubular bells playfully. A steep pull up the bank brought us at last to cultivation, and passing through stubble fields of mountain rice we reached the first huts ; amid the ill-mannered greetings of numerous pariah dogs we sought shelter in one of the smallest.

Ho-wa-ti is a rueful little village of ten or twelve families, though several of the huts are quite roomy. Between them, small garden plots are fenced off, and here grow pumpkins, bigger than a man's head, and runner beans climbing up poles, giving quite a pleasing effect where the huts peeped out of the boscage.

The hut in which we stayed had both walls and floor made of boards instead of matting ; it was wretchedly dark, but improved lighting was easily effected by pulling aside one or two of the boards forming the walls, which are purposely loose, thus letting in shafts of light.

My two interpreters spent most of the following day arranging for porters to take us to the Taron, six days' journey they said, the loads being heavy. For the first time since we had been amongst them, the Lisu showed themselves difficult people to deal with. Atung (*alias* Li), my interpreter, a rough customer well known in the Salween valley, already contemplated treachery.

In the end the necessary porters were secured, a certain amount of food prepared, and the start fixed for the morrow. That night I heard the Lisu singing, shouting and quarrelling in their huts, but by eight o'clock all was silent ; in our own hut the people always went to bed, or I should say rather, lay down to sleep by the fire at seven o'clock and were moving about again at half-past three in the morning.

On November 22nd, the weather did not look at all promising; the sky was overcast, and after opening with a light drizzle we were treated to a sharp shower. The Lisu shook their heads and did not want to start. Rain here meant snow on the pass, they said, but we overcame their scruples, and having come to an arrangement about advance payment, eventually set out at two o'clock, all the morning having been wasted in fruitless argument.

Our porters were a scratch lot. Three or four men were worth their salt, but in addition to these we had two small boys who were naked below the waist, possessing jackets and nothing else, and a woman who was also the mother of a small child; the latter flatly refused to be left behind and was a " passenger," since he could carry nothing. On the contrary, he required food. A young girl and several ancient mariners completed the company.

The Lisu soon gave us a taste of their quality, for we had surmounted no more than two cattle hurdles and crossed a gully, when they sat down for a rest, pulled out their pipes, and lolled back, contentedly smoking and chatting for a quarter of an hour; we quickly learnt patience with the " black " Lisu.

Now on again up the ridge, so steep in places that the porters stop for breath every few yards, till we are many hundreds of feet above the stream, but still the mountain-side is clothed with bracken growing waist high, and oak trees bearing bunches of squat acorns. The halts are numerous, and every time the porters seat themselves, out come the pipes. If anyone has not got one he borrows his neighbour's. How they talk, these people!

At four o'clock we halt at an altitude of 9,486 feet, there being a spring in the forest on the sheltered side of the ridge. Away to the north at the head of the valley a group of bare rocky peaks are visible, and southwards we look down the Salween valley and across to the Mekong-Salween divide, freshly powdered with snow. But the mountains all round us are half hidden in cloud, and showers are creeping down out of the gathering gloom, brushing us as they whisk across the valley.

We manage to rig up a tarpaulin over my bed, and after a supper (boiled rice and pumpkin, with a cup of hot soup, and half a leg of cold chicken) I am glad to get to bed. The men sleep on the ground by the fires as usual.

Towards morning it started to drizzle heavily, but dawn faltering over the Salween valley in an angry sky, now wild with cloud, was magnificent. For a time it looked as though the golden sun would ride the grey billows rolling across the western mountains and triumph over the storm ; but after a tussle the clouds conquered and swamped the gold ; one by one the mountains were veiled.

We were ready to start at 8.30 but had to wait for the mother of the fractious child, she having returned to the village with him on the previous evening. It was nearly ten o'clock before she put in an appearance. Presently a party of Kiutzu came down the ridge and stopped to talk. My men were busily employed killing lice in each other's hair, sitting in rows of four and five while the slaughter proceeded : they looked uncommonly like monkeys.

After leaving this camp we at once entered the forest, all draped in moss. The path was very bad, frequently blocked by fallen tree trunks and masses of rock, over which we had to clamber. Gradually it grew steeper and a thick undergrowth of bamboo brake and ferns on either hand made it necessary to keep strictly to the narrow way.

We had not gone far when it began to rain steadily, till it became impossible for even the bare-footed porters to retain their footing on the slopes. At 11.30 therefore we halted beneath a big tree, though the men had to go some distance down the mountain side for water ; and here we prepared to make ourselves as comfortable as the miserable conditions would allow.

The prospect was not cheerful. On one side of the tree was a hole into which the head of my bed was thrust, the tarpaulin being rigged partly over it. But by the time we had got it all fixed up, nearly everything was already wet. On the other side the ample trunk was hollow, and inside the tree my two men buried themselves, with a fire between them—a cosy enough retreat, both warm and dry, but too smoky for my sensitive eyes.

As for the Lisu, they prepared a place of their own under a big rock further down the slope and we heard them singing away as though they had no cares in the world.

For two hours it rained and then the rain turned to snow. All day, all the evening and all night it continued, sometimes snowing, more often raining, and the steady patter on the leaves and the mournful drip, drip from the branches was the only sound in the deep forest.

Our altitude was about 10,000 feet, and we had to cross a pass of over 12,000 feet, besides which the track through the jungle was so steep and slippery with mud that to proceed was impossible.

I spent the afternoon in bed, as the driest place, reading Shakespeare and writing my diary. It was quite chilly outside though the snow did not lie on the ground ; so I had an early supper inside the tree trunk. But food was scanty and supper dismal in consequence. Then the " Monkey " and I questioned Atung about Mu-wang,[1] and somehow when he told us of the big temples there and the neatly dressed Shans, and the priests and the rice-fields, the gloom was momentarily dispelled, and sunny Burma seemed nearer. Atung himself, however, had never been as far as Mu-wang though he had been to the Taron. As a matter of fact his tale of " big temples " on the Hkamti plain was pure romance, though there are several pagodas such as are seen in any Shan village.

I managed to keep fairly warm and dry under my awning, though the foot of my bed projected beyond cover ; nevertheless I slept badly and woke suffering from rheumatism. Through the rain and swirling cloud I saw the fir trees on the ridge opposite us, white with snow. I was not surprised therefore when the Lisu informed me that it would be impossible to cross the pass for some days, and that as they had not enough food, we must return to the village and wait.

Starting down at 11.30 we reached Ho-wa-ti at 2.15 after only two hours' actual travel. The Lisu were outrageously slack, halting every twenty minutes or half an hour for a quarter of an hour's rest and smoke. It had ceased raining by this time, but it did not look as though the bad weather was finished, and the afternoon

[1] Mu-wang is the Chinese name for Hkamti Long.

was showery. Yet after supper the stars were shining again. Some time in the night it poured with rain so that the roof of our hut leaked like a sieve.

November 25th broke fine and sunny. Snow whitened all the mountains around us and crystalled the fir trees not far above. The Lisu said we should not be able to cross the pass for eight or ten days—a pure fiction by the way—but said they would start again in a week if the weather kept fine.

In the meantime we decided to go down to Sukin and buy supplies, as well as articles such as salt and cotton yarn, to trade with the Kiutzu. We would spend three or four days in Sukin, I thought, and then return to Ho-wa-ti with more porters and lighter loads.

I mended my clothes, and the time quickly passed ; next morning packing the few things I should require I left half my things in the hut, and we set out for the Salween once more.

Taking only three porters and starting at 9.30 we reached Sukin at four in spite of numerous halts and great reluctance on the part of the porters to go beyond Tzu-li.

Sukin [1] is a big sprawling village of nearly a hundred families, mostly Lisu, though at the northern end is a group of Chinese houses, including a couple of shops. At least one merchant there is a comparatively prosperous man.

The Lisu huts occur in little clumps above the rice-fields which for half a mile slope down to the river bank. There is also a small Chinese temple, a most miserable shanty, now used chiefly as a barn. There is a ferry

[1] Known west of the Salween valley as Sekanda. Nowadays Sukin is the residence of the official, as it is more central than Tra-mu-tang.

across to the main road on the left bank, and a rope bridge at the southern end of the platform.

One of my chief amusements was watching the fishing at Sukin. The weather was brilliant now, delightfully warm in the daytime, with a keen frost at night, and walking over the rocks in the river bed was pleasant. There was a little sandy cove on the right bank a few hundred yards below a big rapid, and here the fishing was carried on.

A double cable of some twining plant, rather thicker than whipcord, and forty or fifty feet long, is used, and a heavy stone fastened to each end. Every eight or ten feet the two cables are tied together, and at each joint is attached a hook, baited with a small white grub. One stone is placed on shore and the other carried out in a canoe and dropped in mid-stream, the nearest hook being only a few yards from the bank, which shelves rapidly to clear deep water, with a sandy bottom. At this point the river is not more than fifty yards broad in winter. The current races under the opposite bank, which is steep and rocky. The cable hugs the bottom, the shore end being attached as stated to a big stone, or to a stick firmly planted in the sand. A short line connects this end with another stick firmly planted, on which a stone is balanced, and any tug on the line affects the latter, upsetting the stone which thus acts the part of indicator.

Along three hundred yards of foreshore no less than seven of these lines were out, and quite big fish are sometimes caught, the Lisu of the neighbourhood living largely on a fish diet.

I saw also several U-shaped hand nets attached to two long bamboos, such as are used by the Lutzu at Tra-mu-tang when fishing from canoes.

Besides fish, all firewood is procured from the river,
which for six or seven months brings down big tree
trunks ; piles of splintered timber now lay high and dry
on the sands.

Along the rocky part of the shore were several burrows
from which auriferous sand had at one time been dug,
and one man was hard at work with his primitive cradle
washing for gold ; evidently it was not a lucrative
business. Better results are obtained further west, so I
was told.

Early on the morning of December 1st, the day we
had arranged to start back for Ho-wa-ti, I went down to
the river again to see them pull up the lines. However,
no fish had been hooked, but I saw instead a man netting
fish with a narrow trawl-net weighted with stones and
kept afloat just below the surface by means of bamboos
threaded along the top. One corner is tied to a stone on
shore, and the net is thrust out into the river with a long
pole, and floats upright, fish becoming entangled in the
meshes. One fish had been caught during the night,
but it was just awash and the crows had eaten it.

At this hour, six o'clock in the morning, a bank of
milk-white mist lay over the river like an efflorescence,
and the grass was stiff with hoar frost ; through the
haze overhead I could see blue sky, and the sun was
rapidly lapping up the mist bank. Everything promised
well.

On the previous day several Kiutzu and Lisu had
arrived at Sukin, having crossed the pass since the snowstorm. They reported deep snow, but if they could
cross I supposed we could, especially as they would have
stamped a trail. Every fine day melted more snow, and
the best thing to do was to get over at once before the

next snow-storm. We had bought a supply of salt and cotton yarn during our holiday at Sukin, and a number of Indian rupees.

It was noon before we set out, and we got no further than Tzu-li that day; evidently Atung could not or would not manage the Lisu. However, as I was dependent on him I had to humour him. Going along by the river, I saw several duck, but they kept well out of range on the other side.

December 2nd saw us climbing the steep-sided valley on the way to Ho-wa-ti, still under a cloudless sky. The perspiration rolled off me, and the porters halted more frequently than ever. Flitting about amongst the pine trees were brilliant scarlet fly-catchers.

We had not gone far when we met another party of Kiutzu, and after conversing with them for a time, Atung informed me that hundreds of British troops had arrived at Mu-wang!

This was, of course, an exaggerated account of the British occupation. Though the first column did not actually arrive till January, they were now on the road from Myitkyina.

We reached Ho-wa-ti that evening; the chief was absent, but the people promised to start next day. December 3rd came, but after a lot of talk the Lisu wanted to wait yet another two or three days; it had snowed again last night they said, and they would wait for some Kiutzu who were shortly returning, driving cattle back with them. More Kiutzu arrived from the Taron, and the sky looked muddy in the north, as though preparing for another storm.

Our last hope was the returning Kiutzu, but after all they had their own loads to carry. However, Atung got hold of one of them, and then another difficulty presented itself. They wanted clothes, not silver, and three men exhausted all the blankets and clothes I could part with. Nor did these men seem keen on the business, though that was probably Atung's fault ; Ganton, the Tibetan who had taken me to the Salween in 1911, would, I think, have persuaded them to go, for he had a wonderful way of dealing with the most shy tribesmen.

However, by evening we had collected seven porters, including two Kiutzu, and everything was settled ; three more men were to be found first thing in the morning, and I went to bed with a light heart.

It was a fine starlight night, and a clear dawn followed, but light puffy clouds sailing over from the west presaged wind ; however, the peaks at the head of the valley, now dappled with snow, stood out clearly against the blue sky.

Followed yet another delay, and by noon, instead of the one or two more porters required, we had three less, only four being willing to go. This was due, so I was told, to the news brought by some more Kiutzu who had arrived from the Taron that morning, that the snow was still very deep. But if they could cross, so could we, though, of course, their loads were not so heavy as mine. Moreover, they had to get back again.

But it is impossible to rely on these people. They promise anything at night, when drunk, and forget it next morning when sober. While I was at breakfast a violent altercation broke out between two of them, still apparently drunk from the previous night's carouse. Shouting at the tops of their voices, they fought with long bamboo staves, but in spite of the noise, and praiseworthy efforts at hitting each other over the head while circling cautiously round and round, no damage was done, not so much as a blow struck home.

I was told that the Lisu suspected me of bad faith because in the previous year the Chinese had impressed them and then refused to pay them. But it is hardly likely that the Chinese would have started their adventurous journey to the Ahkyang by alienating the very people on whom they would be most dependent for transport and food, though I can well believe that drastic action would be necessary before they got any work out of the Lisu.

I still had hopes from the Kiutzu, a considerable number of whom had gone to the Salween to buy cattle. But when at midday half the party refused to go at any price, our troubles began all over again. So the day passed, and I ate my two meals of rice and pumpkin, to which I had long been reduced, with a heavy heart.

I had bought a fowl, some eggs, and some bacon fat in Sukin, but at Ho-wa-ti I could get only a little rice, pumpkins, and maize flour. The people would sell me nothing else.

On December 5th Atung exploded his bombshell quite casually. Two days previously a Tibetan runner had arrived with a letter from the official at Tra-mu-tang forbidding the Lisu to carry for me !

The news took me completely by surprise, and it was quite a relief when Atung fell through the rotten floor of the hut into the cattle byre and cut his leg badly. That was all the information I could get. For two days Atung and his friends had known this and had held their peace. They excused themselves by saying that they were afraid to tell me the bad news !

I had now to decide on a plan of action. I still hoped

to get across with some of my baggage, by starting lower down the valley. There was nothing for it but to return to Sukin and try again.

We got as far as Tzu-li that night, arriving at Sukin on December 6th. Meanwhile I had told Atung that we would find two men willing to act as porters, and cross the mountains with light loads, but my valiant interpreter was very reluctant, saying as usual that the path was too difficult. The Chinese cannot understand why anyone should put himself to the labour of crossing mountains merely for pleasure, or in the pursuit of knowledge, which is, after all, the same thing.

Though we reached Sukin at ten o'clock in the morning, there we had to stay for the rest of the day, and every hour was of value now—it might snow again at any moment. However, I made preparations that night, and on December 7th we started down the Salween once more, our objective being a path to the Taron, a day's journey south.

We had not gone far when Atung, who was lagging behind instead of going ahead to the next village to secure porters, and was severely reprimanded in consequence, showed himself in his true colours. For now he blurted out that he was not going to the Taron with me at all, as he was afraid ; he would go down the Salween to Latsa with me and over the pass to the Mekong, but not to the Taron.

This was all very mysterious ; something he had heard from the merchants in Sukin he refused to tell me, though, since the story of the British expedition to Hkamti, it required no acute discernment to guess.

I now perceived for the first time four soldiers keeping level with us on the other side of the river. A few miles

P

below Sukin, where the Lisu porters put my loads down by the roadside near some huts and walked off home without a word, two of them came across in a canoe.

Atung had gone up to one of the huts, ostensibly to look for fresh porters, actually to sit down and have a quiet smoke. I had seated myself on one of the boxes and was eating a piece of chocolate when I was politely accosted. I turned round and saw a tall, rather nice-looking officer in a long military coat standing before me, and having paid my respects, I invited him to be seated and eat some chocolate.

Kao, as he told me his name was, with the rank of perhaps a sergeant, questioned me about my destination, and then unfortunately asked if I had a passport ; to which I replied yes, but had to confess that it was not forthcoming, as I had given it to my servant in A-tun-tzu who was taking my plant collections to T'eng-yueh. We then touched on the matter of Atung, and Kao shook his head when I told him who my interpreter was. Atung, it seemed, had formerly been a soldier ; he was, however, one of the usual type of soldiers on the frontier who are mostly adventurers, ne'er-do-wells, or criminals, impressed men, and was within an ace of being executed for some misdemeanour. Anyway, he left the army, Kao informed me, and launched out on trading enter-prises of his own, enterprises which by reason of his linguistic accomplishments (for he could lie fluently in five tongues) he was amply qualified to undertake. He was, however, a waif and a waster, with neither mother nor family as he had represented to us, though he was welcome at several Lisu huts, and claimed to have numerous friends amongst the people of the villages he had visited. Such was the man, according to Kao, on whom I had relied to see me through a difficult journey.

I told Kao we were going on to Latsa, whither he was himself bound, and saying we would meet again that evening at a village further on he now left me, re-crossed the river, and continued down the left bank.

Meanwhile I and the " Monkey " went up the hill-side to a Lisu hut, where we found Atung peacefully smoking. He informed us that he could get no porters as the people were out in the fields ; but I was wrathful, and, seeing no further use in treating him decently, took away his pipe, telling him to go out and hunt for them. For a moment he looked at me as though he would draw the *dâh* he always carried ; but he went out sulkily enough, and presently some men carrying loads came along the river bank, and we induced them to carry my things to the next village, and return for their own later. The canoe was therefore loaded up, and we went across in two trips, the Lisu dug-outs being much smaller than those of the Lutzu, never carrying more than five men and three or four boxes. The river is sixty or seventy yards in breadth here, with numerous sand shelves and pebble banks which are under water in summer.

The valley below Sukin is fairly well populated, villages of six or eight families being numerous on both banks. Quite a good path led to the village of Chilanda at the mouth of a stream a mile lower down. Kao and his party had already arrived, and we occupied a hut not far from them.

There was an alarming rapid here, and across the river a wide-mouthed tributary valley, the stream from which had built a platform of detritus on which stood a big village of fifteen huts close by the water's edge.

There is a small path up this valley and so over the divide to the Taron.

When we were settled down I sent the " Monkey " across to Kao with a present, as the custom is in this country, with the request that he would find me three porters to guide me to the Taron. Kao sent back a friendly message that we would go on next day, and at a village further down the river he would secure the men for us. Shortly afterwards I called on him, and ate oranges and walnuts while he talked to me about the difficulties the Chinese had in dealing with the " black " Lisu.

" When we come along," he said, " they all run away, and we cannot get porters. We fight with them every year round Latsa, but they hide in the jungle and shoot at us with poisoned arrows, and we never see them. When we do reach the village we find it empty. Everyone hates the Lisu."

" It requires a little better organisation than you possess to cope with them," I thought.

Next day Kao told me we could not start as there were no porters—they had as usual all fled on the arrival of the Chinese soldiers.

XVI

The Monsoon Salween

ECEMBER 7th was cloudy and threatening, and that night rain fell again. Another storm, having its birth in the Burmese hinterland, was mobilising its snowy forces to block the way to the Taron. Early on the morning of the 8th the valley was buried under a canopy of cloud, and though the sun broke later, the day was nevertheless showery, a fresh breeze, backed by an ominous sky, blowing up the valley.

I went down to the river after breakfast, but had no sooner reached the shore, where several fishing nets were spread out to dry, than the unmistakable feeling of lassitude which accompanies fever overtook me. Whereupon I returned to the hut.

While I was consulting maps, Kao came round to see me, and when he had gone I dosed myself with quinine and rolling myself in the blankets lay down ; but not to sleep. At dusk, an early dusk with threatening clouds labouring heavily over this poisonous valley, I got up ; Atung had disappeared, but we were to start again next day and Kao would no doubt look after us.

About three o'clock in the morning I awoke—the rain was pouring down and whining over the sodden thatch. All that day it continued without intermission.

First thing in the morning Kao again came to see me and stayed two hours.

He told us now it would be impossible to reach the Taron before next summer—and what was worse, there was a strong chance of our being imprisoned in the Salween valley, unable to reach the Mekong either. We must stay where we were for the present, as the Lisu refused to travel in the rain. In any case I was too unwell myself to travel.

That evening Atung suddenly turned up, and began to make further trouble. After a preliminary shout, he dashed outside and presently came in again swearing furiously and dragging by the arm my Tibetan, who cringed before him like a child.

I was sitting huddled up by the remnant of a fire at the time, feeling very sick, but this was too much. I went at once to the rescue of the " Monkey," hitting Atung in the face, so that he fell back with a bleeding nose, and let go his hold. Then he sprang past me, shouting for his *dâh* and dashed into the next room, I after him ; but just as I clutched him I tripped in the doorway and fell.

Some women in the next room screamed, two men dashed in between us, pushing me back and I picked up a big stone from the fire-place with which to defend myself and retreated into my own room. Atung was pacified somehow and led outside, nor did he appear again that evening. Later he drowned his sorrows in drink.

It appeared afterwards that he was desperately afraid of Kao, and had determined to leave me, whereupon the " Monkey " remonstrated with him. Hence the scene. Subsequently the matter was referred to Kao, who promised that Atung should see me as far as Latsa, when he himself would get me another man. This quite satisfied me, for I had had enough of Atung.

He had come to me for another advance of pay, which I naturally refused, and it was after that he began to get nasty. But he could not clear out altogether, in spite of his threats, for he had handed over the advance wages I gave him to one of his friends—and the young man had gone off to the Mekong. Now Atung was pressed for money, and two days later he settled accounts with me.

December 10th was dull and threatening, but the rain had ceased. The Lisu had returned to the village, and Kao had secured a couple of porters for himself in addition to those I required ; so he started off first and bade us follow. The Lisu were morose and suspicious ; I did not anticipate an easy time with them.

Our route lay through a gorge, the narrow path impassable for mules ; for at one place we had to climb down about fifteen feet, holding on with our fingers to roots and ledges of rock. Beyond, the river again turns at right angles, and in front is seen a high mountain on the Salween-Irrawaddy divide ; snow was glittering on the fir trees not far above.

Down by the river in strong contrast to the conifer forests higher up, were trees laden with ferns, orchids and Aroids, clumps of giant bamboo growing to a height of 50 or 60 feet and spreading above like Prince of Wales' feathers, Ficus trees, their trunks pimpled with globular fruits, and torn banana leaves flapping in the breeze.

Everywhere the rocks are vertically tilted, and small rapids interrupt the even flow of the green water. There is no granite down here, the rock being nearly all slate, or micaceous shale, but amongst the rubbish shot out of the side gullies, blocks of porphyry are common. Birds were rare, and those I noticed such as grey and white wag-tails, a scarlet-breasted water-wren, crows, kites, and so on, are very widely distributed in Asia.

At midday we halted at a small village, apparently deserted. Sickness was rife in the valley I was told, and the Chilanda porters refused to go a step further. There we were, and there we had to stay for the night, since, with the exception of two or three very ancient men and women who subsequently emerged from their hiding-places, there was no one in the village. My temperature was still 101°, and this, together with a bad headache, made me disinclined to exert myself.

The huts were crowded together in the mouth of a stream which had unloaded a fan of gravel where it pierced the steep-sided range. In summer the river must rise to within a few feet of the platform, but now horsetails and other weeds, bushes of fire-thorn (Pyracantha sp.) and tufts of grass grew amongst the gravel and in the sandy bays of the river bed. The small bushes of Pyracantha, crowded with orange berries brighter than holly, were especially fine; and tufts of feather grass fifteen feet high, their dainty plumes like silver foxes' brushes, were being slowly shaken to ruin by the winter winds. Here and there stood patches of dwarf bamboo, bushes of Cotoneaster and clumps of thorny barberry, but the open hill-sides were as usual clothed with pines, oaks and alders, scattered amongst a rank growth of bracken and other ferns, teasels and bur-marigold, from close contact with which one emerges looking like a distraught porcupine.

Rope bridges stretched between opposite villages, but

they looked very worn and slack ; Atung said they were not used in the winter as there are any number of places between the rapids where canoes can cross in safety. Indeed there are at this season remarkably few rapids between Sukin and Latsa, though the water is probably much more turbulent in summer, as it is further north. Moreover, suitable conditions for single-way rope bridges were becoming rare, as the valley broadened out ; and in some places the two ropes for going and returning were a considerable distance apart. A little lower down slackly hung two-way ropes replace the pair of single-way ropes we were accustomed to see in Tibet.

December 10th ended fittingly enough with more rain, and it never looked like stopping that night.

On December 11th, at last, between broken masses of cloud, we see the sun again ; the storm is passing away. My fever, too, is better and I feel more cheerful. Still, there are no porters, and I have to resign myself once more to passive waiting.

Atung says we shall never get porters here, and that the only way to induce them to come is to pay them beforehand ; he therefore suggests that he and the " Monkey " shall go down the river to the next village and bring back porters—only he must take some money with him. I give the two of them sixteen rupees, and off they go.

I spent the morning by the river, where I saw a woman washing a garment in the stream by the simple process of dancing on it, just as the *dhobies* in far-away Rangoon wash our clothes by beating them against stones till the very fibres are mangled. The glories of soap are of course unknown to the tribesmen or Tibetans, and in many a remote Chinese city a present of soap will be gratefully accepted by the Chinese official and no offence taken. Kao was very pleased with the cake I gave him, and so was the Tra-mu-tang official. As for the Tibetans, their garments do not lend themselves to that sort of treatment. Besides, if a man possesses only one cloak, he can no more have it washed than he can carry out the Scriptural command should it be stolen. But I did once or twice see the " Monkey " performing limited ablutions by filling his mouth with water and squirting it in a thin stream over his bony hands, rubbing them together the while.

The hut in which we stayed was a big one, sixty feet long, and completely divided into three rooms, each with its square hearth in the middle. But as usual the advantage of the high roof was neutralised first by the bamboo rods laid across at the height of the side walls, thus forming a sort of loft for storing tubs of wine, grain, fishing nets, and other impedimenta ; secondly by the racks suspended over the hearths. Though the roof often leaks during heavy rains, yet the huts are substantially built.

In the middle of the afternoon my Tibetan inter-preter returned, and taking me aside, whispered in my ear a dreadful story ; how Atung had inveigled him on to a narrow precipice path ; how, suddenly drawing his *dâh*, he had threatened him with instant death if he did not immediately give up the money I had entrusted to him, and repeat what had been said to Kao concerning him.

"He is a bad man, Excellency," he said confidentially, in order to cover up his humiliation, " be careful ! "

I felt rather inclined to laugh as I pictured the figure my timid and ugly Tibetan must have cut in face of the furious Atung. At that moment Atung himself walked in, and the " Monkey " ceased his confidences. All this was very interesting, but the fact remained that the men had been quite unable to induce any porters to come to my rescue, so I requested Atung to return my sixteen rupees.

"Yes, all right," he replied, "but I had better wait till I can get some men; come on," turning to the " Monkey," " we will go and see if any of those villagers have returned yet." He was gone on the word and I have never seen him since. Till bed-time I was quite confident he would return, but I looked rather silly next morning when we had to start without him, and for many days to come. Yet I think we were both glad to see the last of my dangerous interpreter so cheaply.

The afternoon wore on, and by evening the sky was perfectly clear, with brilliant moonlight. Had the weather set fair again, I wondered? About seven o'clock a party of men did turn up, feeling perhaps somewhat ashamed of their precipitate flight, for they brought me a bottle of wine and promised porters for the morrow, a little kindness which, after our recent misfortunes, I appreciated. All this the "Monkey" and I gathered, for we could not speak Lisu, nor they Chinese.

December 12th broke cloudy till the sun topped the ridge, when the clouds disappeared over the valley; a strong breeze off the snow on the western range made it very chilly at first. Having given the porters some money to begin with, we made a start at 9.30, and climbed a few hundred feet above the river by a narrow path. Still ascending we presently came to an awkward precipice where, the " Monkey " said, he had been held up on the previous day. In order to avoid this narrow path, however, which would have been dangerous for the porters, we descended steeply to the river and were ferried round the base of the cliff in a dug-out, continuing close by the river for the rest of the day.

Just beyond was a small village, arrived at which the industrious Lisu wanted to put down their loads, thinking they had done their day's work, though we had not been travelling three hours. I knew enough of the Lisu by this time to realise that if we changed porters here, we should get no further on our southern march this day. The " Monkey " and I therefore, feeling desperate, decided to try intimidation, and by means of threats and cajolery we for once actually did induce them to go on to the next village ; indeed the " Monkey " became almost violent—but then our porters were mostly women—little vixens too ; and when they realised that we really did not intend to let them go back, they proceeded with a very bad grace.

So we came to Po-la-ti, another village clustered in the open mouth of a gully, this time with high banks on either side, irregularly cultivated. The people, Chinese and Lisu alike—for there were several Chinese families here, were unusually friendly, and we made ourselves comfortable in the house of a headman who, instead of running away, welcomed us. The sun had shone brightly till one o'clock, and in the middle of the day it was quite hot, but the continual western wind had brought clouds in its train, and in the afternoon it was dull and cool.

The river was again broken by several rapids, but the water though swift was generally shallow ; one or two rope bridges we passed were of the two-way variety, and looked much dilapidated.

December 13th was grey and cloudy all day, though the sun made an effort to break through in the morning. I had sent a runner to Latsa on my arrival the evening before, to inform Kao of Atung's desertion and our difficulties. He returned early in the morning with a message of condolence from Kao and a request that we would stay at Po-la-ti, where there were several Chinese traders from whom we could buy food, and not come on to Latsa where we could get nothing. But I did not want to miss seeing Latsa.

However, so far the thought of returning to A-tun-tzu had not entered my head, though I was not unwilling to cross to the Mekong by the Latsa pass, if progress westwards was finally barred. The people here said that the pass to the Mekong could not be crossed for several days, but there is no doubt that had I waited a week or ten days, I could have crossed ; westwards, however, everyone said it was not possible to go, or if they admitted the possibility of it, they were not willing to attempt it. As a matter of fact, there would have been no insuperable difficulty in crossing the 12,000 foot pass into the Ahkyang valley, and reaching Hkamti Long, or following the 'Nmai hka valley to Myitkynia.

On the night of December 13th the rheumatic pains from which I suffered awoke me about two o'clock after a very vivid dream, and suddenly everything seemed straightforward. I decided that we must return all the way up the Salween valley and try and cross to the Taron by the Tibetan pass from Trenge, just below Lakora. But first I would go to Latsa. All this I thought out elaborately step by step as I lay awake that night after my dream, listening to the rain pouring down. It seemed extraordinarily simple, but it proved quite otherwise. Presently I fell asleep again, and woke full of confidence, my ardour in no wise damped by the mist and rain which filled the valley.

Starting in the rain at ten, the " Monkey " and I reached Latsa in two-and-a-half hours, by a narrow slippery path which in some places had slipped away altogether ; we were very soon drenched to the skin, not only by the rain but with brushing through the wet tangle of vegetation.

What a dreary sight was this valley with its sodden ruined crops bowed in the fields, its empty huts and dying people, the grey shrunken river lapping against the pebbles, the misty clouds clinging to the tree-tops, and the snow on the firs higher up ! Were we really imprisoned here until the spring ?

We had not gone far when we found the villagers burying someone, at a spot where a number of fresh graves stood ; it was more dismal than ever to see these yellow clayey mounds with the poor little household goods, which would never be used again, lying idle at the gravehead, and the tattered paper birds swinging to and fro over them in the wind.

We passed through a couple of villages, and saw huts on the right bank, but the valley was less populous here than further north. At last we caught sight of Latsa fort, a square log building, arrow-proof but decidedly not bullet proof, standing close beside the river : no village was visible, the people having removed their huts higher up the mountain when the Chinese soldiers came. There were two buildings, a larger one for the accommodation of the men and a smaller, a few yards distant, which was a combined office and kitchen ;

close by flowed a stream where a woman was diligently washing some clothes.

Walking across the compound, which was surrounded by a low bamboo fence a dog could have broken through, we entered the larger house, and found ourselves in the men's quarters. Here thirty or forty of them slept like rabbits on low benches round the walls. I had been a little puzzled as to how forty odd soldiers, said to be posted at Latsa, could be accommodated in so small a building, but now I understood.

However, scarcely had we entered before Kao came along and rather unceremoniously bundled us out, inviting us more politely to come into the smaller house—a mere room it was—where, he said, we should be more comfortable.

This then was the renowned Latsa fort of which I had heard so much. It was a log house, neither barricaded nor loopholed for defence, so that the advantage of a clear field of fire up and down the river was rather wasted. It was certainly commanded from the slopes above and from across the river. However, it was evidently good enough to keep the Lisu to the south in check.

Kao had a good deal to say, and was quite obviously relieved when I told him I had come to ask his permission to allow me to return to Tra-mu-tang. He said he had tried to find men to take me to the Taron, but had been unsuccessful ; it would be impossible to go there until next spring, and the pass to the Mekong was also blocked. Our only chance was to go up the Salween into Tsa-rong and cross by the pass on the great Tibetan highway. " But you will have to obtain a special passport from Tra-mu-tang for that," he added, " it is Tibetan territory."

Then we talked about Atung, and Kao gave that gentleman short shrift. " He shall be executed," he said bluntly, and at once gave orders to that effect. A clerk wrote busily in the corner. I suspect that condemning Atung to death was easier than carrying out the sentence.

I said what a pity it was I could not take a boat and float down the Salween ; I should soon reach T'eng-yueh that way. But Kao, in sudden panic at the suggestion, immediately filled the river with enormous boulders over which the water dashed in regular cascades. I made enquiries about the path down the valley, and Kao again came to the rescue of its reputation, saying that it was very dangerous, as one had to crawl along narrow ledges in the gorges, and cross gullies on tree trunks, with Lisus shooting poisoned arrows from behind the bushes ; at least that had been their experience, whenever they went on the warpath in that direction.

There were several carcases of pigs hanging from the roof, the winter's supply of meat for the soldiers, and before I left Kao kindly ordered one of the men to cut me some pork chops, which I was very glad to accept as I had eaten no meat for some time.

We took three hours over the return journey. The rain had ceased, but the valley looked as gloomy as ever, and it poured again after dark. I felt better for the walk, though the fever was still hanging about me, and every night now, when I lay down, I suffered agonies from the most distressing rheumatism. The Chinese at Po-la-ti were all asking me for medicine, complaining of ague ; but the Lisu are sceptical as to the beneficial effects of medicine and say they do not need it, though apparently they were dying like flies this winter. After dark they carried a small child into the hut to show me. He was dying. Only the whites of his rolled-up eyes showed, and his breath came in short gasps ; the flush of fever darkened his brow. I could do nothing for him.

That night I had a square meal—soup, boiled pork, pumpkin and boiled rice, and afterwards sat round the fire with the Lisu while they brewed liquor. A large iron *kuo*, or open pan, was set over the fire, and several spoonfuls of sticky, musty rice stirred into the bubbling water. This rice had been fermenting for weeks, tightly bunged up with leaves in a big earthenware jar. After simmering for ten minutes the thick milky liquid was ladled into cups, together with a good deal of rice, and we drank it hot, like soup. It was sour and heady so that I found one cup enough for me ; but the " Monkey " drank himself to sleep and was soon nodding by the fire. I was very tired that night, and slept soundly, though I awoke aching in every limb.

December 15th turned out quite fine, and at night the sky was cloudless. Kao had promised to send us a soldier as interpreter, and on the 16th we were to start back. In the course of the day several soldiers from Latsa theatrically armed with swords and ropes passed through the village in quest of Atung, but whether that slippery warrior was ever caught or not I cannot say ; I doubt it.

The idea of starting back next day filled me with joy. To be up and doing, that was the great thing ; inaction was cloying my brain.

Q

XVII

Back to Tra-mu-tang

O N the evening of December 15th our interpreter arrived, and at nine o'clock on the 16th we set out, accomplishing the journey to Chilanda in five hours. The men travelled fast enough now, scarcely halting except at the ferry, eating nothing all day, though they smoked incessantly. I have already inveigled against the slackness of the *hê* Lisu, but there is no doubt that when they have a mind to travel they can. For these three days they displayed a stamina for which I should never have given them credit. With but two or three brief rests they marched for five or six hours carrying fifty pound loads. The two meals a day which they allow themselves consist principally of maize porridge. No doubt *pan*,[1] which they chew, acts as a stimulant, and smoking makes them stubborn to the pangs of hunger, but practice from childhood is the real secret of their endurance. The women, too, carry their babies on their backs all day long while working in the fields. The baby is wrapped up in a filthy goat-skin supported by two bandages

---

[1] In the eastern tropics *pan* leaves (*Piper betel*) are chewed with betel nut (*Areca* sp.), but in the Burmese hinterland where the *pan* grows wild and there are no betel palms, the fruits of the *pan* itself are chewed. Where neither *pan* nor betel nut can be obtained, tobacco is chewed.

crossed over the mother's shoulders and tied round the waist. Often there is nothing of the baby visible, not even the top of its head, so that the mother appears to be carrying round an inanimate bundle. But sometimes the baby's head peeps out from the skin and lolls back weakly, the attitudes into which the unfortunate child is shaken as the mother moves about and bends over her work suggesting that if it survives it will be able to put up with any imaginable discomfort in later life.

To return, then, to the journey. There had been a heavy dew during the night which just froze in the small hours, and a long bank of cloud floated low down upon the river ; but the sun soon came through and a glorious day transformed the valley. Now through gaps in the range we could see the snow sparkling on the fir trees, and rejoice.

In a gully we crossed I saw some Clematis in flower, and the purple Crawfurdia, and on one of the sandy patches by the river, where horsetails were growing amongst the gravel, I picked up an extraordinary little mole (*Parascaptor leucurus*) and made a museum specimen of it that evening with nothing more technical than a pocket knife. He was given a bamboo tail and stuffed with compressed cotton-wool from my medicine chest. The Salween was still falling, the water becoming cleaner and greener every day.

The start from Chilanda on the 17th was delayed by the truculence of the Lisu, who, having demanded an exorbitant price for porters, wanted the money down in advance. As it was these very people who had only done half a day's journey, after receiving a day's wages in advance, I refused, whereupon the chief, a very powerful man, threw down his load in a rage and began untying the bamboo head strap.

"Not so fast," I said, and held his arm. He turned on me like a wild cat, and I caught him by the neck as he gripped hold of my shirt. For a moment it looked as if there was going to be a free fight, and it would have fared ill with me, for the chief, though a short man, had the arms, chest and shoulders of a Hercules. Then the angry faces of two other men were thrust menacingly into mine, a fist was clenched, a *dâh* was bared, and I let go, while my pacific Tibetan danced round shrieking in an agony of apprehension, and the soldier stood by afraid to say a word. Evidently these people had not forgotten my hammering Atung, and thought me a dangerous person ; on the other hand, there is nothing more to be feared than a frightened tribesman. One cannot hope to succeed with such people till one has gained their confidence.

After this little argument had been settled, we started, the Lisu promising to go as far as a small village just beyond Sukin, but on our side (i.e. the left bank) of the river : we would not cross to the right bank till higher up.

I was much struck by seeing such common English wayside weeds as stork's bill, Potentilla, knotweed, shepherd's purse, stitchwort, violets and so on, in the fields, while on the rocks were shrivelled plants of Didissandra, and in the gullies grew pink-flowered Begonias and numbers of tropical plants. The path on the left bank is better than the one we had come down by, and above Sukin there are none of those high cliffs which had cost us such a waste of time on the way south.

We reached some poor huts above the valley leading to the Yuragan pass at five o'clock, after a cloudless day, and hunted up fresh porters the same evening.

There was a sharp frost in the night again, and splendid weather followed. An easy march up and down, sometimes in the river bed, brought us to Yuragan in the afternoon, and here we had to stop, as no porters could be found; the following day would be our last amongst the Lisu, after spending a month in their company.

There were several Chinese soldiers billeted in houses at Yuragan. This is a favourite method of controlling the tribes with the Chinese, and I had found soldiers at Chilanda as well, though there were none at Sukin. The object is to keep an eye on the people and maintain communications between the posts of Tra-mu-tang and Latsa. The soldiers act as relay runners when a message is required to be sent; otherwise they simply loaf and learn the language.

On December 19th we climbed several hundred feet above the river, passing through groves of leafless oak on which grew epiphytic Dendrobiums, a queer combination of tropical and temperate vegetation it seemed.

Pong-ta, the first Lutzu village, was reached in two hours and then came a long delay while we sought porters. However, I was so overjoyed to pay off the last Lisu porters that I did not mind, and spent the time eating oranges in the hut of a friendly Lutzu. Eventually we did induce porters to go, though the halt had been so prolonged that night had fallen before we reached Bibili. First we crossed to the right bank in a canoe so small that we had to make six trips before we got our eight porters and loads across ; even then the gunwale was almost awash each time, and we had to paddle cautiously. Each trip took five minutes there and back, so that more than half an hour was spent at the ferry. Just here the river was dark olive-green and very deep, flowing sluggishly between sand-banks.

In the gorge above, the foliage was limp with dew, and frost still whitened the open hill-side ; but across the river the south-facing pine-clad slopes were dry and brown. It took us three hours to reach Bibili from the ferry; I timed it carefully because a small boy, aged nine, carried a man's load all the way !

We were now only a few miles from Tra-mu-tang. Starting in good time on December 20th, we reached the ferry at Choton in a couple of hours, and were gladdened by the sight of Tibetan dancers performing in front of the huts. Here, too, were scarlet roses in bloom, and trees golden with oranges. How broad and green the valley looked ! It seemed like a new world we had entered !

The weather was still fine and sunny, the shade temperature at noon being 47° F. and at 2 p.m., 55° F. At the next village there was a feast in progress—a lama was exorcising devils, and we could hear him praying and tinkling his bell upstairs. I gave the people some money, and at once a Tibetan invited me to the feast, nor was I slow to accept. I had not eaten bread for three weeks, and the buckwheat cakes they put before me tasted delicious ; I had also wine and meat, as much as I liked, and walnuts.

An hour later we set out for Tra-mu-tang, now only a few miles distant ; my plan was to get porters there the same evening and start for Tsa-rong early on the following morning.

We reached our destination at 4.30 and went straight up to the house of the Lutzu chief, who received us with symptoms of embarrassment. A soldier sat by the fire. He greeted us coldly, then left—to report my arrival at the *yamen*. From the chief we learnt that the bad season which had decimated the Lisu lower down the valley had made itself felt here too ; but at Tra-mu-tang it was the animals which had suffered. One man had lost all his cattle from disease. The sky had clouded over ominously towards evening, and that night the temperature dropped to only 37° F. Next day, December 21st, I learnt that we could get no porters from the Lutzu chief—I must go and call on the official.

My interview with the official was not hopeful. I asked for a couple of porters and a guide to take me to the Taron, but this was politely refused. The official was indeed politeness itself throughout the interview, with that old-world courtesy which gently disarms impatience at any lack of Western understanding. Alas! that the revolution should have so far discouraged this oriental charm of manner ! And now I was requested to explain my object in visiting the Salween valley, in view of the new regulations. These, which emanated from Li-kiang, were to the effect that Europeans were not permitted to take photographs or make maps on the frontier, or do various other things in the manner of acquiring knowledge. One might have thought that the Yun-nan frontier was fortified, mined and garrisoned, so elaborate were the instructions on these points ! I was also required to surrender my photographs ! As regards my future movements, only one loop-hole of escape from the Salween valley was left me—I must return to the Mekong by the big road over the Londre-la, and so to A-tun-tzu. No protestations of mine availed.

Realising that I was now practically a prisoner I went straight back to the house where we were living, gave some instructions to my man, packed my boxes, put some food and silver into a Tibetan skin bag, and with this, a blanket and a few necessaries, set out at four o'clock in the afternoon for Kieunatong. The day had been dull, and darkness fell swiftly, so that having traversed the gorge above Tra-mu-tang between the towering limestone cliffs, in which deep gloom prevailed, I had some difficulty in reaching even the first village, where I arrived at seven o'clock. Entering a hut I found the ashes of a fire, but no one at home except a baby, fast asleep, and being more tired than hungry I quickly rolled myself in the rug I had brought and lay down on the floor.

About an hour later my host and hostess returned, and I made them understand that I proposed to billet myself on them for the night, and that I wanted some food. The fire was therefore resuscitated, the family pot of maize meal set boiling, a clean straw pallet procured and laid on a rough bench, and some fresh eggs brought in. After supper, I once more wrapped my rug round me, and taking off my boots lay down to sleep on the straw pallet ; the house people then spread an extra cover over me, and I slept fairly well in spite of the baby's protestations during the night.

I was up at six next morning. It was still dark, and after a hasty meal, I set off at seven. Rain had been falling and moist clouds filled the valley with dank gloom. I reached the ferry in an hour, but the boat was on the other side, and shout as I would I could get no response from the huts above.

At last I gave it up and started back for the rope bridge, hoping to cross there : the people were all up the mountain ; it was useless to wait any longer.

At the rope bridge I saw a canoe with two people in it fishing, and having at last attracted their attention, I climbed down the cliff to the river and got aboard. For some distance they hugged the right bank, pushing against the cliffs with their paddles, but presently, coming to a place where there was good landing on the other side, they shot across and put me ashore. I found myself just below the rapid and not far from the ferry above, which was reached with a loss of two solid hours.

Turning up the side valley towards Kieunatong, I reached the French mission at noon. Here I was warmly welcomed by Père Genestier, who, when he heard my story, sat me down to a sumptuous meal, perceiving no doubt that for the moment, at any rate, this was the thing I was most in need of. My object in going to Père Genestier was to enlist his help and ask his advice. But when I spoke of the Taron, the father shook his head and pointed down the valley and across the Salween to where the snow lay low on the mountains. There was a sullen look in the sunless sky.

" It will snow again very soon," he said ; " you could get to the Taron now, probably, but the men would not be able to get back till next summer." We discussed every possible project, but in the light of the Tibetan situation Père Genestier advised me to return to the

Mekong as the Chinese authorities wished; and as every path and pass, as well as the vagaries of the weather were intimately known to the intrepid father, I decided to take his advice. So bidding him farewell, I set out on the back trail.

I left Kieunatong at two o'clock, and in spite of crossing the river promptly on my arrival at the ferry, it was dusk before I emerged from the gorge, and dark by the time I reached the paddy terraces below the monastery at Tra-mu-tang. Here I lost myself completely and wandered about for an hour before I found the path across the deep gully which yawned at my feet. Meanwhile rain had begun to fall heavily, and I was just anticipating another night in the nearest hut when, after nearly tumbling over the cliff, I suddenly struck the path. Crossing the gully and several ploughed fields on the far slope, I reached our house at seven o'clock.

My Tibetan, who did not know where I had gone nor whether I was coming back or not, was quite relieved to see me, as was also the Lutzu chief: the soldier who was billeted in the house to watch me had gone off to the *yamen* earlier, I suppose to confess that he had somewhat neglected his trust. After a good Tibetan meal with plenty of boiled milk, for I was very thirsty after my eight hours' walk, I turned in, and paying no heed to the rain which pattered down faster and faster, was soon sleeping like a child.

It was nearly midday, December 23rd, before I got up, to find a steady drizzle falling. Nevertheless we started down the river for the ferry at Choton and got as far as the first village, where we had enjoyed a meal on our arrival three days before; here we were accommodated in a Lutzu hut, and I was given a small outhouse, a few yards from the building, to myself.

All night it poured with rain, and the outlook on December 24th was very dismal. None of the porters would start while it rained like this, so here we had to remain, prisoners in the hut, while the rain fell steadily. What a sad Christmas Eve! Even the fire smoked and sulked, for the wood was all sodden. A little cold chicken and bacon, a cup of soup, and some boiled rice and pumpkin was my dinner that evening, after a day which dragged with leaden footsteps to a dreary close.

Christmas day dawned as dismal as ever, and when I saw the valley full of steamy cloud, and the mountains hardly a thousand feet above us white with snow, hope almost left me. There were 5000 feet of rock between us and the Mekong, by the lowest pass.

When the " Monkey " came in to get me some breakfast I asked him if the porters would go to-day, but he looked at me and replied : " Bimbo, the Lutzu say now they dare not cross the pass for ten or fifteen days— the snow will be many feet deep on the pass; a fortnight ago three Tibetan porters carrying loads for the Chinese soldiers were caught in a snowstorm and frozen to death."

Ten or fifteen days! And supposing it snowed again before ten days had elapsed, as it probably would!

I was eating my breakfast by the smoky fire, when the door opened and in walked the " Monkey " with two Lutzu chiefs and the official interpreter from the *yamen ;* and they brought me a Christmas present! The official had sent a message to say that as it was impossible to

cross the Londre-la, the people might take me back to
Tsa-rong, and so to A-tun-tzu over the Chu-la, the way
we had come! I danced round the room with joy!
Such a rush and scurry to pack up my few belongings
and get out of this miserable hut—we were to start at
once and return to Tra-mu-tang! Back we went by the
now familiar path, and across the deep gully, to take
up our quarters in a hut just below the *yamen ;* in a day
or two we would start for Tsa-rong, the interpreter said—
as soon as he could collect porters, in fact.

After all I did not spend such a bad Christmas night.
The " Monkey " made up a big fire in my little room,
and I brought out the tin of mincemeat I had kept all
these days for Christmas fare, a luxury I had kept for
nearly two months though I had often been hungry.
After my boiled rice and pumpkin, and a little bacon fat
and a cup of soup, I called in the " Monkey " and we
nearly finished the mincemeat between us ; the Tibetan
pronounced it excellent, though they do not as a rule
like sweet things.

So I sat by the fire in the semi-darkness of the hut,
and looked into the glowing logs and thought of them
all at home and the merry Christmas evenings we used
to spend in the dear old country, till the evening's
candle gave a last flicker and went out.

On December 26th the official sent me a pound of
butter and a fowl. This day the clouds lifted and broke,
and the sun looked through wanly, but at 9 p.m. the
temperature was still 42° F.—not cold enough for fine
weather. However, on December 27th a change really
did set in, for after a cloudy morning, with a temperature of 40° F. at 7 a.m., the sky began to clear in the afternoon, the clouds gradually disappeared in the east, and

the snow on the divide glowed in the rays of the setting sun. By eight o'clock at night the temperature had fallen to 38° F. and the stars sparkled like jewels.

In the morning I went to see the official and stayed with him for an hour. While I was there, who should arrive but a tax collector from the Taron, who told us how he had been caught in the big Christmas snowstorm, and of ten porters, three had perished in the snow. They had been eight days coming from the Taron, he said, but this I could hardly believe, since in ordinary weather it takes only four days, and they could easily have returned to lower altitudes if the snow had proved so serious an obstacle. He described to us how the dead men had looked on the following morning, seated on the ground, legs drawn up under them, lips parted in a frightful sort of grin, hands clasped.

There had been an ugly story in A-tun-tzu of a Tibetan girl, carrying a load for a Chinese soldier, who had died of sickness and exhaustion on the Londre-la in the spring. But the Chinese soldiers are relentless. They are cruel masters and the greatest hardship falls on the porters, who are treated more like animals than men and women. Yet the Tibetans laugh at the Chinese soldiers who come into their country, and ask how they can expect to cross the mountains in winter when they have no clothes— a just enough jibe, for these men are certainly most ill-clad in thin cotton cloth, woollen socks and straw sandals—a poor outfit for such a climate.

It will be noted, however, that all these passes can, as a rule, be crossed up to the end of January, though after November it is necessary to choose one's time ; the heaviest snowstorms occur in February and March.

On December 28th the sky was again completely over-cast in spite of the brilliant starlight when I turned in the previous night : the temperature only fell to 34·5° F. I spent most of the day in bed, not feeling well. There was an acrimonious discussion as to who should accompany us back to Tsa-rong, but finally I agreed to the Tibetan interpreter from the *yamen* and one soldier.

XVIII

Through the Granite Gorge

"DECEMBER 29th. At 7 a.m. barometer 25·19 in.; temperature, in shade, 31° F.; a sharp frost on the ground; sky cloudless, a beautiful morning, and so it remained all day." So says my diary. There was some delay after an early breakfast, but we were ready to start by noon.

Chang, the mandarin, came to see me off; nothing disturbed his equanimity or made him depart a hair's-breadth from his kindly courtesy. To some extent his attitude disarmed me—it was impossible to be un-scrupulous in one's dealings with such a man. In the maelstrom into which rudderless China is being rapidly sucked, her rulers will do well to pause in their haste to replace tried men of the old school by hot-headed fanatics with bees in their bonnets. But Chang knew little of Western thought. He was ignorant, old-fashioned, conservative, bigoted, obstructive and—a gentleman. Tra-mu-tang is not a place of great strategic significance, and never will be; such places are best left to the wise and beneficent rule which the genius of China had evolved when, as they are fond of reminding us, our ancestors dressed in skins.

That day we crossed the Salween by ferry and reached the small village on the left bank just below the Kieuna-tong valley. It was delightfully warm in the sunshine, but a sudden chill fell on the earth as soon as the sun was behind the mountains, and by 7.30 the temperature had fallen to 38° F. Some Tibetans we met here, on their way down the river with salt, told us it would be necessary to keep along the river as the pass above Kieunatong was snowed up.

The weather had now set in fine for January, during which month it very rarely snows in the mountains. There were no porters to be had yet, so next morning the " Monkey " and I went up to the mission house to see Père Genestier and discuss the situation ; he believed that the Tibetan pass to the Taron might still be open, but if not, the Zayul route from Menkung certainly would be ; it was open all the year round, he said. " There is a rich family at Trenge who have just got back from Lhasa ; they will have all the news ; perhaps the Tibetan question is settled by now; you may be able to go to Pomed." Thus the brave old priest heartened us. There was, however, the question of the two men supplied by the *yamen* to be considered. The interpreter did not matter ; he was half a Chinaman, but his dress was Tibetan, and he would almost have passed as one.

The soldier, however, a lad of only seventeen, made no attempt to be anything but what he was, and having scared him as to the true state of affairs in Tsa-rong, where, we said, a Chinese soldier ran the risk of sudden death, I left it to the " Monkey " to rub it in. It was not likely, however, that either of them could be induced to help us to go anywhere but to A-tun-tzu as they had received strict orders to see us back there.

We remained where we were all December 31st, while the soldier went back to Tra-mu-tang for something ;

nobody seemed in any hurry, least of all myself. I spent the day making a collection of ferns, finding twenty-five species. Other plants included a Spiraea in flower on the slate rocks in the river bed. The shade temperature rose to 55° F. after a sharp frost, but the children still went about naked in the middle of the day.

While here, and subsequently at Saung-ta, I measured the heights of several Lutzu, with the following results. The average height of thirteen men drawn at random from various villages, both *hê* and *pai* Lutzu, was 64·8 in., with extremes of 60·25 in. and 68·5 in.; but this does not include two dumb and otherwise abnormal dwarfs, only 57·25 in. and 57·75 in. high respectively. The average of thirteen women chosen similarly was 60·8 in., with extremes 56·5 in. and 63·25 in. These figures are sufficient to give a good general idea of the stature of the Lutzu.

The average height of six Tibetan women of the Salween valley I found to be 62·4 in., showing close agreement with the Lutzu in this respect; and though the numbers dealt with are too small to be of much value, still the result is in accordance with my idea that the Lutzu are a cross between the tall Tsa-rong Tibetan and the dwarf Nung; and further, that the Tibetan women of the Salween valley, as at Jana, are not pure Tibetan at all.

New Year's Day, 1914, with a temperature of 29° F. at six o'clock. We were one porter short of the required number, but we started nevertheless and got a little way. The limestone and slaty rocks met with previously here give place to granite, and we halted on the mountain side a hundred feet or so above the river, amidst slabs and boulders; the porter did not turn up, however,

R

so we camped for the night. The "Monkey," who had stayed behind with the abandoned load, also failed to turn up. In the afternoon long plumes and streamers of thin white cloud, pulled out by the wind, hung stretched across the valley from the west. I did not undress, but slept as I was, in my blankets, on the ground.

Soon after seven next morning the "Monkey" arrived with the missing porter, and we started at eight, immediately entering a granite gorge.

For a couple of miles the path, through scrub forest, soon two or three hundred feet above the river, was easy enough, but presently we came to a series of terrific granite precipices and matters became more difficult. Smooth walls of rock 20 and 30 feet high faced us, and to negotiate them long thin tree trunks, with notches for steps, led from ledge to ledge. The first of these ladders we came to was 30 feet in height and we had to descend. One by one the porters disappeared over the brink and my turn came. I did not like it at all, there was nothing to hold on to, and I was several steps down before I realised that the ladder was jammed so tight against the cliff that it was impossible to get a grip on it even with one's fingers; moreover, I could only just fit my toes into the notches, and they slipped on the smooth sloping wood. The position was perilous; half-way down, gripping the notch above with my fingers as firmly as possible, moving one foot at a time with the utmost caution, I looked behind me and perceived that if I fell I should not stop on the steep and narrow ledge below, but roll off it and over the next precipice, perhaps into the river. Now I looked up and saw a figure bearing down on top of me almost hidden beneath a load—he was descending rapidly. At last I was down

and thankful to be alive, and when we reached the next
ladder I sat on the edge and, to the amusement of the
men, took off my boots and socks, so that I could supple-
ment the feeble grip of the hands by a good purchase
with the feet.

Presently we reached a deep cleft spanned by two
logs lashed together with a creeper, and sloping steeply
down to a ledge below us.   There was no hand-rail,
nothing to hold on to, even the wall on our right being
out of reach ; we could tumble over either side and drop
down 100 feet before we should hit against anything.
I squatted down and slithered and crawled across somehow, feeling uncommonly sick before I reached the other
side.   No wonder the natives prefer crossing the mountain
to going through the granite gorge !   But there were
greater difficulties in store yet !

Thus we traversed these precipices several hundred
feet above the river, on the other side of which the
granite cliffs rise steeply for a 1000 or 1500 feet.

Picture this gorge fringed with thick forest along the
water's edge, with pines clinging grimly to the precipices ; down below the water tumbles and foams over
boulders some of which are as big as houses, and its
song soars up between the grey old walls and is flung
back in broken echoes beneath the turquoise sky of
Tibet.   Looking down the gorge, the dark olive water
suddenly breaks out into emerald-green where, at a turn
in the river, the afternoon sun glances into the valley ;
and in the foreground a shaft of silver marks where a
stream leaps over the precipice and flies into spray
before reaching the river.   What more beautiful
gateway could one have into the glorious land of Tsa-
rong !

Towards evening we came right down to the water-side, clambering over boulders in the river bed, and then up through jungle again. Presently we camped. It was quite cool now, for the sun is out off the valley by one o'clock in winter, so that it only receives about four hours' sunshine altogether; and though the noon temperature was 51° F., at night it went down almost to freezing point, even under the trees. We did not build shelters, for it was dark when we halted and there was no need for them; but we piled up big fires. In the forest it was warm at night and cool by day. Covering the piles of broken rock on either side of the river were ferns, orchids, creepers and shrubs making a tangled undergrowth, through which ran a well-marked if not a well-made path. We were still in the monsoon region, and several bushes and rock plants were in flower, notably the beautiful pink-flowered Luculia, which is so astonishingly fragrant. In the dead of night I awoke as usual and heard the roar of the river below us, very loud.

On the following day we continued up the gorge by a path only a little less perilous than that of the previous day. Our route lay through the forest, up and down over boulders half hidden beneath masses of vegetation, then down into the river bed again where stark boulders lay bleaching in the sunshine, and the going was difficult. From mid river rose a gigantic block of granite standing up quite 40 feet above the present level of the water, which swirled round it in violent eddies. In summer the river must engulf this boulder and pour over the top.

After a time we leave the river bed and ascend again, the left bank here broken up into tors and smooth slabs of rock sloping steeply to the river, with tremendous precipices behind; pines and small bushes are scattered along the broken ridges, and jammed into the crevices.

Only small streams enter the river, and every one cascades down from a considerable height—we come to one which descends hundreds of feet in three leaps. Boiling rapids thunder between the walls, though the water is far below its summer level; in some places the cliffs have been eaten away by enormous pot-holes, and many of the boulders are literally honeycombed with smooth-walled tunnels and concavities, white like chalk.

Late in the afternoon we reached a sand-bank, and abruptly the jungle ceased, its place being taken by a thick shrub growth. At the upper end of the bank a canoe was drawn up, and round one fire sat eight ancient Lutzu women; while round a second fire were gathered a party of Tibetans guarding numerous bags of salt. They had just been put ashore from the canoe. The Tibetans brought bad news. Menkung, they said, was full of soldiers, the Chinese were again advancing by the main road, and all was confusion.

Presently the canoe was loaded up with our luggage and most of the porters, the Lutzu crew, seizing each a paddle, sprang aboard, and the canoe conveying all my boxes and fifteen people was taken a few hundred yards up-stream and paddled across to the other side, where the party landed; meanwhile the rest of us had been sitting round the fire on the sand-bank roasting yams—the sausage-shaped tubers, some of them a foot long, which the natives had grubbed up in the jungle. They tasted like sweet potatoes.

It was evening now, the sky very pale, a chill breeze making the leaves flap and rustle and rattle together in the jungle; the mournful song of the Lutzu came to us from across the water and down below the sand-bank we heard the water raging amongst the boulders.

Presently the canoe returned and we jumped in, the Lutzu women standing up in the bows; the long bamboo rope was also paid out and coiled up forward ready for immediate use. Away we went with a swish of paddles, beneath the towering cliffs which hemmed in the river, till we came to a big pebble bank over which the shallow water tossed and raced, rattling the pebbles together as a retreating wave does on the steep shingly shores of England. Bump! went the heavily laden canoe, and the ill-clad girls leapt over the gunwale into the icy water and ran ahead with the long rope. The water swirled around their knees and wetted their tightly bound skirts, the canoe rocked and yawed as they pulled this way and that, hauling us slowly through the rapids while the men pushed with their paddles, and the sound of a million rattling dice echoed from cliff to cliff. At last we were hauled and pushed into deep water again, the women being in nearly up to their waists before they came aboard, and shortly afterwards we ran ashore on the right bank where was a sandy cove; the canoe was unloaded and pulled ashore, and all hands went to collect firewood from the forest which thinly fringed the cliffs behind.

A cutting wind blew down the valley, and we sought shelter in a trough of the sand, and built wind screens with faggots, and lit the fires. My bedding was laid out on the sand, and as the stars began to glitter above

the great Salween river, the "Monkey" brought me
my supper and we sat down to talk.

Opposite us the granite cliffs tower sheer from the
water for hundreds of feet, the rock face broken by
ledges and crannies, where deformed pine trees cling
with desperation to their precarious hold. Beneath the
cliff the water swirls along rapidly, caressing a big snag.
On this snag, the people tell me, the canoe was upset
last year when coming down laden with salt, and three
men were drowned. I am not surprised ; the river is
full of visible and invisible dangers, and the Lutzu are
reckless navigators. They seem to fear nothing—can
they even swim, I wonder?—and would it be any use
if they could, once in this water ?

Now it is dark ; the Lutzu women sitting in a circle
round the fire, their knees drawn up, their feet and legs
bare, their wet skirts pulled tightly round them and an
extra wrap thrown over their shoulders, look like ghouls.
How cold they must be ! The temperature is down to
38° F. now, and their clinging garments are scarcely
warmed by the blaze. Yet they do not seem to mind.
So they sit in a ring, from time to time filling their wooden
bowls with hot maize porridge from the bubbling iron
cauldron in the centre. Gradually the talk flags, then
ceases ; one by one the ill-clad crew nod, a head droops
on a breast, and then another, till, sitting as they are
in the cold sand and crowding closer and closer to each
other for warmth, they sleep.

We were awake early on January 4th. A faint glow
of orange suffused the sky as the stars faded, and daylight
began to creep gently into the valley ; across the cold
grey water dozens of monkeys scrambled and gambolled
on the barren cliffs. At half-past six we are having break-

fast, the shaded thermometer showing two degrees of frost, though there is no ice on the river, the temperature of which is still 38° F. Now the canoe is loaded again, the boxes being stacked in the middle, with a rug spread out for me to sit on just behind the crew, who stand forward ; in the stern sits the pilot and captain steering with a paddle.

There were fourteen of us on board, the canoe drawing about a foot and a half, thus laden to an imaginary Plimsoll line, which, in rough water at least, is the gunwale ! I was scared in some of the rapids, but trusted to the Lutzu. The canoe was made from a single hollowed fir trunk, 25 to 30 feet in length and 2 feet in the beam, with a depth of 12 inches.

The porters, however, continued along the left bank of the river, where the going in that firm sand was quite good. At one place they had to climb over a cliff by a difficult path. The soldier, two interpreters, myself and another Tibetan, with the crew of nine, made up the boat's party.

It was nine o'clock when we pushed off, the sun already sparkling on the waves, blue sky overhead, limpid green water beneath, and on either hand the gaunt grey precipices. Looking north and south we could see the snow glittering on the divide which stretched, an impregnable barrier, between us and the Taron. Soon we were out in mid river, the little waves, driven by a fresh breeze down the valley, slapping musically against the gunwale. Now the women stood up to paddle, and drove us along at a fine pace where the water was smooth, singing at their work and banging their paddles against the side of the canoe, while the sunshine glistened on the flying spray.

Presently the cliffs closed in again, and we approached a line of rocks round which the water broke angrily : so we hugged the shore, pushing against the rocks with the paddles. The canoe seemed to stand still while the water boiled and heaved round us, the waves knocking against the cliffs and scattering spray everywhere ; the steersman aft stood up and shouted, the crew pushed desperately. Inch by inch we ascended a smooth bank of green water, and shot suddenly into a quiet bay. And so it went on, first under one bank, then across to the other side, now paddling along merrily in smooth water till at last, after two hours, we ran ashore on a sandspit and disembarked, to give the crew a rest.

It was now about eleven o'clock and delightfully warm, the shade temperature being 50° F. and the sun so powerful that the sand was heated to 64° F. Here we lolled on the soft beach and watched the water hurrying through this stone passage, so utterly different to the arid region a few miles further north, or the jungle region a few miles to the south. We stood on the frontier of two climates : behind us, the monsoon rains, though muzzled by the great mountain range to the west, pour down in summer ; in front, they fail, and soon cease altogether.

Little breezes skim across the water wrinkling the surface with a thousand ripples ; brilliant little fly-catchers dart hither and thither amongst the scattered pines.

After half an hour's rest we embarked once more, and paddling through a passage emerged between tremendous portals at the upper end, to see the river pouring several feet over a fall ; the noise here was terrific. We landed again on the right bank and it being impossible to haul the canoe through such a cataract, it was taken right out of the water by eighteen men, and carried bodily over the boulders to a safe point above the fall. In summer the river here where it enters the gorge must be a wild sight. It is then of course quite unnavigable, and indeed the path my porters had followed up the right bank is, for the most part, under water.

Our porters were now ferried across to the left bank, where a good path continues to Saung-ta, only half a mile distant; already the straggling line of huts was visible along the high bank and a herd of cattle tended by two small boys were feeding in the scrub. The granite gorge is no more—the rock here is all schist, the mountain sides very barren. So we paddle up to the left bank, and the nose of the canoe is thrust into a small sandy cove, and made fast. We are back again in Tsa-rong, and the river sings its little chattering songs as it sweeps past the dun-coloured cliffs beneath the eternal turquoise sky.

We found the Saung-ta chief's house filled with sacks of salt. Next day the canoe would start back through the gorges laden with this merchandise to be landed on the lower sand-bank, the downwards journey being easily performed in a day. For two or three months the boat's crew live on the sand-banks in this manner and navigate the rapids for these first three miles of gorges, going to and fro between Saung-ta and the beginning of the jungle region. In summer the route is impracticable.

There were no porters available at Saung-ta and though we arrived there at one o'clock we got no further. But I did not mind. After a meal I called the " Monkey " aside, gave him two hundred rupees, and told him to go

to the next village, Laungpa, just at the entrance to
the upper gorge. There he was to seek out the chief,
tell him our circumstances, and ask him for three men
to guide me to the Taron via the Trenge route; the
men were to receive fifty rupees each for their trouble.
Meanwhile the other interpreter had sent the soldier
back to Tra-mu-tang with a stick on which he had cut
several notches and a cross; this was cypher message
to the official announcing our progress (no mystery;
only because he could not write Chinese).

One of the first men we met in Saung-ta was a Tibetan
from Menkung who had accompanied the mission which
turned us back at Jana, two months before. He seemed
surprised to see us again, but on hearing our story, he
was able to hold out no prospect of a reversal of sentence
on our return. "There is much trouble in Tibet" was
all he said, shaking his head sagely—like Lord Burleigh
in "The Critic," and doubtless implying as much left
unsaid.

There was a sharp frost in the open that night, but
on January 5th the temperature actually rose to 61° F.
in the shade at two o'clock and then fell again rapidly
with the setting sun. After breakfast my escort was
perturbed by the non-appearance of the "Monkey"
and complained to me that he had not slept in the house
on the previous night. At first I feigned indifference,
but then I said:

"Did you not send a messenger to Tra-mu-tang
yesterday?"

"Yes!" he replied.

"Well, I also sent my man to take a message!"

It was nearly midday before I espied the "Monkey"
coming along the river path with two men; this, and

the delay, seemed to me good omens for the success of the mission, and I went out to meet them so that we could discuss things in the open, unheard. Alas ! There was a path to the Taron, said the Laungpa chief, but it was only open six months in the year—no one could find his way through the snow now. Even in summer it took men eight days from the Salween to the Taron ! Not a man in Laungpa would go for any sum I offered— it was impossible ! Besides, the chiefs would not allow any stranger to cross the Salween. I did not believe the snow was so deep that it would have been impossible for Tibetans to cross the mountains, but when they said it took eight days to reach the Taron, I was less sceptical ; it is probably an exaggeration—six days should be enough, but there can be no doubt that between the Salween and the source of the Taron to the north, there is a tremendous double or treble range of mountains. The views I obtained from the passes above Jana and Saung-ta confirm this. Probably there are longitudinal valleys inhabited by the tree folk !

So we stayed on at Saung-ta, and that afternoon the soldier returned, bringing with him another *yamen* parasite wearing a black tunic with scarlet Chinese characters sewn on to the chest. He stepped into our little room like a figure from a mediæval fairy story, and made his bow to an astonished Englishman.

I refused to travel on January 6th, and spent the day looking for plants. In the deep gully behind the village I found a barberry in flower, but nothing else, though there were bushes of Buddleia, Pistacia, Hydrangea, oak, roses, raspberries and such like, besides orchids on the rocks. In the evening I told the interpreter I would not go on any further till the soldiers went back. " This is Tibet," I said, " not China." He did not like that, nor did his soldiers, as they had very little money or food ; I felt I could soon wear them down. Unfortunately I had hardly any food myself and was unable to renew supplies here, as the entire village had gone down the river with salt ; some maize cakes and a little meat I had bought from the Tibetans the day we arrived were already finished and I was back on the old diet.

We sat tight through January 7th, but on the 8th, some people having returned, I decided to go on as far as Laungpa and wait there. Starting at 11.30 we reached the next village soon after one, and settled down again. The weather was still perfect, with frosts at night though it was quite hot in the early afternoon ; very rarely the sky clouded over from the west during the day, but by sunset it was always clear again. Light breezes blowing down the valley kept the air cool even in the sunshine, but we had none of those furious dry up-valley winds which are such a feature of the arid regions throughout the summer.

The opposition, whose money and supplies were now running inconveniently short, held a council of war that night which resulted in the second *yamen* scallywag starting back for Tra-mu-tang next morning ; nevertheless we rested another day at Laungpa, and I spent the time collecting a few of those ephemeral weeds which are to be found in flower all the year round on the English countryside—a mallow, shepherd's purse, a purple dead nettle, stitchwort, and so on. Fancy going to the Tibetan Salween to find shepherd's purse !

I still wanted the first soldier to return and not accompany us amongst the Tibetans ; as for him he was between the devil and the deep sea. " I dare not go

back, sir," he said : " the official will beat me." " All
right," I replied, " the Tibetans will shoot you. I
don't mind—but they may shoot me too. I dare not
go on." Then the interpreter, who was an opium maniac
and had already exhausted his supply, begged me to
proceed. " We will stop here," I said. " When the
soldier's money is finished he will have to go back ;
I will give him neither money nor food. I do not want
his company."

However, the food problem was almost as acute for
me as for him ; and the Lutzu had nothing. Once
amongst the Tibetans we could get abundance and
variety of food, but here they had no butter, eggs, milk,
or rice, and hardly any meat. It was, of course, a tremendous relief to get maize-meal cakes and salted tea
again ; but it was not enough. Having by strategy got
rid of one *fusung* therefore, I decided to go on to
Trenge, the first Tibetan village, at the upper end of
the gorge above Laungpa, and stop there till I had starved
the second into compliance.

On January 10th we embarked in a canoe once more
for a two hours' voyage through the gorge to Trenge.
The scenery here is not so fine as in the granite gorge ;
the cliffs are barer, with none of those fantastic pines
clinging in freak attitudes to crevices and ledges, and
there is only one rapid, though the river twists and turns
between frowning cliffs. In some places the rock is
conglomerate with a curious pitted or vesicular structure
like lava.

Presently we were able to get out and walk along the
shingly shore while the crew tracked ; only once was
there any difficulty in getting the canoe over a small
rapid, the men jumping out and hauling us through a bit

of rough water which, owing to our having slewed round
broadside on, for the moment threatened to capsize
us. The path is on the left bank and climbs up several
hundred feet above the river. At noon we reached
Trenge, and found a crowd waiting to welcome us,
news of our progress up the valley having preceded us.

XIX

The Rise of Tsa-wa-rong [1]

A S we drew in to the left bank opposite Trenge, we were met by two of the most curious little men I have ever seen. They were not ill-looking, and were dressed in Tibetan attire to the very pig-tails bound round their heads ; that was the incongruous part of it, for neither was more then 4 feet 10 inches high.

There was, as I have said, quite a crowd here, with several ponies, and the ferry was still plying to and fro. I ought, perhaps, to have felt flattered at this greeting— the preparations were all for me, so that I need not waste time. But I was not flattered, and refused to allow our cargo to be discharged.

" Land on the other side, we will go up to Trenge to-day," I said peremptorily. There was a deadlock, and the men looked blankly at each other, but the " Monkey " backed me up and the Lutzu dared not disobey, though their Tibetan masters were scowling.

Now occurred one of the funniest things I have ever seen. We were still close inshore, and at this moment

[1] Tsa-rong (㙰 𐨐 i.e. the hot valley), a sub-prefecture in the Salween valley. Spelt Charong on some maps of Tibet. Its capital is Menkung. Tsa-wa-rong (㙰 ꡍ 𐨐) is a district in S.E. Tibet, and includes Tsa-rong. I think Mr. Teichman accidentally confuses the two. (See *Travels of a Consular Officer in Eastern Tibet*.)

the plump little seventeen-year old soldier stood up
in the stern to look round him.   Immediately two twin-
like dwarfs, Tweedledum and Tweedledee, rushed down
to the water's edge and spread before the warrior a stone
jar of wine, some butter wrapped in a leaf, a piece of
bacon, and several maize cakes.   The Chinese soldier
had to be placated at all costs—the Englishman did not
matter !   Who was the more embarrassed, the soldier
who could not speak a word of Tibetan and was ignorant
of Tibetan custom, or the twins, I cannot say, but if the
former thought he was going to get his bribe without
paying for it, he was woefully mistaken ;   the delicacies,
after due exhibition, were whisked away not less sum-
marily than the pudding to which Alice was introduced.

I now gave orders for the canoe to go across to the
right bank, though the "Monkey" told me the Tibetans
did not wish me to go to Trenge.   We, however, went
across nevertheless and landed in the teeth of dumb
protest, and the Lutzu having emptied the canoe, made
haste to push off and hurry back to their own village
before they got into trouble.   The Trenge people,
seeing that their little game had fallen flat, now returned
to their own side of the river, and having sent on a man
ahead to prepare the great chiefs, reluctantly shouldered
my boxes and carried them up to the village.   This
stands on a half-moon shaped platform high above the
stream and a few hundred yards up the ravine.   There is
an excellent path, and the view of the big houses with
the flags fluttering right along the crest of the rocky
spur opposite, the thundering white torrent, and the
emerald-green fields and clustering trees set amongst
the barren mountains makes one of those odd contrasts
so typical of these arid valleys—an oasis in a wilderness.

s

I went to the biggest house in Trenge, that of a rich slave-owner, and was given a cosy little room to myself, where I was very comfortable. The chief was quite friendly and brought me eggs, meat and bread; he did not like the Chinese soldier being there, but had no objection to the " Monkey " or myself.

" We have orders, Bimbo, that no one must cross the Salween ; you may stop here a day or two to buy food, but if you stop longer the Menkung chiefs will hear of it and make trouble." This was the bulwark of Tibetan strategy, to defend at all costs the line of the Salween against the Chinese advance, while at the same time strenuously opposing them further east, on the line of the Mekong. The latter river, however, would be more difficult to hold, for Chamdo on the north road at the Mekong bifurcation was still in Chinese hands.[1]

South of the Mekong confluence the Chinese were attempting to force a passage into Tsa-wa-rong from Chiangka and Samba-dukha, where fighting was reported. But the pass from here over Damyon to Drayü-gomba is, or should be, impregnable, and we could therefore eliminate the possibility of a Chinese advance into Tsa-wa-rong from the east or south.

Now it is of the greatest importance to the Tibetans to hold the Salween against the invader, because it controls two of the high roads to Lhasa, one through Drayü and Shobado, the other through Menkung and Sanga-chutzung ; while so long as the Chinese advance by the single road through Ba-t'ang and Chamdo, it is impossible to protect their flanks, and their communications can be cut with the greatest ease, as in fact happened during the Chinese revolution. It must not be forgotten

---

[1] Chamdo has long since been recovered by the Tibetans.

that the only part of Tibet which is likely to profit the Chinese lies south of the Ba-t'ang–Chamdo road. By pushing on to Lhasa from an advanced base at Ba-t'ang along three converging roads, the advantage to the Chinese would be enormous in spite of the great difficulty of maintaining lateral communications. But with Tsa-rong stemming the tide of invasion and covering two roads the Tibetans have the advantage, especially since the British occupied Hkamti Long, thus protecting the southern frontier of Zayul. Had the Yun-nan troops been co-operating at this time, they might have gained a footing in Tsa-rong via the Shu-la (our route), or up the Salween from Tra-mu-tang, or over the Dc-kar-la, though in the face of resolute opposition it would be impossible for any considerable body of troops to force the passes. The fact that they did not do so only shows how firmly established is provincial autonomy in the far west.

Co-operation on a large scale between the provinces, even with an empire to be divided between the victors, is still an Utopian dream. Nevertheless I am far from denying any complicity to Yun-nan in the Tibetan adventure, and am disposed to regard quite seriously the statement of the Chinese prisoners taken by the British expeditionary columns in the Burmese hinterland in 1914. These men said, in defence of their being, an armed force, in British territory, that they were seeking the quickest route from Yun-nan to Tibet. Anyone who has the slightest acquaintance with the North-East Frontier knows of course that any attempt to open up communication with Lhasa say from Tra-mu-tang via the Irrawaddy sources is, under present conditions, fore-doomed. But if one ignores mountains and rivers and certain aspects of climate, population and transport, which is just what many people wishing to find the quickest route from A to B would do (I have often done it myself), there is no doubt that it is not very far from Tra-mu-tang to Lhasa. In fact, the Chinese raid into the Burmese hinterland, countenanced by the Yun-nan government, was not so much a threat to Burma, nor an end in itself, but a means to an end. That end was Tibet. At the same time it *was* a very real threat to Burma.

It is then apparent that so long as the Tibetans hold Tsa-wa-rong, the Chinese stand a very poor chance of conquering Tibet, even if they once more succeed in reaching Lhasa.

Tsa-wa-rong is the key to the most fertile and most thickly populated part of the country. But, as already pointed out, the last line of defence is the Salween, and if terms are arranged which will allow the Chinese to control the country as far west as that river, Tsa-wa-rong falls into Chinese hands. To this sacrifice, even for the sake of peace, the people of Tsa-wa-rong, who have had the wolf in their fold, would never tamely submit. Moreover Tsa-wa-rong, east of the Salween, controls no less than five trade routes into China, all but one of them caravan roads, and it would be a serious thing for a great trading people like the Kampa to have their best trade routes wholly in enemy hands. It would mean that in any future war the Chinese could pour as many troops as they liked into the province with its excellent roads and comparatively well-populated valleys without opposition. There would be a choice of numerous points at which the Salween passage might be forced, instead of only one as now.

There are, however, other considerations, apart from questions of strategy, which make it very unlikely that Tsa-wa-rong would yield should the Chinese claim territory as far west as the Salween.

After the six weeks we had spent in the monsoon Salween amongst the tribesmen, nothing forced itself more strenuously on my notice, during this second journey across Tsa-rong, than the high degree of civilisation attained by the Tibetans of Kam. They have splendid roads, fine houses, good and varied food, clothes and jewellery; the people are intelligent, law-abiding, hard-working, generous and religious; they do not smoke, nor drink to excess, nor take opium. The men are physically strong, splendid specimens often, the women pretty. I never saw a beggar nor a robber in Tsa-rong. Nor is the country cursed with those huge monasteries which suck the blood from other parts of the country. Are such a people going to permit the Chinese armies of Ssu-ch'uan, which it must be confessed contain not a few adventurers, swindling traders, robbers and the off-scourings of happier cities on the plains, to steal and ravish their women, destroy and rob their monasteries, and batten on them in their own houses, without striking a blow for freedom? I think not.

China has made a very great political blunder in her attempt to conquer Tibet with the men she could best spare from her own country. Had she realised more fully that in this fanatical land, the power being all in the hands of a priestly hierarchy, the common people were sadly oppressed and ground down, she might, by fair dealing and just treatment of all, have influenced a large body of Tibetan public opinion in her favour.

But her methods have been more barbarous than those of the Tibetans themselves, and it is natural to submit more readily to oppression from one's own people than from strangers. An army not given over to rapine and murder would have disarmed the common people of Tibet in a very short time, and a wise kindly rule have been of much greater advantage to the country than the present despotism.

But China has lost her chance by employing men who, judging from what I have seen of the garrisons of Ba-t'ang, A-tun-tzu, Latsa and other places, are simply pork butchers, and officers who are unfit for their job. These latter are altogether too young and ignorant for the responsible positions they hold, and their vision is blinded by the glitter of their own brass-buttoned uniforms. They are men of some education and understanding, who are living amongst people with neither one nor the other, and consequently they soon get an inflated idea of their own cleverness which, through inanition, is actually deteriorating. These men do not study their profession.

I have no admiration for the Chinese governing class. The Chinaman was not born to rule empires. He is peaceful and law-abiding, and so loyal a slave to custom that he will make the most intractable do as he does rather than adapt himself to new surroundings. The Chinese are the great stimulants of the Asiatic pulse, the precious antitoxin to the latent poisons of the East. They will infuse their blood into the lazy Burmese race, into the uncouth Tibetans, into the indolent Malays, and new empires will arise. But the Chinese themselves will not again stride to world power—they have had their day.

To return to Tsa-wa-rong. I have asked myself why it is that the men of Kam are so highly civilised in this dour land, and the answer I found was, because they are great travellers ; their horizon is unbounded. They go far into China to trade, and far into Tibet to worship. They see other civilisations—China, India, even Burma, and other peoples ; exchange goods with them, bring back new ideas. They go to Lhasa to pay homage to their own pontiffs and visit their own holy places. They are a pastoral people who have settled down to an agricultural life without ever losing their nomadic instinct ; but the calls of trade and religion have usurped necessity, and drawn them further afield than ever did their flocks.

Yet there must be something underlying these things, some one principle more fundamental than trade or religion, which can be singled out as the first cause of this great and growing civilisation of Tsa-wa-rong. And this principle, following Bagehot, I take to be the system of slavery prevalent all up the Salween valley at least, and probably throughout the provinces of Zayul and Pomed as well. The great boon that any system of slavery confers upon a people is leisure, which alone allows an agricultural or pastoral people time for contemplation ; and by contemplation are developed those abstract ideas of religion, ethics and justice which remain so crude in savage races. All the great world religions have arisen in the East, where men need not work hard for a living, and consequently swarm, and are slaves, just as criticism and mechanical invention have arisen in the great cities of the West under the pressure of competition.

Again, with leisure from work, people are enabled

to trade, and are no longer dependent upon their own resources ; they can travel to other lands with the surplus products of their own soil, and bring back new things, and, still more precious, new ideas. Thus we see how slavery has helped the Tibetans by stimulating thought beyond merely theological speculation. But since the first breath of heresy amongst a vagabond people would have scattered the sheep from the fold for ever, there has arisen a rigid tyranny of religious custom ground with an iron heel into the brains of a people whose mode of life is conducive to superstition.

While then a love of travel as well as speculation has grown up hand in hand with slavery, religious custom has played the part of a magnet, so strong that, however far the votaries of trade may wander from the fold, they cannot get outside the field of force whose poles are Lhasa and Shigatse. Again, prowess in war is the ultimate factor in the building up of civilisation. It is obvious that of two savage tribes warring against each other, the one that wins will take slaves and advance its civilisation by this means, as shown above. But here the case is not so simple, for the people who occupy Tsa-rong must always have been superior in arms to those who, presumably of necessity, occupied, or were driven across into, the monsoon jungles to the west. There is a very sharp line between the civilisations of Tibet and of the jungle folk all along the frontier from where the Brahmaputra makes its southward bend to where the Salween also turns. The Tibetans of Kam were no doubt always strong enough to raid the Taron valley or Zayul, and carry off slaves, for the Tibetan is instinctively a fighter ; but as a matter of fact, their knowledge of the art of war is comparatively poor, and such as it is undoubtedly comes from China. Yet I believe that they are a people almost apart amongst the heterogeneous Tibetan race, whose genius has been, and will be still further quickened by their standing four square against two oppressions. The one, that of the Chinese from without, the other, that of their own rulers, from within.

During the last few hundred years they have probably seen no little fighting of a sort. First, perhaps, against the western tribes whom they have gradually driven southwards into the Irrawaddy valley; secondly, against the Chinese; thirdly, against a too harsh central government; fourthly, against the English, who at the time of the Lhasa expedition found the levies from far away Kam at least not inferior to any other Tibetan troops; and now once more against the Chinese. I cannot believe that they have reached their present degree of civilisation without this much clash of arms.

While it is true that amongst a primitive people slavery is a great civilising force, it can hardly be doubted that later on in their history people begin to degenerate under its influence. Slavery allows time, as already pointed out, for contemplation : but it also allows time for indulgence in any vice to which a people are prone. Thus the Shans of Hkamti Long, all of whom keep slaves, are certainly degenerating as a result, since they spend the leisure thus obtained in drinking opium and sleeping. But the Shans were civilised long before they came to Hkamti and kept slaves. The truth is this. Amongst a primitive people who are accustomed to snatch a living from the soil, slaves won as a result of prowess in war enable the fighting race to turn to peace and still further advance their prowess in war, and hence their civilisation; while amongst a people already civilised, and no longer threatened by superior civilisations, recourse to slavery gives men so much leisure that time begins to drag.

That the Chinese, even with their superior organisation and arms, will beat their more mobile enemy under present conditions I think most unlikely. So long as the Tibetans hold the Mekong, Tsa-wa-rong is safe, and on Tsa-wa-rong hangs the fate of Tibet. At present the Chinese troops are just as likely to throw in their lot with the Tibetans as remain loyal, and with a little organisation and training, the latter could never be beaten.[1]

[1] Recent events seem to justify this belief.

XX

The End of the Journey

WE spent two days at Trenge. There is an excellent path up the ravine, which evidently crosses the mountains to the Taron. I saw a mule caravan setting out in that direction, and there can be no doubt that this is one of the main Tibetan roads to the Taron. It was opposite this point that the brave and luckless Captain B. E. A. Pritchard was drowned while fearlessly attempting to swim that river after the destruction of the rope bridge by the Nungs. Another road follows the right bank of the Salween northwards to Menkung, and from the summit of the spur opposite the village, a good view is obtained up the main valley to the pass above Jana.

This spur is a holy place. We climbed up there one morning and walked right along ; it was like walking along a wall. Prayer flags fluttered, and fragrant pillars of smoke rolled up from the little white brick censers where the people burn conifer branches. The holy formula is cut deeply into the limestone rock on every hand. Amongst the tattered bushes which half clothe the nakedness of the mountain slopes here, I picked up numerous Gasteropod shells belonging to several genera ; the same species are also common amongst the granite rocks above Pang-tzu-la, on the Yangtze.

On January 12th the weather clouded over heavily

from the west and it snowed on the mountains. We heard that the big canoe had again been upset in a rapid below Saung-ta ; this disaster seems to be an annual event. On this occasion only one man was drowned but several bags of salt had been lost.

I still refused to continue the journey unless the soldier went back, and having come to the end of his resources, he gave in, though protesting that he would be beaten by the official. However, the alternative was starvation, so he chose the lesser evil.

On January 13th therefore we were once more ferried across the Salween, the soldier started southwards down the valley and we set out northwards, the loads being carried by dwarf Nung slaves, both women and men. The former were tatooed with indigo from between the eyes in a broad wedge over the shapeless flat nose and round the mouth. They were very shy and I was unable to measure them, nor would they face the camera squarely. It is these dwarfs, not the Naingvaw [1] we had met at Sukin, who live in the tree-tops ; the women in particular were repulsively ugly and some of them had very ape-like faces.

It was a brilliant cloudless morning, but gradually a heavy haze, suggested rather than seen, began to overspread the valley and presently resolved itself into thin banks of cloud floating between the river and the mountains. Looking up or down the valley now was like peering through a London fog, and the view at sunset was particularly striking, the spurs looming through a red mist as though seen by firelight.

[1] Probably there is no great difference between the Naingvaw of the 'Nmai hka and the Nung of the Taron. The name Kiutzu applies equally to both.

Soon after we reached Lakora a party of pilgrims from the Do-kar-la arrived : they were all dressed in long sheepskin coats, the greasy wool next their hot skins, their feet and legs protected by long cloth boots, from the leather soles of which their toes frequently projected. So it was still possible to cross the Do-kar-la ! but they had had a bad time in the snow, which was several feet deep, and quite soft. Seated round an enormous fire on the river bank the pilgrims took their frugal supper of tea and *tsamba*, and presently when the long ribbon of sky above the valley glittered with stars, there was mingled with the splash of the river the drone of prayers uttered in sad monotonous tones.

On January 14th we continued up the valley, halting at the hot springs for lunch. Here another band of twenty pilgrims, including several women with babies on their backs, and others with compact loads in bamboo racks, passed us. In the evening we arrived opposite a couple of huts on the far bank, where a canoe was tied up, but shout as we would the people took no notice of us, and as it was impossible to make Jana that night, we had to camp on the river bank as we were. Here some of the pilgrims joined us.

The temperature rose to 52° F. at 2 p.m. by the hot springs, and we had a pleasant ride up the valley, but it is too long a stage from Lakora to Jana in a day, though I had done it in 1911. In the morning, after a warm night, the temperature falling only to 36° F., some men came over from the houses across the river and brought me a present of eggs. Of course they had heard our shouts the previous evening, but evidently they did not wish to see me on the right bank of the Salween again.

We reached Jana next day and rested there on January
16th. Here there are not such sharp frosts as we had
experienced on fine nights in the monsoon region ;
it only just froze on the ground, but there was of course
hardly a trace of frost ; at Sukin, on the other hand,
whenever the night sky was clear the grass had been
stiff with rime. One would naturally have expected to
find it colder here, in the arid region, for though the
rocks are heated by day, they radiate this heat very
rapidly at night. Probably the haze checks radiation,
and it must not be forgotten that in the monsoon region
the snow comes down much lower on the mountain
side, and helps to keep the air in the valley cold, while
the vegetation, though it checks radiation also prevents
the valley warming up in the day time. It was never
really cold in the Salween valley here except when in
the evening a light breeze blew from the north.

Starting again on the 17th, having given up the idea
of going to Menkung in view of the serious situation
in Tibet, we retraced our footsteps through Lumpu,
where I had some excellent dove shooting over the fallow.
Then climbing up once more through the woods we
reached the pass overlooking the Wi valley. A bitter
wind off the mountains numbed us and the snow lay
thick under the trees on the north side of the pass ;
indeed the steep track was like an ice run, for the snow
had thawed and refrozen ; so in spite of the utmost
caution we slipped about badly, the ponies nearly coming
to serious grief. Several caravans had been over since
last snowfall, but they had made the path worse instead
of better.

At the clearing half-way down, where we had halted
for lunch six weeks before, I wanted to stop for the night ;

it was dark now, the path more dangerous, but the men said there was no one here now so we pushed on.

The abandoned huts, dark against the snow, and the forest of black pines beyond looked very desolate in the vivid moonlight.

Presently we emerged from the forest, but the path was still ice-bound and we slithered down towards the Wi-chu under a sky which seemed alive with fiery meteors. I was quite tired out by this time, having had several nasty spills, besides plenty of work to do holding on to a pony's tail; so instead of going on to Rata we scrambled down the steep slope to a small village just off the road and on the river bank. The people received us very kindly, and I was soon seated down to buttered tea and *tsamba* by an enormous fire in the big dark room. How I enjoyed it all, back again in Tibet amongst a kindly people with plenty to eat and a comfortable house !

Whilst breakfasting next morning I saw some doves feeding over the bare fields, which as usual in these steep valleys comprise a series of terraces bounded by low stone walls sloping gradually to the river. I was to a large extent dependent on my gun for meat and never missed an opportunity of bagging a brace of doves. On this occasion, however, I only succeeded in wounding one, which swooped drunkenly across the river, entered a hole in the gravel cliff, lay down and died.

I went down to the river bank and looked at the clear icy cold water hurrying between the high banks. At one point the river was deep but not very swift, while just below it was broken up into rapids, but shallower; the breadth was about twenty-five yards. I decided to try the former first. Taking off my boots, socks and trousers and keeping on my shirt, waistcoat and jacket, as a protection against the cold wind, I stepped into the river just above the rapid. The water was a beautiful deep green, and I could count every stone at the bottom, but it ran more swiftly than it appeared to and I had to proceed gingerly; moreover the pebbly bottom hurt my feet and stones gave way, threatening to bring me down, a prospect I did not at all relish. Considerably less than half-way across the water reached nearly to my waist and progress becoming both difficult and hazardous, I returned to the bank, to renew the attempt after a short rest. At each step into deeper water I involuntarily caught my breath; but it was no good, and I returned to the bank again.

Now I put on my boots. This, I thought, would both steady me by the extra weight and prevent my slipping; certainly I got yet further so equipped, almost to mid-stream, in fact; but there the depth and rush of water became alarming and I was forced to retreat once more. Indeed the crystal clearness of the water made the depth very deceptive. I now tried at the rapid, where the water, though flowing swiftly, appeared much shallower. But stepping into a hole I was almost swept off my feet, barely saving myself from a nasty accident. After that I gave it up, consoling my chagrin with the reflection that after all it really wasn't worth it; there were plenty more rock-doves on this side.

I was now quite numb with cold and the colour of a boiled lobster, so without waiting to dress, I seized my clothes and ran up to the house where I was soon drying in front of the fire and drinking buttered tea amidst the amused smiles of the Tibetans.

This incident taught me how really difficult it is to

ford even the smallest Tibetan river, however easy it may appear. The cold, the rush of water, the roar which fills one's ears and the insecure footing afforded by stones all tend to distract and confuse one's direction. With mules, or even with two or three men holding hands, it would be easy to ford the Wi at this season, choosing one's place, but it certainly could not be done in the summer. Afterwards I discovered that there was a two-way rope bridge a little above where I had tried to cross.

We now set out again, reaching Kapu in an hour, and after lunch I successfully stalked a large flock of doves which, with curious waddling gait, making their heads oscillate, as in those grotesque Japanese toys, were walking over the fallow. I bagged four with one barrel, much to the admiration of the Tibetans, and was now well supplied with meat for a couple of days. We did not stop at Kapu as I was impatient to get back to Pitu. But nowhere was the Tibetan news good, and there came now rumours of a fight at Samba-dukha for the passage of the Mekong, in which fifteen Tibetans had been killed, and the Chinese soldiers were said to be only two days' march from Drayü itself.

In the next village, Wábu, out of which we had been hustled so unceremoniously two months previously, we found the people still disposed to be truculent and not at all anxious to receive us. However, after our representations at one or two houses had met with the cold shoulder, we got tired of it, and ignoring the frigid looks bestowed on us at the house selected, and the bellicose attitude of a whole squad of dogs, we forcibly took possession and made ourselves at home. Immediately the demeanour of the Tibetans changed ; we were made

welcome, the most comfortable quarters were assigned
to me, the room swept and garnished, tea and twisted
bread brought out, and everything possible done to make
us comfortable.

A dozen dark columns of fragrant blue smoke rose into
the crisp air from the house-tops. These issued from
little whitewashed incense burners, each like a small
square chimney-pot standing on the low parapet, where
dry juniper branches flared and crackled. The occasion
was some religious festival. We left Kapu the same
morning, and soon reached Chu-mi-la-tung at the foot
of the pass.

At sunset I climbed up the Wi ridge in order to see
night creep down once more over that savage landscape
in which the twin peaks of Orbor are set like diamonds.
There was more snow about now, but the sky was gloomy
with storm clouds, and a thick dust haze enveloped the
mountains. On the following day, however, the air
was clear again and the sunshine glittered on the snows.
At seven o'clock in the morning the temperature was
29° F., a cold wind blowing down the valley. On the
way up to the pass we were overtaken by a dozen pilgrims
who were returning to Drayü-gomba near Chamdo;
they had heard of the fighting at Samba-dukha and were
troubled in consequence. In a couple of hours we reached
the Wi-chu again and crossed by the wooden bridge;
there were quite a number of birds about down here—
finches, creepers, thrushes, tits—I even saw a parrot,
which must have lost itself.

On the right bank we passed a stone hovel built on the
mountain side. It was roofed with logs and turf, with
a tiny entrance leading into one small room half underground, where the family lived. Round about the scrub

had been cleared and the ground broken up for the spring crops. Three children, the eldest seven years old, were even now working hard, dragging heavy logs and collecting firewood. A few goats wandered over the barren soil, a cat meandered carelessly distant from the hut, and a woman stood waving her arms at an eagle which soared in short circles low down over the little homestead. Suddenly it swooped with lightning-like rapidity, and next moment it was working its way up in ever-growing spirals into the blue vault of heaven. Black against the sun, with widespread pinions, it looked just like some strange Jurassic bird come to life, for from between its great claws a long tail hung down. Poor pussy had been caught napping.

We reached Pitu in good time, the lolling monks outside the monastery gate staring curiously at us as we approached and put up in the old house. The inebriated lama had gone, and a very brisk soldierly looking man met us. He was an officer from Lhasa come to rouse the people of Tsa-rong, and the living Buddha had betaken himself to the mountains to pray in solitude for a Tibetan success. That evening sentence was pronounced. We might rest a day in Pitu, no longer. The country was up, every family was giving one or two men in the fight for liberty, emissaries from Lhasa were riding east and west and south and north collecting levies, arms, money and food. Any day the Chinese might appear in Drayü, to the north, and overrun Tsa-rong. The situation was desperate. From three o'clock next morning drums and gongs were beaten and trumpets blown inside the monastery; sleep was impossible, so I got up and dressed. A cold north wind was blowing and presently snow began to fall.

The bare brown terraces, white houses and leafless trees amongst which flocks of white-necked crows roosted looked terribly dismal under the lowering sky.

The chiefs sent me a present of food, and later I visited the military official in his room. The first thing that caught my eye, hung on the wall, was a modern magazine rifle, which had been taken from the Chinese driven out of Lhasa in the previous year. So the day dragged to an end and next morning we started back for A-tun-tzu, travelling down the Wi valley road.

We reached Jalung on January 24th after a short march. I found a pretty little pink-flowered Pertya actually in bloom by the stream here.[1] It was a small shrub not more than a couple of feet high with rolled needle leaves, and heads of flowers, a typical heath-like plant of the arid region. The weather remained fine and it was plain that even the Shu-la, in spite of its 16,000 feet, would present no difficulty.

On the 25th we marched along by the Wi river and in the evening turned off up the stream to our old camp beneath the trees. So cold was it here that I was glad to work hard dragging big logs up to the fire. The stream was everywhere covered with ice, and icicles hung from the banks and trees; beneath its glassy roof you could see the free water slinking. At 7.30 the temperature was 30° F., and after supper I rolled myself up in the blankets and slept on the ground by a huge fire.

Dawn, and nearly 14° of frost; it was hardly light as we sat round the fire having our breakfast—how I was enjoying Tibetan tea now on these cold mornings ! Its great merit lies in the fact that, though the tea

[1] *P. monocephala*, sp. nov.

itself is of the coarsest kind and always the same, yet
the soup comes from the churn in almost as many
flavours as our own tea-blenders produce, varying with
the amounts of salt and butter used and more especially
with the age of the latter. Now came the big climb,
first 2500 feet up the steep spur through the oak forest,
then gradually ascending and traversing towards the
Shu-la. The weather was perfect, and our last views
of the Tsa-rong mountains were grand beyond description. Nevertheless I found the climb exhausting, and
lagged behind, for it was too cold to ride my pony;
I was thankful to rest at the spring where we had
halted on the way down, and eat some lunch. Here
lying back in the warm sunshine—though we were
nearly 14,000 feet above sea-level—I gazed for the last
time over these gigantic snowy ridges surging like
foam-crested waves beneath the turquoise sky of Tsa-
rong; far away a few flecks of cloud rested lightly on
peerless Orbor.

It was three o'clock when we stood on the Shu-la.
The sun was already low down, and the wind stung our
hands and faces. The eastern slope of the mountain lay
in shadow and here the snow was piled several feet deep,
but luckily a good path had been stamped in the powdery
mass. Colder and colder it grew; the last rays of the
sun slanted across the gap and struck the blood-red
cliffs, crimsoning their summits. Then we turned our
backs on Tibet. On our way down we met a tea caravan
of sixteen mules from Chung-tien, and at the foot of the
cirque, where the little stream spread out in a broad
sheet of ice, a few pilgrims were encamped; they
had erected wind screens of brushwood and settled
down on the iron ground by a big fire. It would be

very cold here, in the open, without the protection of
trees, yet I wished I were going with them.

Three magnificent black and white eagles circled over
the desolate mountains. Lower down the snow had
melted and refrozen, and ever-widening slopes of green
ice lay spread out over the valley bottom, making the
path difficult and dangerous. Ice in a hundred fantastic
forms locked the stream between its bush-grown banks.
It was nearly dark when we reached our old camp, and
finding that the snow lay deep under the trees we camped
in the open where we looked straight down the valley
to the east, and beheld a belt of light in the sky in which
all the most magnificent stars glittered at the same time.

Eighteen degrees of frost in the night, and the stars
shining brilliantly. When I awoke before dawn the
fires were down, but it was too cold to crawl out and
revive them, and the Tibetans were asleep. It was the
last camp of our long journey, on which I had set out
three months ago. The veil of night lifted slightly
in the east and the long ragged chain of the Yangtze-
Mekong divide appeared, black against the coming
dawn ; the great stars which all night long had patrolled
the sky were setting ; new ones waned, and vanished
as they rose. The stream was hushed, frozen solid ;
not even a breeze whispered through the forest. Now
the Tibetans begin to stir ; presently they sit up, and
the fires are quickly attended to while snow is melted
in the iron pot for tea. At last I crept out from my
blanket nest, pulled off my woollen gloves, slipped into
a woollen dressing-gown, wrapped myself in an enormous
chupa, and sitting by the fire drank cup after cup of
foaming tea. Then the sun appeared over the mountain
rim like a ball of burnished gold, and by eight o'clock

we were off, picking our way cautiously down the steep path and over the smooth green ice-slides which confronted us.

Under the trees where the snow lay the going was easy, but in the open it was terrible, especially where we had to cross the glassy stream which had welled over in broad, smooth steps. Beautiful were the sun shafts shining red through the long tattered strips of bark, wrenched from the birch trees, and the streamers of green lichen which danced in the breeze. Lovely little crested tits hopped amongst the branches ; and when at last, leaving the dark forest we emerged into the arid gorge to find ourselves looking down once more on the Mekong, now blue as the South China sea, it was impossible to feel anything but gay.

We reached Meri at one o'clock, and the first person to hail us from the house roof was that odious little boy-soldier whom I had forced to return to Tra-mu-tang! He had crossed by the Londre-la and would go back by the same route, he said ; even that pass is open intermittently after the new year.

Next morning we reached Lu-ting-ch'iao, and crossed to the left bank by the rope bridge ; there are two huts still standing here, but the village is on the right bank, and the people promised to come across early the next morning with ponies, for the last stage to A-tun-tzu.

January 29th, our last march. We rode slowly up the gorge with fine views of the Salween divide behind us, to A-dong where we lunched.

The ride up from A-dong to A-tun-tzu was dismal. As we climbed higher, gusts of bitter wind came shrieking down the narrow valley and I was almost perished on my pony. At last we reached the pass and saw the snow

lying on A-tun-tzu mountain, and monastery hill, and
the whole valley black and silent. All the familiar places
where I had collected plants—how strange they looked
under this winter mantle ! Presently I was riding down
the almost deserted street : the shops were shut and
coloured papers fluttered from the closed doors. It was
the Chinese New Year. Now I entered the silent
house : the old grey-haired woman sitting by the fire
drinking as usual, welcomed me with astonishment, but
I did not wait her volume of questions. Tying up my
pony, I fled to Peronne's house and was welcomed with
true French hospitality. First a meal, then a long talk
in his cosy sitting-room over the *ho-pan*, my story briefly
told, Peronne's news of the latest revolution, and last—
my three months' mail. I read till far into the night,
then slept like a corpse till the sun was high in the
heavens, to awake in the familiar bare room.

XXI

The Return

OWING to the New Year carouse I was compelled to remain in A-tun-tzu for five days, neither men nor mules being immediately available. The sun had no power now and the nights were frigid ; snow lay deep under the trees, and silence reigned in the thickets which three months earlier had throbbed with life. Scarcely was there even a bird to be seen, and the woods slept serenely under their snow blanket ; the friendly chatter of the stream was long since hushed. On the hill-side, steeped in the daffodil sunlight, the coral-budded willow shoots glowed warmly as though conscious of the life which stirred within them.

On February 4th we started south by the Pai-ma-la, camping at 13,000 feet. Instead of putting up the tents, we all slept on the ground by the fire, and though we had 10 degrees of frost, towards morning it snowed and this extra blanket sufficed to keep us warm ; still it was unpleasant putting one's nose outside at dawn.

That morning we were trudging through snow in the teeth of a wild gale on Pai-ma-shan, and next day were basking in the sunshine amidst fields of green barley by the Yangtze.

It was interesting to observe how the evergreen trees on these high ranges rid themselves of an excessive burden of snow. The Picea trees, by the downward sweep of their branches, shoot it off as soon as the amount tends to become excessive ; but the smooth leaves of Rhododendron roll up into cylinders and hang modestly down, refusing to harbour any at all ; and the flattened branches of *Thuja orientalis*, standing edgeways, also deny it support.

My loads were carried from village to village by porters. One night the soldiers who had accompanied me from A-tun-tzu as escort, gave a lot of trouble by lagging behind and getting drunk. When, after dark, they reached our village, they began to abuse and bully my Tibetan porters, and one of them drew his knife when I objected. After that we had a fight, and finally this warrior tried to brain me with a brick. However, in the end peace reigned.

The Tibetans had a quaint way of drawing lots for the loads, some of which were more awkward to carry than others. Each person handed to the headman who had summoned them a symbol; one gave a feather, another a piece of rag or a stick, a third offered a walnut shell, and so on. Then the headman shook them all up, and walking round, placed each on one of the loads ; and the person whose symbol it was, claimed that load.

I was examining the now distant Yangtze-Mekong divide through my field-glasses one day, when an old Chinaman came up and asked me if I could see A-tun-tzu through the " thousand *li* glasses," well though he knew that A-tun-tzu lay on the other side of the snowy range ! The fact that the European's eyes are large and set far back in his head, giving him a mysterious look, is probably the origin of the once-universal belief that he can see into the heart of a mountain and discern gold and precious stones beneath the surface; and further, that with the aid of his " thousand *li* glasses " he can plainly see not only the prodigious distance implied by the name (some 300 miles), but penetrate any object in the line of sight—a belief which still commonly prevails in country districts.

We halted but two days at Chung-tien; then from the stark plateau, its marshes teeming with duck, its frozen pastures dotted with herds of yak grazing head on to the driving snow-storms, we gradually descended once more to the genial warmth of the Yangtze valley. In four days we stepped from winter to spring, from the austere mansions of the Tibetans to the little grey-roofed walled houses of the Chinese, hidden in jasmine-scented lanes.

The duck were flying south now, and on the ploughed land we saw pheasants. Beyond the clearing where we had lost the mules nine months before we found a collection of six huts in the forest. Some Lisus had founded their homes here two months ago; already paths had been made, forest trees felled, and the steep mountain sides ploughed for the spring crops. No Chinaman could have wrung a living from a soil so barren. The huts were painfully crude, tiny one-roomed cells with wooden palings for walls, the cold earth for floor, and bamboo matting for roofs; but we were glad to avail ourselves of one rather than spend a night in the open.

Our Lisu pioneers boasted only the scant clothing of the Yun-nan muleteer; on their shins they wore wooden pads, like the shinguards of the professional footballer.

On February 18th we reached Li-kiang and saw again the green fields and terraced rice-ponds in which the blue sky was placidly reflected; by the cobbled roadside were lodes choked with rafts of bubbling Confervae, and lilac-flowered Primula.

If the day ever comes for the publication of a Tourist Guide to Yun-nan we may expect to see something like this :

" Visitors to Chien-ch'uan should look out for the fragrant *Primula nessensis,* a pretty wayside weed flowering in early spring. A day should be spent here (supper, room and breakfast 100 ' cash '—about a shilling—straw pallet and wooden pillow provided) on the lake. There is good duck shooting—no licence required. If time allows, an interesting excursion may be made to the salt mines of La-chi-mi (four days ; sedan chairs $4)."

Or thus :

" From the pass an extensive view is obtained of the Li-kiang range (highest peak 20,000 feet) which has hardly received at the hands of climbers the attention it merits. Guides cannot be obtained locally, as the people do not mountaineer."

And so on, in the style of Baedeker.

And now the rugged snow-clad mountains of the north were beginning to slope down to the fertile valleys, till one evening we spied on the horizon the dimpled hills of the Tali plain darkening from crimson to purple and from purple to indigo in the setting sun. We were going down, down with the great grey weary rivers to the plains where men dwell. Hedges of canary-yellow jasmine, as yet leafless, covered the raw-red sandstone with scabs of shrill colour. By the sapphire lake the air is heavy with the scent of bean-fields, myriads of bees drone round the sun-lit mud walls of the houses, and pigeons coo softly in the temple roofs ; presently the breeze sends waves of glassy green rocking across a sea of yellow mustard, a rain of pink peach blossom glimmers through the naked orchard, and in the silver rice-fields the cypress trees grow fuzzy.

Tali-fu was reached on February 23rd. There had been a serious mutiny of troops, aided by students, in December, and several officials had been murdered ; but all was now quiet again. However, it was evident that the Republic had not yet established that era of universal contentment which had been anticipated.

At Hsia-kuan I inspected some simple reclamation works, consisting of a network of shallow pans, like rice-fields, protected with mud walls on which are planted willow trees. Silting up at this end of the lake is proceeding apace.

Arrived at Yang-pi two days later, an official who was on his way to the capital called on me. He had travelled widely, visiting England, America, Germany and even Lhasa, and of course politely, but falsely, raved over the beauties of England and deprecated the uncouthness of China.

Primula malacoides was in flower by the wayside. The whorls of rose-pink flowers are charming, and the plant is as beautiful in fruit when tier on tier of silver dusted fairy cups replace the fragrant flowers. It grows in the fields like speedwell at home, but prefers a rich moist soil shaded from direct sunshine, when it will reach a height of eighteen inches. One plant I noticed had already sent up from a jungle of sea-green foliage fourteen flowering stems, and there were nine more coming on. Occasionally I saw white-flowered plants, but they were

rare. People were engaged in mending the road here—
an uncommon display of public spirit ; at one spot they
were actually constructing gutters, excellent gutters,
whose only fault was that the water would never run
into them, as the camber on the road happened to slope
the other way. Now we began that long succession of
ups and downs across the corrugated surface of Yun-nan
where the bold rivers of Tibet grind a passage through
the three-ply country. Every afternoon there would
appear a contour map of the land in the sky, long billows
of cloud grappled to the mountain crests, fading and
fraying towards their edges ; and troughs of deep-blue
sky between, marking the valleys. These clouds surged
slowly out of the west, and disappeared after sunset.

The gorge of the Mekong was gay with flowers, the
roadside bordered with bushes of sky-blue *Ceratostigma
Griffithi*, the cliffs smothered with gushes of lilac-
flowered Strobilanthes ;   while everywhere sprawled
Caesalpinia nepalensis, its gawky brown arms writhing
in all directions, seeking support with their hooks, or
where no complacent neighbours could be found,
making a half-hearted attempt to twine. Fountains of
its daffodil-yellow flowers shot up from a sea of tossing
leaves. Another pretty shrub now in bloom was a species
of Abutilon, its tawny bell-shaped corollas dangling
amidst downy leaves drawn out into slender drip-tips.

After that we crossed the Salween, over whose enchanted waters hover the five-coloured mists. In this
valley we find a mixture of tropical and temperate
vegetation, an Indo-Malayan flora mingled with an
Eastern Asiatic. *Bauhinia variegata* was coming into
flower, and the white-barked Erythrina trees flourished
their scarlet keels.

One evening, as we rode into the village where we intended to halt for the night, we saw a party of Tibetans camped under a hedge. They took no notice of us, till my cook, who spoke Tibetan well, playfully addressed them in their own tongue; immediately a dozen faces looked up and smiled at us. Later, whilst the mules were being unloaded, two of them came across to the inn and made themselves useful, then took me back with them to their friends. Being invited to join the circle round the fire, I crossed my legs and sank down amongst them, Tibetan fashion. The hubble-bubble was passed round, and every man and woman took a pull at the coarse tobacco; they brought out wine, too, full flavoured and of a most villainous strength.

What a set of scarecrows they were to be sure, tricked out in horrible horsy old check caps pulled down over their foreheads, second-hand blankets, and frayed reach-me-downs picked up at a Bhamo auction! They were from Chung-tien and had gone right away down to one-time royal Mandalay, selling ponies.

As we climbed out of the deep Salween valley next morning we heard the gibbons hooting and calling one to another in the forest below us: " coo-ee ! " " coo-ee ! " and then a storm of yelping would break out and gradually die away till here and there a single cry broke the stillness.

We reached T'eng-yueh on March 10th and left two days later, following the road to Myitkyina, as we had come. A good deal of rain after leaving the well-paved roads of the T'eng-yueh plain made progress slow, and on a streaming night we reached the Ta-ho, and camped in a Yawyin hut, the owners of which were absent. It was still raining furiously, and doubts were entertained of our crossing the river on the morrow.

However, next day the weather was fine again, and we engaged Lisus to carry our loads over the steep bamboo bridge while the mules went two miles up-stream to the ford.

These Lisus,[1] or Yawyins, who dwell along the Burma frontier, call themselves Hua-pa. They differ in some respects from the Lisus of the Salween valley, but are essentially the same people. The Yawyin women have a peculiar dress of their own ; the skirt is made with broad strips of buff, red and brown cloth embroidered at intervals with cowries, and the short jacket is almost entirely concealed beneath waves of blue bead necklaces hanging to the waist. Twisted round the head is a scarf with harlequin-coloured strips as in the skirt, finished off with tassels. Cloth gaiters are worn and loads of heavy ornaments, wrist bangles, ear-rings, or metal tubes and finger rings. Round the waist are girdles of cowries or coils of rattan fibre, and there is frequently a band of small silver plates sewn down the breast.

It was no easy matter crossing the bridge, which arched steeply over a natural sluice in the rocks, through which the water poured with a roar ; the footway was extremely narrow, and it was necessary to pull oneself up by the flimsy hand-rails which threatened to collapse and precipitate one into the cauldron below. After a stiff climb up from the river, towards evening we stood once more on Kambaiti pass, and saw Burma lying at our feet, its forested mountains awash in a golden mist, its valleys already sunk in night. Eastward we looked over ridge

---

[1] For an account of the Lisus see A. Rose and J. Coggin Brown, *Memoirs of the Asiatic Society of Bengal*, Vol. III, No. 4.

beyond ridge to the towering Salween divide, boldly enamelled on a background of gun-barrel blue.

Three marches brought us to Sadon, where I met Colonel Willoughby,[1] formerly military attaché at Peking.

With the opening up of the Htawgaw hill tracts north-east of Myitkyina, this road to T'eng-yueh may become much used; the first necessities are to carry it over a lower pass than Kambaiti, and to bridge the Ta-ho. Another possible route to T'eng-yueh is via the Htawgaw road to Chipwi, thence by the low Panwa pass into Ming-Kuan and down the Shweli. This would be a round-about way between Myitkyina and T'eng-yueh, never-theless it is likely to be much used. The upper Shweli valley itself—the district called Ming-Kuan, is well populated, and with the opening of a good road between Myitkyina and Htawgaw, local trade between the three centres will be stimulated.

And now we were nearing the end of our long journey. A twenty-five mile march through the rippling hills next day brought us after dark to the edge of the plains, only to find the bungalow occupied. However, Mr. Dawson, of the P. W. D. who was in possession kindly fixed me up in comfortable quarters near by, and then gave me dinner.

The rest is soon told. Starting early next morning, we covered the remaining ten miles to the Irrawaddy before the sun gained power, and crossed to Myitkyina; and on March 22nd I left for Rangoon by train.

[1] Now General M.E. Willoughby, C.B., C.S.I., C.M.G.

U

APPENDIX

THE MYSTERY RIVERS OF TIBET

OF the three great Asiatic rivers referred to in the text, the Yangtze (Kin-sha) is the largest, the Mekong the smallest; the Salween, though considerably smaller than the Yangtze, is bigger than the Mekong.

Nothing is known of their proportionate discharges in their upper courses, but where the three flow parallel to one another, the Yangtze is about twice as big as the Salween, which in turn is perhaps half as big again as the Mekong. Their respective sizes here might be represented by the numbers 5 : 3 : 2 ; but this is only a rough estimate suggested by their *apparent* sizes, not a calculation based on measurement. However, it cannot be wildly out of proportion.

All three rivers rise far up on the great frozen plateau of north-central Tibet, known as the Chang Tang ; and in that particular mountain range, averaging 17,000 feet above sea-level, known as the Tang-la.

The headwaters of the Yangtze, here called the Mur Ussu, rise from the northern slopes of this range, the headwaters of the Salween (called Nag Chu) from its southern slopes. Between them, but further east, rise the headwaters of the Mekong.

There is evidence to show that the Himalayan mountain system formerly extended eastwards far into China ;

and that it was broken through, possibly by earth movements, possibly by rivers cutting back at their heads. At any rate, the narrow belt between 95° and 100° E. long. and 27°–30° N. lat., where the great Tibetan rivers change direction and converge to roll through the mountains, jammed into the narrowest possible space, represents a breach in the great east-west divide. The broken eastern end of the Himalayan system forms a huge bluff, overlooking the plain of Assam. The broken western end can be picked up somewhere in the Tibetan Marches, east of the Yangtze. The two ends are connected by an arc of snowy peaks which, springing from the Salween-Brahmaputra divide, enclose the headwaters of the Irrawaddy.

That at one point the three rivers should flow within fifty miles of each other, the Mekong in the centre being 28 miles from the Yangtze and 20 miles from the Salween, is one of the geographical wonders of the world.

The Yangtze

The headwaters of the Yangtze have been to some extent explored by Prejevalsky, Wellby, Rockhill, Sven Hedin, and others ; but the ultimate source still remains unknown.

This great river rises in about 34° N. lat., 90° E. long., presumably amongst glaciers. It was formerly considered to be about 3000 miles in length, but the discovery of the great bend at Li-kiang, and recently of another bend, north of Ba-t'ang, by Mr. Oliver Coales, have added hundreds of miles to its length. It is safe to say that it is not less than 3500 miles long, and may be nearer 4000 miles.

North of Ba-t'ang the main river is little known, its affluents less. The most recent explorations in this region are those of Mr. Oliver Coales and Mr. Eric Teichman ; but hundreds of miles of the upper Yangtze must be written off unexplored.

Between Ba-t'ang and Li-kiang the course and appearance of the river are fairly well known ; but beyond the great bend, as far east as Sui-fu (the head of navigation, and about 1500 miles from its mouth) it flows through more or less unexplored country at the bottom of a terrific gorge. This portion also is therefore largely unknown.

From its source in Tibet the Yangtze flows east for 500 miles, then bends round to the south, flowing close to the Mekong for some 200 miles. Then comes the great double bend, as sharp as a V round Li-kiang ; after which the river, having touched its most southerly point (lat. 26°), flows north-north-east, and north-east to Sui-fu.

It seems probable, from the work of Professor J. W. Gregory and others, that the Kin-sha—that portion of the upper Yangtze with which this book deals—formerly continued on its southward course and reached the Gulf of Tong-king.

The further course of the Yangtze, the great river of China, from Chung-king to the sea, near Shanghai, is too well known to require comment.

THE MEKONG

The Mekong is the centre one of the three rivers. Its ultimate source is unexplored, but it rises in the Tang-la, in approximately lat. 32° N., long. 95° E. The name of the luckless French explorer, Dutreuil de

Rhins, who was murdered in Tibet, will always be associated with the headwaters of the Mekong which he discovered and mapped.

Between 29° and 31° N. lat. the appearance of the river is practically unknown, though of its actual course there is little room for doubt. Mr. Eric Teichman, however, has done valuable work hereabouts, especially in clearing up some of the problems connected with its affluents.

At Chamdo (lat. 31°9′, long. 97°20′), the Mekong divides into two, of which the more northern is the main stream.

South of Tsa-kha-hlo the Mekong has been explored almost as far as Tong-king, but in many places can scarcely be called well known. It flows into the China Sea near Saigon, following a direction slightly east of south. Thus, except for its east and south-east course in Tibet, and some big twists in Tong-king, it has none of the sensational changes of direction which distinguish the Yangtze.

The length of the Mekong can be stated with no more degree of accuracy than was that of the Yangtze; it is between 2000 and 2500 miles long.

THE SALWEEN

Of the three rivers, the Salween is the least known. It rises in about lat. 32° N., long. 92° E., and flows east and south-east for over 300 miles, before bending south to roll through the great gap. But all this part of its course, besides its source, is unexplored. The little we know of its headwaters we owe to Rockhill.

In its straight north to south course through Yun-nan, the Salween flows in a deep and difficult trough, filled with jungle, and rendered the harder to explore by its unhealthy climate. About 100 miles of the river here is quite unexplored.

The Salween continues almost due south through Yun-nan into Burma, and finally enters the Bay of Bengal, near Moulmein. Although over 2000 miles in length, it is a remarkable thing that, in over 1000 miles, it receives only one big affluent—the Shweli—and that it is navigable for barely a hundred miles from its mouth !

It is not so many years since great controversy raged as to whether the Nag Chu of the Tibetan plateau was the headwaters of the Salween in Burma, or of the Irrawaddy. The question was finally decided by the exploration of the Irrawaddy, although previous to that it had been satisfactorily, if indirectly, shown that neither the Tsang Po of Tibet (now recognised as the upper stream of the Brahmaputra) nor the Nag Chu, could be reconciled with the lower Irrawaddy.

But the exploration of the upper Salween still remains to be done, and especially that portion of it where it changes direction from east to south, to cut through (presumably) the breached Sino-Himalayan axis.

INDEX

314   Index

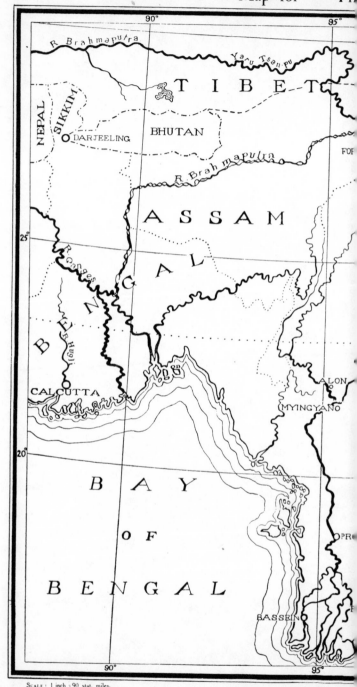